WALTER SCOTT: THE MAKING OF THE NOVELIST

JANE MILLGATE

Walter Scott:
The Making of the Novelist

UNIVERSITY OF TORONTO PRESS

Toronto Buffalo London

© University of Toronto Press 1984
Toronto Buffalo London
Printed in Canada
ISBN 0-8020-2527-7

Canadian Cataloguing in Publication Data

Millgate, Jane.
Walter Scott : the making of the novelist
Includes bibliographical references and index.
ISBN 0-8020-2527-7
1. Scott, Walter, Sir, 1771–1832 – Criticism and
interpretation. I. Title.
PR5341.M54 1984   823'.7   C83-099231-6

43,445

Part of chapter seven of this book appeared in an earlier version in *Nineteenth-Century Fiction* 34, no 4 (1980) 379–96 (© 1980 by the Regents of the University of California) and is reprinted by permission of the Regents.

Publication of this book is made possible by grants from the Canadian Federation for the Humanities, using funds provided by the Social Sciences and Humanities Research Council of Canada, and from the Publications Fund of University of Toronto Press.

Contents

Preface

Everyone has heard of the Waverley Novels. There they sit, ranged on the shelves, as many as forty-eight volumes, affirming by their uniform bindings an inescapable kinship one with another. The general title gives legitimacy to the least distinguished members of the family: *The Black Dwarf* and *Count Robert of Paris* possess a status that derives in part from *Rob Roy* and *The Heart of Midlothian*, while *Rob Roy* and *The Heart of Midlothian* labour under a burden not of their own making as separate texts. If the title Waverley Novels had been thought of only at the end of Scott's career as a name for the collected edition of 1829–33 that he liked to refer to as the '*magnum opus*,' the problem offered by the novels as a 'set' would not really amount to much. But because each of the Waverley Novels was, so to speak, to the name and the manner born, such analogues as the Charles Dickens Edition, the New York Edition of Henry James, or even the Wessex Edition of Thomas Hardy fail to attain the kind of collective identity possessed by the sequence that served as their model. To be sure, the achieved effect is partly a product of the introductions and annotations of the final collected edition, the autobiographical and other peripheral matter that carries over from one volume to the next and insists on the links between them, but it also derives from an echoing relationship developed among the novels at the time when they were first written.

The term Waverley Novel is itself older by a decade or so than the *magnum opus* edition; it was current not only among Scott's close associates but among general readers on both sides of the Atlantic by the early 1820s, and its beginnings can in fact be traced to that moment in

1815 when Scott determined to issue his second novel, *Guy Mannering*, not entirely anonymously (like his first) nor over his own name (as his friends urged) but as a new work by the Author of *Waverley* – a conventional descriptive phrase that was shortly to gather to itself extraordinary nominative power. The first collection of the novels, the twelve-volume set of 1819, put the official seal upon the concept. Entitled *Novels and Tales of the Author of Waverley*, it included all the fiction up to *A Legend of Montrose* – not only, that is, the works which had originally been ascribed to the Author of *Waverley* but also the three series of *Tales of My Landlord* whose title-pages bore the name of Jedediah Cleishbotham.

From virtually the beginning of his career as a novelist the linkage between each new work and its predecessors and potential successors became an inescapable fact of Scott's creative life. The insistence on anonymity was something far more than a publishing gambit, capable of exploitation for economic advantage; it was also in some special way essential to Scott as a novelist, so much so that even when the financial crash of 1826 compelled him to acknowledge the novels as his own, he continued to issue them over the name of the Author of *Waverley* and not that of Walter Scott. The publicly proclaimed connections among the novels acted as a challenge for the earliest readers; in attempting to identify the Author of *Waverley* they sought, when confronted with each new novel, to define both its likeness and its unlikeness to the rest of the series. But the very phalanx-like solidity of those multivolume sets has deflected the attention of twentieth-century readers away from the varying and subtle interrelationships within the sequence as it developed over time and led them instead to think of a collective entity (bearing, all mysteriously, the name of a railway station) with whose individual parts they have little direct acquaintance. Where one novel is known – say, *Ivanhoe* – the others are assumed to be much the same.

If I exaggerate a little here it is in order to emphasize the need to take a fresh look at Scott's career as a novelist as an historical phenomenon taking place over a period of time. Recent attempts to rescue Scott from the prison of his own collected fiction have missed the point in certain important respects. The Scottish novels are the most frequently discussed by modern critics: *Waverley, Guy Mannering, The Antiquary, Old Mortality, Rob Roy, The Heart of Midlothian, The Bride of Lammermoor,* and *Redgauntlet.* Since 'historicalness' is usually combined with Scottishness as a criterion for selection, *Guy Mannering* and *The Antiquary* are sometimes excluded; sometimes, by broadening the scope of inquiry beyond the historical boundary-point of the late seventeenth century that seems to have marked for Scott the limits of the directly accessible, the list is extended to include *The Fortunes of Nigel*, for example, or even *The Fair Maid of Perth*. But to concentrate on a group of novels selected from the total range and then to regroup them according to technical or thematic subcategories is to forego those insights that derive from the awareness of sequence and interconnection as factors in both the genesis and reception of the novels as first published.

The novels I will be examining in the present study overlap to a large extent with the central texts of what might be called the current Scott canon, but they will be approached in a different and even somewhat old-fashioned way, as members of a series. By taking each novel published between 1814 and 1819 – the group, running from *Waverley* to *A Legend of Montrose*, included in that first collected edition – and viewing it as a separate text that nevertheless possesses an additional dimension deriving from its membership in the Waverley sequence, I hope to throw light on the dialogue Scott was conducting with himself and with his first readers about the conventions of the new fictional subgenre he was in the process of creating. Although I have organized my discussion around the separate texts, my concern is also with a career – with the creation of an authorial persona, the Author of *Waverley*, and the development of a corporate entity, the Waverley Novels.

An approach that lays emphasis on the *career* of the Author of *Waverley* must, however, take into account the fact that in 1814 the career of Walter Scott was already at mid-point. When *Waverley* appeared Scott was on the eve of his forty-third birthday and not only firmly established in his legal position as Clerk to the Court of Session but famous as a poet and editor and deeply engaged in numerous publishing ventures with the Ballantynes, Constable, and others. Since the pattern of what followed was to some degree shaped by what had gone before, it has seemed necessary to begin with a brief consideration of certain features of Scott's first career as editor and poet. To pursue the connections between the editing, the poetry, and the fiction is one way of counterbalancing the effects of the twentieth-century insistence on Scott's status as 'onlie begetter' of the historical and regional novel, his position as the master of romance against whom nineteenth- and even twentieth-century novelists – realists and romancers alike – found it necessary to define themselves. Though it is certainly true that Scott's literary-historical importance inheres in this marking-out of the historical and regional territory that the later nineteenth-century novel was so thoroughly to colonize, his achievement in this respect should not distract attention from one of the most fascinating aspects of this great originator – his profound distrust of innovation.

Because of his determined commitment to anonymity Scott's letters offer very few statements of his ideas on fiction, and it is easy to be misled by asides to the Ballantynes about the commercial desirability of novelty in matters of subject or setting or by his apparent readiness to concede in an anonymous self-review that all his heroes were much the same. These were in their different ways evasions, substitutes for analysing the degree to which each of his works played a part in the creation of new conventions and in the evolution of a very sophisticated art of repetition with variation. Scott seems, at some deep level, to have been afraid of confronting his own originality. When breaking new ground he needed the reassurance that his innovations were not in fact radical but merely variations upon, or extensions of, what was already venerable and familiar. The career as a novelist that began with one of the most amazing right-angled turns in literary history, when the man who had been the most famous poet in Europe shifted to an almost total dedication to prose fiction, was only sustained by a complicated balancing of the new against the old that had its origin in his earlier literary experience – and perhaps even in the legal training that taught him to move forward only upon a solid basis of precedent.

But he made of this personal need a brilliant literary advantage. The subtle interconnections and variations among the novels in the first great phase of the Waverley sequence generated a cumulative effect that modified each text, whether considered in isolation or as part of the group. The entire career of the Author of *Waverley* took its shape and direction from the achievements of 1814–19, and, despite the shift in historical focus in *Ivanhoe* and the pressures created by the financial disaster of 1826, the later novels did not break the established pattern. The sequence of novels became its own flexible but coherent category, for which the complex and continuing relationship between the Author and his readers provided a controlling context. By focusing on the interconnections among the early novels as well as on the individual texts themselves I hope to show how narrative possibilities were created and narrative boundaries established for all of Scott's fiction, and, indeed, for much of the work of his literary heirs.

Parts of chapters two, seven, and nine of this book appeared in earlier versions in *The Review of English Studies*, *Nineteenth-Century Fiction*, and *The Bibliothek*, and I am grateful to the editors of those journals for permission to reuse them here. A section of chapter four was given at the conference on Scott and His Influence held at the University of Aberdeen in August 1982, and I should like to thank the organizers, Dr J.H. Alexander and Dr David Hewitt, for giving me the opportunity to exchange ideas on Scott with scholars from many different parts of the world. I wish also to thank Edinburgh University Institute for Advanced Studies in the Humanities for appointing me to a fellowship during my work on this study, and the Social Sciences and Humanities Research Council of Canada for its generous support of my research.

The librarians of the following institutions have kindly allowed me to consult Scott manuscripts in their collections: the Berg Collection of the New York Public Library; the British Library; the Brotherton Library, Leeds University; the Edinburgh University Library; the National Library of Scotland; the Morris L. Parrish Collection of the Princeton University Library; the Pierpont Morgan Library; the Signet Library. I am particularly grateful to Mr Alan Bell, formerly of the National Library of Scotland, Mr Herbert Cahoon of the Pierpont Morgan Library, Mrs Lola L. Szladits of the Berg Collection, and Miss Marjorie G. Wynne of the Beinecke Library, for their unfailing patience and courtesy in dealing with my written queries about Scott and with my repeated visits.

This book has benefited from the writings of many scholars and critics, and I have tried to indicate in my notes the most important and specific of such debts. I should like, however, to take this opportunity to record my particular appreciation of the assistance of those who have shared with me their knowledge and wisdom about matters critical, historical, and textual, or who have read parts of this study while it was in progress: Professor William Beattie, Miss Catharine Carver, Professor David

Daiches, Professor David V. Erdman, Dr Peter Garside, Professor W.J. Keith, Miss Claire Lamont, Professor George Levine, Professor Hershel Parker, Professor Alexander Welsh. Above all, I am indebted to my husband, Michael Millgate, whose encouragement and scholarly counsel have sustained me at every stage of my work.

Textual Note

Since this is a study of a career as it developed, quotations from Scott's works are taken from the first editions. On occasion, however, I also cite textual changes in later editions or quote from the introductions and annotations Scott supplied to the collected editions of his poetry and fiction published at the end of his life. The first reference to each of Scott's works, including the 1932–7 edition of his *Letters*, is accompanied by a full citation in the notes; subsequent references to these texts are incorporated within parentheses in the text.

WALTER SCOTT: THE MAKING OF THE NOVELIST

I

Editorial Strategies:
The *Minstrelsy* and the *Lay*

The story of the remarkable success of *Waverley* is well known. Lockhart's biography contains the classic account – a thousand copies sold within five weeks of the publication date of 7 July 1814, a second edition of two thousand sold within seven weeks more, four editions in all within the first six months, and many more in the years that followed. But Scott did not, like Byron, wake one morning and find himself famous. He already enjoyed an enormous reputation as the author of *The Lay of the Last Minstrel*, *Marmion*, and *The Lady of the Lake*, and in one sense, indeed, *Waverley* marked a diminution of his fame. Scott's disappearance for a trip around the northern lighthouses immediately upon its publication has acquired in retrospect a symbolic significance, and by the time his final major poem, *The Lord of the Isles*, appeared in January 1815 he had been outstripped not only by Byron – whose beating him at poetry he was himself entirely willing to acknowledge[1] – but also by the new prose romancer, the Author of *Waverley*.

The continuing perception of Scott the novelist as having suddenly and absolutely eclipsed Scott the poet has tended to obscure the possible relevance of seeing his later career in fiction as a continuation of his earlier career both as a poet and, earlier still, as a translator, collector, editor, and annotator. And yet the later career was necessarily built upon the first, and many of the habits of mind and imagination that contributed to the shaping of the sequence of Waverley Novels are already detectable in the themes, structures, and techniques of Scott's poems and editorial enterprises. Even in a brief survey of his pre-*Waverley* career it is possible to identify not only specific elements that were to be taken up in the novels but, more pervasively, the kind of emphasis he placed from the very beginning upon the importance of locality, the sense of regional identity and historical continuity, and the authenticating significance of editorial and other 'framing' devices.

Above all, perhaps, one can see how persistently Scott's innovative genius was counterbalanced by a kind of late-Augustan respect for established forms, how gradually he in fact moved, through a prolific sequence of separate works, in the direction of that imaginative freedom he finally achieved in the world of his fiction, and how successfully he concealed from himself the radical nature of the journey he was taking. It was clearly of the utmost importance to him that the movement from amateur antiquarianism, through editing, to poetry, and on to fiction, should be capable of rationalization not just as a series of variations on standard forms and conventions but also as a sequence of happy accidents, the work of conspiring circumstance rather than of genius thrusting towards its necessary outlet.

Although Scott published a few translations from the German in the 1790s and four of his poems were included in Monk Lewis's *Tales of Wonder* in 1801, his literary career began in earnest with the publication in 1802 of the first two volumes of *The Ministrelsy of the Scottish Border*.[2] This collection of Border ballads, supplemented by a few modern imitations, was a project of Scott's own devising, and he was himself responsible for writing the long introduction, composing the annotations, and making the final decisions about content, sequence, and text; he also supplied some of the imitation ballads from his own pen. The *Minstrelsy* was, of course, the product of much collaboration, and Scott himself, through numerous acknowledgments at once specific and generous, was always ready to indicate his debts, citing the diverse sources from which he derived his materials – correspondence with collectors in various parts of Scotland and England, manuscript collections, printed works, the indefatigable searches of his friends John Leyden, William Laidlaw, Robert Shortreed, James Hogg, and others, as well as his own journeys in pursuit of surviving fragments, the famous Liddesdale 'raids' of the 1790s. Yet it remains one of the most intensely individual of Scott's productions, demonstrating as it does his ability not only to draw on the skills of very different men and organize the most diverse kinds of material but also to appear, almost simultaneously, in several guises – as antiquarian, scholar, historian, critic, and poet. These varied elements are accommodated without any sense of strain within a work whose loose yet continuous structure supplies them with an appropriate expressive form.

At the time when volumes I and II of the *Minstrelsy* appeared, Scott was the recently appointed Sheriff-Depute of Selkirk, the son of a respected Writer to the Signet, a rising young barrister, and a married man. But he was still deeply imbued with the impressions received in childhood when, in the home of his grandparents at Sandyknowe, he first listened to the ballads and legends of Border raids, in some of which his own ancestors figured in roles more or less heroic. The scenes of ballad action were at that time all around him, and the half-ruined tower of Smailholm established a physical connection with the stories from his own family past; ballads and tales alike belonged to an oral culture, still in Scott's childhood enduring side by side with the knowledge derived from books and schools. The ambitions of the young Edinburgh lawyer of literary tastes and some poetic accomplishment, not averse to making a name for himself provided it did no injury to his professional prospects, coexisted with a deeply felt personal attachment to the ballads and Border lore he had been storing up over a period of twenty years or more.

The desire to claim the ballads as part of a personal and regional heritage is insisted upon in Scott's letters to Bishop Percy: 'An early partiality to the tales of my country, and an intimate acquaintance with its wildest recesses, acquired partly in the course of country sports, and partly in pursuit of antiquarian knowledge, will, I hope, enable me at least to preserve some of the most valuable traditions of the south of Scotland, both historical and romantic.'[3] Throughout the remainder of his life Scott repeatedly stressed the emotional power of place, especially when associated with some personal, historical, or legendary occurrence, and for him, as he told Anna Seward at the time of the *Minstrelsy's* appearance, the 'peculiar charm' of the ballads derived from their locality: 'A very commonplace and obvious epithet, when applied to a scene which we have been accustomed to view with pleasure, recalls to us not merely the local scenery, but a thousand little nameless associations, which we are unable to separate or to define' (*L* I, 146). Place was, moreover, a controlling factor in the structure of the anthology. By confining himself to ballads current in the south of Scotland, Scott gave his collection a unity and coherence not found in his model, Percy's *Reliques of Early English Poetry*.

In the *Minstrelsy* all aspects of Scott's rootedness make their appearance – references to personal experience, anecdotes of his ancestors direct and collateral, claims advanced in terms of that ancestry for connection with the oldest families in the land.[4] The volumes are dedicated to the Duke of Buccleuch, and it would be easy to interpret this as merely a shrewd gesture on Scott's part; the Duke had, after all, helped obtain for him the post of Sheriff and might be expected to assist his career in other ways. But Scott was not, in fact, being disingenuous in stressing the Duke's role as head of the Scott clan; he saw him, quite simply, as the living representative of that Border tradition to which the *Minstrelsy* itself served as an act of witness.[5] Scott was claiming his heritage, seeking to be true to his past and his place – in personal, familial, and historical terms.

There was ample precedent for the role of antiquarian and editor through which Scott sought to affirm this claim, most notably, of course, that of the *Reliques*. The example of Percy was of considerable importance to Scott, as the careful prose of his letters to the Bishop sufficiently suggests. Percy's credentials as gentleman-antiquarian were unimpeachable, and this was of consequence to a young lawyer who did not wish in any way to lose caste. But the excitement created by his first encounter with the *Reliques* had been one of the great landmarks in Scott's imaginative development, and the *Minstrelsy* was in its way the direct product of the shock of recognition he then experienced. The well-known passage recalling that moment is worth quoting again for the vividness with which it conveys the enchantment felt by the young Scott in contemplating not merely the marvellous substance of Percy's collection but the entire endeavour represented by the *Reliques*:

I then first became acquainted with Bishop Percy's Reliques of Ancient Poetry. As I had been from infancy devoted to legendary lore of this nature and only reluctantly withdrew my attention from the scarcity of materials and the rudeness of those which I possessed, it may be imagined but cannot be described with what delight I saw pieces of the same kind which had amused my childhood and still continued in secret the Delilahs of my imagination

considered as the subject of sober research, grave commentary and apt illustration by an editor who shewed his poetical genius was capable of emulating
the best qualities of what his pious labour preserved. I remember well the spot
where I read these volumes for the first time. It was beneath a huge platanas
tree in the ruins of what had been intended for an old fashioned arbour in the
garden I have mentioned. The summer day sped onward so fast that notwithstanding the sharp appetite of thirteen I forgot the hour of dinner, was sought
for with anxiety and was still found entranced in my intellectual banquet. To
read and to remember was in this instance the same thing and henceforth I
overwhelmed my schoolfellows and all who would hearken to me with tragi-
cal recitations from the ballads of Bishop Percy.[6]

In the years that followed his first encounter with the *Reliques* Scott
made himself master of the apparatus of editorial possession by familiar-
izing himself with the full range of late eighteenth-century scholarship
on ancient ballads and romances and with historical accounts of his own
Border region. The General Introduction to the *Minstrelsy* shows that he
learned his lessons well. He deploys with ease and aplomb all the
paraphernalia of academic history: the citation of sources, the quotation
of authorities, the inclusion of the regulation quantity of Latin and early
forms of English. The style – what was to become Scott's basic prose
voice for the remainder of his career[7] – emerges as lively but in no way
idiosyncratic; the manner, deliberately adopted, is that of the historian
and scholar rather than the enthusiast; and the local and personal touches
are controlled by the prevailing detachment. Having sought to place the
ballads within an historical frame, he goes on, in a final section, to
describe the arrangement of the anthology and justify its procedures,
delicately negotiating the treacherous ground where the acrimonious
Ritson had been doing battle with Bishop Percy over the latter's editorial
sins.[8] The appendices that follow the Introduction incorporate fairly
extended passages from documents, memoirs, and poems illustrative of
points taken up earlier. They draw on both manuscript and printed
sources, and their aim is clearly to assert the seriousness of the volumes by
freighting them with solid documentary matter. Scott amplified this
material in subsequent editions; he also corrected and rearranged the
ballads, added new ones, and expanded some of the annotation. The most
important changes had been made by the edition of 1806, but the

Minstrelsy remained an ongoing enterprise right to the end of Scott's life, and as late as 1830 he wrote two important additional essays for inclusion in a new edition.[9]

This continuing involvement with the *Minstrelsy* helps to confirm the importance Scott placed on Border material and on his own editorial achievement in making this region, its past history, and its literature part of the common poetic heritage of cultivated readers everywhere. For him ancient poetry and regional history were mutually illuminatory, and in an *Edinburgh Review* article of 1806 on Ellis's *Specimens of Early English Metrical Romances* and Ritson's *Ancient Engleish Metrical Romanceës* he insisted on the importance of this complementary relationship:

To form a just idea of our ancient history, we cannot help thinking that these works of fancy should be read along with the labours of the professed historian. The one teaches what our ancestors thought; how they lived; upon what motives they acted, and what language they spoke; and having attained this intimate knowledge of their sentiments, manners and habits, we are certainly better prepared to learn from the other the actual particulars of their annals.[10]

What Scott was here preaching he had already practised in terms of the alternation of historical narrative and poetry in his own anthology. The *Minstrelsy*, indeed, deliberately exploits the mixture of modes: the texts are enhanced by introduction and annotation, but they also serve as illustrations of the basically historical material that surrounds them. In many instances the effect is of an interwoven narrative thread running from the historical account in the headnote through the text of the ballad itself and on into the minor expansion and commentary in the supplementary notes. This orchestrated effect of parallel narration, expansion, and ornamentation is most ample in respect of the historical ballads – though it occurs in connection with the romantic and imitation ones as well – and it reaches new levels of development in the third volume, published in 1803 after the initial success of the first pair. Scott was now in his stride, at ease with the mixed form he had adopted and ready to move confidently beyond the original sixteenth-century terminal point he had set for the historical ballads. By including a group of five ballads relating to the Covenanting conflicts, he had passed from the realm of Border legend into that of history proper, and it is hard to escape the feeling that the emphasis has tilted slightly, that these ballads are included less for their own sake than for that of the surrounding commentary – with its masterly evocations of the career of Montrose, of the Cameronian temperament, and of the characters of Claverhouse and John Balfour of Burley. The editorial framework of the group provides a continuous narrative within which the poems are set as illustrations, forming an historical sequence that begins in the 1640s with 'Lesly's March' and extends into the 1680s with 'The Battle of Bothwell-Bridge.'[11]

This is the stuff out of which Scott would later develop *Old Mortality* and *A Legend of Montrose*, and if the *Minstrelsy* is seen as part of the prehistory of the Waverley Novels, it becomes very easy to point to motifs, anecdotes, even phrases that were to recur in those later texts. From the Introduction alone one can pick out such examples as the comment on Francis Stuart's grandson serving as a common soldier in the service of the later Stuarts, a fact made use of in the plot of *Old Mortality*, or the citation of the tag, 'A king's face should give grace,' that was to be invoked so powerfully, but in a very different context, by Jeanie Deans in *The Heart of Midlothian*. Lockhart, in a prefatory Advertisement to the 1833 edition of the *Poetical Works*, expressed in slightly exaggerated form what has since become the standard position on these 'premonitory' elements: 'In the text and notes of this early publication, we can now trace the primary incident, or broad outline of almost every romance, whether in verse or in prose, which Sir Walter Scott built in after life on the history or traditions of his country.'[12] But the emphasis on the *Minstrelsy* as a hoard of primary materials does not go to the heart of the matter; since Scott's remarkable memory rarely allowed him to forget anything, recurrence is not in itself a surprising phenomenon. It is the fusion of historical commentary and poetic instance in the *Minstrelsy* that needs to be stressed, rather than its anticipation of the historical fiction in details of incident or phrasing.

The editorial strategy of the *Minstrelsy* raises, of course, the issue of language, so central to twentieth-century critical debates about Scottish literature and cultural history. It seems unnecessary to enter at this point into the question of what happened to Scottish literature – not to mention the Scottish sense of national identity – following the loss of Scots as an available literary language, or to examine the different timing of that

loss in respect of poetry and prose. The classic statement of felt depriva-
tion is contained in Edwin Muir's *Scott and Scotland*.[13] The fact of loss can,
however, be clearly observed in the *Minstrelsy* in terms of the relationship
between texts and commentary. Put quite simply, the ballads are the
product of an oral, folk tradition and are mostly in Scots; the commentary is the product of a written, literary, and scholarly tradition and is in
conventional English. It would be perfectly easy to argue from this for a
deep split in Scott's own imaginative and cultural experience, and
perhaps in that of late-eighteenth-century educated Scotsmen in general.[14] But what seems most pertinent here is the degree to which the
form of the *Minstrelsy* afforded Scott easy expression for both Scots and
English elements within the scope of a single work.[15] The integrative and
orchestrative effect of the commentary, as it embraces, expands, and, as
it were, projects the ballad material, constitutes a repossession of that
material by the educated, anglicized side of Scott.

In the *Minstrelsy* the two elements are thus held in balance: the
significance of the Scots material is enhanced, its value celebrated by the
prose commentary, while the historical and scholarly impulses behind
that commentary are directly connected to the living oral culture. Two
kinds of access to the past exist here side by side – that of the folk
tradition and that of written history. Both forms of knowing and telling
find expression as Scott moves with ease around the edges of his historical and ballad material, weaving the diverse strands together through
renarration, illustration, and explanation. When Scott harks back to the
Minstrelsy, as he does so often in his later poetry and fiction, he is
deploying as a source of authenticating reference a work which is itself
self-authenticating. The *Minstrelsy* is thus both the starting point for a
lifetime of self-allusion and a model for the many variations Scott was
subsequently to devise, as annotator, editor, and self-commentator, in
both the narrative frameworks and the actual texts of his poems and
novels.

Elastic though the *Minstrelsy* was, its framework proved incapable of
containing all the projects generated by the editorial and creative ener-
gies it released. Both the edition of the romance of *Sir Tristrem* from the
Auchinleck Manuscript and the original verse romance that grew into
The Lay of the Last Minstrel were originally intended to form part of the

Minstrelsy. Work on *Sir Tristrem* had begun early in 1801, and by March of that year Scott's associate John Leyden was already well advanced with the transcription. The text of the poem was set up in type by October 1802, though by this time the decision had already been taken to issue it separately – 'the minstrelsy is to be compleated altogether independent of the Preux Chevalier who might hang heavy upon its skirts' (*L* XII, 221). The autumn of 1802 also saw the commencement of the *Lay*, and as late as December 1802 it was still intended for inclusion in volume III of the *Minstrelsy*, a plan only abandoned the following month when it had become clear that the poem, already possessed of its own framework of the old minstrel, would be 'very long' (*L* I, 175).

Recognition of the interconnectedness of the *Minstrelsy*, *Sir Tristrem*, and the *Lay* is necessary to an understanding of the stages by which Scott felt his way to a full-scale career as a poet. It is also important to keep in mind that he believed all three works to have had their roots in the Borders. It is true that the claims put forward by Scott for the primacy of the Scottish *Sir Tristrem* have not withstood the examination of later scholars, but the claims themselves are what matter in the present context. Scott nailed his editorial colours to the mast within the pages of volume II of the *Minstrelsy*, published in January 1802, in the shape of the announcement included in the headnote to the modern third part of 'Thomas the Rhymer':

Thomas the Rhymer was renowned among his contemporaries, as the author of the celebrated romance of *Sir Tristrem*. Of this once admired poem only one copy is now known to exist, which is in the Advocates' Library. The editor has undertaken the superintendance of a very limited edition of this curious work; which, if it does not revive the reputation of the bard of Erceldoune, will be at least the earliest specimen of Scotish poetry hitherto published.
(II, 283)

If *Sir Tristrem* seems now to have been the least worthwhile of the three linked enterprises, requiring as it did enormous amounts of research, correspondence, and time-consuming labour, that should not lead to an underestimation of its importance in Scott's own development. To read the lengthy correspondence with George Ellis about *Sir Tristrem* is to recognize an element of the obsessive and the simply stubborn in Scott's determination to win over the English scholar to his own view of the poem's origins and status. From the first letters early in 1801 through numerous extended pieces of argument in 1802 and 1803, on to the announcement of the volume's publication in May 1804 and even beyond that date, Scott never relaxes in his passionate determination to prove his basic case: *Sir Tristrem* in the Auchinleck Manuscript is for him indisputably 'Scottish & of great antiquity' (*L* XII, 176); moreover, it is a version of the poem originally composed by Thomas the Rhymer of Erceldoune and the basis for certain French texts of the Tristram story rather than derivative from such texts.[16] The same arguments, amplified by new material gleaned from his own continuing researches and from information supplied by Ellis and other antiquarians such as Ritson and Douce, were deployed with considerable ingenuity and forensic eloquence in the Introduction to the published volume.

Subsequent scholarship has demonstrated that the Auchinleck *Sir Tristrem* derived from continental originals rather than being their source, and that Thomas the Rhymer and the Thomas invoked as authority in several of the Tristram versions were far from being one and the same. Some of the arguments and evidence now accepted were familiar to Scott, but he maintained his original position through all the editions published in his lifetime.[17] Whether he might have partially recanted had he written an autobiographical preface to *Sir Tristrem* at the end of his life remains open to doubt, since what was involved was quite as much loyalty as logic: a change of heart was required as well as a change of mind.[18]

It is plain that at the outset of his literary career Scott did not sharply separate issues of scholarly debate from those of local feeling. He had earlier allowed local loyalty to have a shaping influence on his scholarship in using the cache of Romantic ballads, obtained from Mrs Brown, that so greatly altered the final make-up of the *Minstrelsy*. Mrs Brown's texts were of Aberdeenshire origin, but Scott had no hesitation in preferring them over the broken and incomplete texts of some of the same ballads that he had been able to collect in authentically southeast Border versions. While he omitted the poems that 'seemed to be the exclusive property of the bards of Angus and Aberdeenshire,' he nevertheless blurred what has seemed to subsequent ballad scholars an important distinction between two streams of transmission and did not scruple to use Aberdeenshire texts for 'various readings' and 'supplementary stanzas' (I, cvi).[19] He clearly felt it was his duty to represent the Border minstrelsy at its best; thus, while insisting that 'No liberties have been taken either with the recited or written copies,' he added an important qualification by noting that, where alternative readings were available, 'the editor, in justice to the author, has uniformly preserved what seemed to him the best or most poetical reading of the passage' (I, cii). The editorial soundness of such a policy has since been loudly and frequently challenged, although the charge that Scott made up substantial portions of the ballads out of whole cloth has been demonstrated to be false.[20] What remains clear is that the controlling impulse was to present the public with the old ballads at their finest. Scott was himself capable of passionate feeling about even the most defective ballad scraps, but he did not wish to try his readers by too much exposure to the fragmentary. His mission was to open up the world of the Border past, expose its poetry to a wider audience, and induce that audience to share his own especial delight in such material.

In the case of *Sir Tristrem* something of the same missionary zeal was certainly at work. If the gospel was to be preached it was essential that the genuineness of the text, its authentically Scottish origins, be demonstrated, and much of the apparatus of introduction and annotation is devoted to that end. The resulting edition has formal affinities with the *Minstrelsy*: prose introduction, edited poetic text, modern imitation in the supplied conclusion, annotation. But it lacks the reciprocating inter-woven texture of the earlier work – that echoing response of note to text, the carrying over of the narrative from one mode to the other. The poem itself, written in what Scott himself acknowledged to be 'a strange and peculiar stanza,'[21] is much less accessible and attractive than the contents of the *Minstrelsy*, and Scott's own continuation is simply pas-tiche, with none of the genuine revivification of an old form found in some of his imitation ballads. It is understandable that Constable and Longman should have been unwilling to weigh down the 'skirts' of the *Minstrelsy* with so ponderous an item. Scott's own appetite for Border material and for romance remained undiminished, however, and despite the recalcitrance of *Sir Tristrem* as editorial subject and metrical model he was unwilling to abandon entirely that bonding of the poetic and the historical afforded by the framing strategies of the editor.

When, therefore, *The Lay of the Last Minstrel* appeared in January 1805, the large format and handsome printing proclaimed the confidence of the author and his publishers in his role as poet, while the expansive annotation signalled a link with Scott's earliest efforts as editor.[22] The poem was not allowed to stand alone but provided with a prose Advertisement to serve as the reader's first introduction to a poetic text that was itself equipped with a narrative framework. The Advertisement, a direct address by the poet, offers to locate the romance in historical and technical terms by commenting on certain of its narrative and metrical features. Scott here attempts to combine many of the standard arguments used by eighteenth-century scholars in defence of romance into a rationale for his own poetic enterprise, but in shifting about between arguments based on historical illumination and those relating to poetic technique and narrative structure, he ends up with a somewhat incoherent document whose appearance of logic is largely a syntactical effect. It claims that the poem 'is intended to illustrate the customs and manners which anciently prevailed on the Borders of England and Scotland' and that the combination of 'pastoral' and 'warlike' habits in this region provides material 'highly susceptible of poetical ornament.' The 'plan of the ancient metrical romance' has been adopted for the sake of the 'greater latitude' it allows in describing scenery and manners, since such descriptions, rather than 'a combined and regular narrative,' have been the author's main object. The same generic precedent is invoked to justify metrical flexibility and the inclusion of supernatural material, which 'would have seemed puerile in a poem which did not partake of the rudeness of the old ballad, or metrical romance.' 'For these reasons,' the Advertisement confidently concludes, 'the poem was put into the mouth of an ancient Minstrel, the last of the race, who, as he is supposed to have survived the Revolution, might have caught somewhat of the refinement of modern poetry, without losing the simplicity of his original model.'[23]

The minstrel framework is thus presented as somehow holding together the various impulses within the poem by providing a dramatized figure whose presence simultaneously justifies the poetic mode adopted and links two distinct historical eras. Scott the author-editor, speaking in the Advertisement, blurs the distinction between the separate processes of poetic and historical connection. The creation of the old minstrel is made to seem the product of a literal-mindedness that the author believes his readers will share, an unwillingness to make the kind of imaginative leap encountered at the beginning of, say, *Christabel*. It is as though, like the Thomas the Rhymer of the ballad, neither author nor reader can enter the land of faery without some intermediary to conduct them there. In the account of the old minstrel's arrival at Newark Castle in the 1690s and his subsequent recitation of his 'lay' to the widowed Duchess of Buccleuch and Monmouth and her assembled court, the fictional and the historical are made to commingle. Actual historical figures and existing locales, possessed of a reality that extends outwards to the annotations and on into history books and maps, are juxtaposed to the fictional and semi-fictional beings (such as Lord Cranstoun, William of Deloraine, and Lady Scott of Branksome Hall) who inhabit the tale itself.

The discontinuities of the 1805 Advertisement are symptomatic of Scott's uneasiness as editor and critic with the creative processes that made this melding of fact and fiction possible. The Advertisement represents, in fact, an initial attempt to establish for the *Lay* what we might call a fable of composition, and thus to deflect certain anticipated criticisms – even self-criticisms. In subsequent elaborations of this fable the process of developing a *modus vivendi* for Walter Scott, Esq, advocate, and Walter Scott, poet, is extended by the placing of the creative achievement within a context of autobiographical anecdote, thus making what was for Scott a characteristic substitution of narrative sequence for analytical examination. This strategy has more than a biographical fascination, since it is clearly the *post hoc* rationalization of the aesthetic method by which Scott enters his fictional world. The presence in his works of explicit frameworks is indicative, together with his habitual recourse to imitation, allusion, or generic variation, of the degree to which his creative powers depend for their release upon staged proce-dures that ostensibly bridge the gap between the world of his own fictions and the world of external reality – or, alternatively, that other pre-existing world, scarcely less real to Scott, composed of the corpus of earlier works of literature.

In the final version of the fable – anticipated privately as early as March 1805 in a letter to Anna Seward, publicly in the form of the published Introduction of 1830 – Scott took a tack somewhat different

from that of the Advertisement of 1805, employing an ostensibly autobiographical account of this early career and of the *Lay*'s origins to conduct
his readers from the modern, known world of shared experience into the
fictional realm of the poem. The stress now is less on the poem's form as
metrical romance and on its 'appropriate prolocutor,'[24] the old minstrel
– these having long won acceptance from readers – than on the inclusion
of Gilpin Horner, the goblin page. Scott insists that the *Lay* was begun in
direct response to a request by 'the lovely young Countess of Dalkeith'
(*PW* I, xix) for a ballad on Gilpin Horner, the subject of a Border legend
she had recently heard: 'thus the goblin story, objected to by several
critics as an excrescence upon the poem, was, in fact the occasion of its
being written.' He goes on to characterize as a 'chance' event (*PW* I, xxi)
his first encounter with the metre of *Christabel* and to describe how he
composed a few stanzas of the *Lay* and then burned them when the
response of his friends William Erskine and George Cranstoun seemed
unenthusiastic – only to be surprised by subsequent eager inquiries from
these same friends as to how the work was progressing. Even the
framework of the minstrel is accounted for anecdotally, as the result of a
friend's suggestion that 'some sort of prologue might be necessary, to
place the mind of the hearers in the situation to understand and enjoy the
poem' (*PW* I, xxvi). This narrative of happy accidents represents the
origin of the *Lay* as a natural and inevitable process almost beyond Scott's
personal control, each stage connected to the next by interventions not of
choice but of chance.

Although the essentials of this version are followed by Lockhart in the
Life, it seems in fact to be as open to question as the version it replaced.
Gilpin Horner, said to be the 'occasion' of the poem, does not put in an
appearance until late in canto II, nor is he mentioned in any of the letters
from the end of 1802 and the beginning of 1803 in which the *Lay* is
discussed. Surviving documentary evidence suggests in fact that the
Countess's suggestion was not made until mid-January 1803, when the
poem was already well under way, and that the decision to incorporate
the goblin page had probably not been taken even at the end of that
month.[25] Scott is simply restructuring his fable: the placing of the
Countess's request for a Gilpin Horner poem before the beginning of the
Lay not only makes a much better tale; it also builds on to the poem yet
another in the sequence of frames – the story of his responding to the
appeal of his 'lovely chieftainess.'[26]

It is possible that the elaboration of the story about the Countess of Dalkeith owed a good deal to Scott's memories of another poem written in response to the request of a noble lady. The earliest mentions of the *Lay* in Scott's letters frequently associate it with the imitation ballad of 'Cadyow Castle,' which he wrote in 1802 at the instigation of Lady Anne Hamilton and included in volume III of the *Minstrelsy*. In 'Cadyow Castle' Scott adopts the role of a modern minstrel singing at the request of a 'noble maid' a tale of her ancestors associated with one of their traditional strongholds: 'You bid me tell a minstrel tale, / And tune my harp, of Border frame' (III, 387). It is a short, if crucial, step from this point to the creation of a dramatized ancient minstrel singing to a noble lady of the doings of her ancestors at a point in time when such a performance was still historically possible. The shift from a metaphorical to a dramatized minstrel undoubtedly had a liberating effect on Scott's poetic powers, and the stiffness of the modern minstrel convention in 'Cadyow Castle' is absent from the *Lay*; yet he seems to have continued to yearn for a further frame that would make explicit a connection between the poem and his own world, one in which Walter Scott as modern minstrel performed in response to Lady Dalkeith's prompting. By borrowing from his memory of the fairly extended discussions with Lady Anne Hamilton about her poem, he colours his story of the part played in the *Lay* by Lady Dalkeith and so achieves – privately in 1805, publicly in 1830 – the effect desired.[27]

This autobiographical extension to the sequence of frames makes of the young Countess of Dalkeith and the poet a further parallel with the Duchess of Buccleuch and the old minstrel within the poem. The wife of the latest representative of the Scotts of Buccleuch takes, in the 1830 Introduction, her place beside the Lady Scott within the minstrel's story and the Duchess in the sequence framing each canto. The process of transcending the limitations of the fiction through historical and biographical annotation is thus given a new variation; the weaving together of present and past, of real and imagined worlds, through the continuing associative power of the local is provided with a new metaphor. The manner of the 1830 Introduction is that of the confidential reminiscence, but its purpose is not essentially different from that assigned to the old minstrel himself; it too serves 'to place the mind of the hearers in the situation to understand and enjoy the poem.' Personal anecdote is used to reconfirm the essential structure of the *Lay* – that pattern of teller-tale-audience which ostensibly connects the poetry to the world of experience.

In both the *Lay* and its immediate successors the frameworks and annotations seem almost to derive from an uneasiness on Scott's part with poetry in its naked condition – as an artifact detached from the world of rational discourse. The apparatus looks like an attempt to contextualize and explain, to ground the world of the imagination in that of actual history and geography and so render it 'safe.'[28] The subjection of his own poetry to the kind of editorial treatment normally reserved for ancient texts serves to modify the authorial role itself, to detach Walter Scott, Esq, in some degree from the troubling figure of the poetic creator. But it is important to recognize that the desire to frame and contextualize is not a purely retrospective activity, restricted to the act of editorial repossession by which Scott seeks to accommodate the poetry to the world of prose; it is with him intrinsic to the working of the creative impulse itself. Attractive though it may be to account for the elaboration of frameworks in purely developmental terms, pointing to their origins in the apparatus of the *Minstrelsy*, it remains necessary to recognize the framing impulse as a complex process both of containment and of liberation; the very devices that insist on the connection of the work of art with its regional and historical sources also act as markers establishing its freedom *as* work of art.

The external structures of Scott's poems and novels habitually enact a process of transition and mediation, but the effect created is curiously double, drawing the reader into the world of the poem even while continually reminding him of its fictionality. The presence of a mediating figure like that of the old minstrel serves to point out the stages by which the imaginative journey from present to past, or from the realm of experience to that of fancy, can be made, but it also emphasizes the distance between those different worlds. Scott himself described the introduction of the old minstrel as serving to 'remind the reader at intervals, of the time, place, and circumstances, of the recitation' (*PW* I, xxvii), but such interruptions also tend to set off what is recited, confirm its separate identity as text, and place a boundary between the story told, the situation of its telling, and that further narrative circle which the author Walter Scott, by means of his Advertisement and annotations, throws around the entire work.

2

Variations on a Method:
Marmion to *Rokeby*

To move from the *Minstrelsy* to *Sir Tristrem* and on to the *Lay* is to have an increasing sense of each stage of a career leading surely to the next, of Scott always keeping one foot firmly on the old ground as he steps forward to the new. And the pattern apparently continues, success with a verse romance in 1805 prompting the commencement, as ironic response, of a novel whose young hero suffers from a surfeit of such works. One can even argue that it was the experience of editing and completing Strutt's turgid historical novel *Queenhoo-Hall* that made Scott think, in 1810, of going on with *Waverley*.[1] Most authors, of course, proceed to some degree along a creative line that starts with influence or model and moves through imitation or reaction – acknowledged, unconscious, or concealed – towards new creation. As we have already seen, however, what is remarkable about Scott when compared with other nineteenth-century authors is the stress he himself placed on the process, preferring always, when arguing the critical case for his own writings, to cite a model or source rather than claim originality – even asserting that he introduced the old minstrel into the *Lay* lest he be himself 'suspected of setting up a new school of poetry, instead of a feeble attempt to imitate the old' (*L* 1, 243). To be sure, the gulf between the conclusion of *Queenhoo-Hall* and the completed *Waverley* of 1814, like that between the end of *Sir Tristrem* and the beginning of the *Lay*, is enormous; even so, a substantial case can be made for a step-by-step progression within the first half of Scott's career.

Plausible though such a version of Scott's development may be, it requires in fact a good deal of refinement and modification. As is clear from his descriptions of the genesis of the *Lay*, it is dangerous to accept without question Scott's own *post hoc* accounts of creative events. His preference for a narrative of his career based on a combination of imitation, association, and happy accident should not be allowed to obscure the large part that was in fact played by deliberate experimentation with a wide range of forms. The first dozen years or so of his literary career saw the production of an astonishing variety of literary exercises. He began with translation and ballad imitations, but in 1799 he tried his hand at a play of his own, *The House of Aspen*, which he attempted to have produced in London in 1800 and thought of including in a collection of his short poems in 1805. The years that saw the publication of the *Minstrelsy*, *Sir Tristrem*, and the *Lay* also marked his debut as a reviewer of works as different as Southey's *Amadis of Gaul*, Thornton's *Sporting Tour*, and two books on cookery. In 1806 he published the first separate collection of his *Ballads and Lyrical Pieces*, in 1808 *Marmion* and the eighteen-volume edition of Dryden (including a life of Dryden), in 1809 the beginning of the *Somers Tracts* edition, in 1810 *The Lady of the Lake* and an edition of Anna Seward's *Poetical Works*, and in 1811 *The Vision of Don Roderick* and more editions. Meanwhile he continued to turn out reviews and articles on many different topics, edit the *Edinburgh Annual Register*, work on his edition of Swift, try his hand at autobiography, carry on a continuously expanding correspondence, and, as a matter of sheer necessity, write summaries, opinions, and judgments in the course of his legal duties as Clerk to the Court of Session and Sheriff of Selkirk.

This eager appetite for every kind of literary exercise represents the obverse of the conservatism that needed always to claim some existing textual landmark as the point from which it had started out. It is true that the works of these years were often far from innovative – Scott brought nothing especially new to the art of reviewing, for example – and that there is thus a sense in which the variety does not of itself constitute a contradiction of his avowed position as imitator rather than innovator. But the verse romances, no matter how firmly connected to an earlier tradition they were made to seem, did break new ground for English poetry, while the sheer range and exuberance of Scott's activity can be recognized in retrospect as symptomatic of a need for some as-yet-undiscovered outlet for his immense literary energy. Hindsight, indeed, makes one want to say that Scott was searching all the time for that adequate mode of expression he would only attain when he turned to the novel. But the necessity for such a development was far from apparent at the time. The 1805 chapters of *Waverley* were taken up in 1810 only to be set aside again when they failed to arouse any enthusiasm in James Ballantyne, and Scott's creativity continued to be directed primarily towards the composition of long poems.

The major poems that followed the *Lay* all came equipped with a body of annotation worthy of Scott's beginnings as antiquary; they also continued to assert the connection between his own romances and the texts he had edited in the *Minstrelsy* and *Sir Tristrem*. It is true that the *Lay*, *Marmion*, and *The Lady of the Lake* do not present the reader with that counterpointing of formal English prose against older Scottish poetry which characterizes the *Minstrelsy*, but by working a series of variations on the framework transition Scott nevertheless retains in these three poems something of the foregrounding effect previously achieved by embedding the ballads in prose commentary. He moves from the old minstrel of the *Lay* through the extended modern verse epistles of *Marmion* to the briefer exercises in Spenserian verse used to introduce the cantos of *The Lady of the Lake*. And in each case the framework, ostensibly employed to establish connections with the actual world of the poet, serves to mark off as literary artefact the text it encompasses.

The framing device employed in *Marmion* raised doubts in the minds both of indulgent admirer and of hostile critic. Scott's friend and fellow antiquarian Ellis, to whom the epistle to canto v was addressed, greeted the appearance of *Marmion* in 1808 with a word of regret for the absence of one who, 'though the last,' was 'by far the most charming of all minstrels,' and wondered whether this loss was entirely 'compensated by the idea of an author shorn of his picturesque beard, deprived of his harp, and writing letters to his intimate friends.'[2] Jeffrey was less gracious, noting in his review in the *Edinburgh* that the minstrel's 'prologuizing' function was 'but ill supplied' by the epistolary introductions.[3] Ellis and Jeffrey were both registering, though not relishing, the deliberately contrastive effect Scott had sought. 'Each canto is to be introduced by a little digressive poem' (L I, 347) he told Anna Seward during the early stages of the poem's composition, and the digression afforded by the new framework was in a direction away from the historical fable and towards the contemporary world of the author and his friends.[4]

The setting for the epistles to the first four cantos is Scott's country home at Ashestiel in the valley of the Tweed, but though the tale and the act of telling thus share a common Border setting, the fable is constituted much more deliberately as poetic fiction than was the fable in the *Lay*. The contexts afforded by the epistles, with their exemplification of a different poetic mode – modern and meditative where Marmion's story is historical and narrative – are literary and aesthetic. In the opening epistle to William Stewart Rose, Scott uses the late autumn landscape round his home to achieve a metaphoric transition into his meditation on the wintry state of the nation in 1807, bereft of its three greatest men, Nelson, Pitt, and Fox. The excursion into public poetry in praise of these lost leaders serves as a kind of negative poetic example, and helps to define the poet's true subject, to confirm 'How still the legendary lay / O'er poet's bosom holds its sway.'[5] The shift into the realm of romance is effected through an argument from poetic tradition. Scott still moves, in his characteristic fashion, by stages and by example, but the mediators and models deployed here differ from those in the *Lay*: instead of the old minstrel and the Duchess of Buccleuch, Spenser, Milton, and Dryden are invoked as practitioners, or would-be practitioners, of romance. The 'legitimization' of *Marmion* is thus literary rather than historical.

Even in the epistle to canto II, which stresses the continuities implicit in such activities as hunting – the modern experience differing very little from that of earlier generations engaged in the same pursuits in the same localities – there is a countervailing stress on that knowledge of the past which comes from something other than re-enactment. To see the same sights, perform the same rituals, is one way of getting in touch with the past, but such activity provides access only to the continuous aspects of human experience. To know the regional past in its difference, to recapture particular events and individual men, requires listening and telling rather than doing – as is reflected within the epistle itself in the evocation of Scott's repeating the local legends to an audience of children.[6]

The places of the past and the places of his own childhood were for Scott, as for other Romantic writers, essentially similar in their power to evoke a poetic response. But what gives a special quality to all Scott's Border writing is that the two things come together: the act of memory

links the present with the personal past, while the Border tales link the
present with history. The epistle to canto III makes such connections
explicit:

> Thus, while I ape the measure wild
> Of tales that charmed me yet a child,
> Rude though they be, still with the chime
> Return the thoughts of early time.   (125)

Some lines on the power of place might almost be by Wordsworth:

> Yet was poetic impulse given,
> By the green hill and clear blue heaven.   (125)

But this is pure Scott:

> And still I thought that shattered tower
> The mightiest work of human power;
> And marvelled, as the aged hind
> With some strange tale bewitched my mind,
> Of forayers, who, with headlong force,
> Down from that strength had spurred their horse.   (126)

For anyone interested in Scott's personal and artistic development
these verse epistles are revealing documents of a kind not encountered
again in his published work until the series of autobiographical statements
initiated, after his financial crash, by the Introduction to *Chronicles of the
Canongate* in 1827. Through the epistles, as he told Ellis, he parades 'a plur-
ality of hobby-horses – a whole stud, on each of which I have, in my day,
been accustomed to take an airing' (*L* II, 22), and the freedom with which
he expresses his delight in the Border countryside, his personal happiness
in the life of Ashestiel, is the product of a period still recalled more than
twenty years afterwards as a peculiarly happy one. In the 1830 Introduction to *Marmion* he remarked upon the wealth of personal references to
his 'domestic occupations and amusements' and attributed them to 'a
loquacity which may be excused by those who remember, that "out of
the abundance of the heart the mouth speaketh"' (*PW* II, vii–viii).

Clearly the autobiographical impulse was strong upon him at the time he was writing *Marmion*; his fragment of prose autobiography dates from the same period, its contents overlapping to some extent the epistle to his lifelong friend William Erskine that introduces canto III of *Marmion*.

Erskine was a key figure in Scott's personal history and imaginative life,[7] and the epistle Scott addressed to him dramatizes their friendship through the confiding tone of the verses, their open expression of his keenest personal joys, and the frankness of the debate that is staged about the best form for Scott's poetry to take. That Erskine is assigned the worst of the argument is not really important; his role as foil is what counts. His suggestions that Scott write verses on the allied commanders or adopt Joanna Baillie as his model may not seem especially felicitous, but their function is precisely to be rejected and thus provide a springboard for the celebration of Scott's delight in romance. Here, with the *Marmion* story in mid-flight, vivid expression is given to Scott's faith in the interlocking functions of personal memory, communal tradition, regional associations, and the romance impulse. The childhood world of Smailholm is again evoked, an actual locality rich in personal, family, and historical associations, along with the experience of coming into imaginative possession of that world within the secure context of deep family affection – 'endured, beloved, carest' (128). The Smailholm scenes of childhood, with their loving family judges, are assimilated to the world of Ashestiel and to the presence of Erskine as critic and friend:

> From me, thus nurtured, dost thou ask
> The classic poet's well-conned task? (129)

The answer is not in doubt, but Erskine's role as refiner of Scott's poetry and indulgent witness to his necessary commitment to romance is still important:

> Still kind, as is thy wont, attend,
> And in the minstrel spare the friend[.]
> Though wild as cloud, as stream, as gale,
> Flow forth, flow unrestrained, my tale. (129)

The epistle ends with an argument won, and with a transformation of the physical details of the opening evocation of the world of Ashetiel into metaphors for the poetry which follows.

The relationship articulated by means of the epistles between the modern world of autobiography and the lost world of *Marmion* is one of continuities delimited and defined by the registering of important distinctions. Here is the world of the present, of the poet and his audience, of questions of critical judgment on subject-matter and treatment; there, separate yet responsive, is the tale. Here is the nineteenth century, there the sixteenth. This placing, at once personal, critical, and historical, provides another enactment – different in form from that in the *Lay* but not totally dissimilar in function – of the stages by which Scott moves into his romance world. In the *Marmion* epistles, however, he is probing much more deeply the sources of his creative life, the imaginative processes by which he moves into his poetry.[8]

The desire for some kind of placing frame finds expression even within the tale itself. Scott always seems to need to establish a locus of observation. Over and over again he identifies an observer from whose point of view, at least initially, a scene or episode is perceived – the warder at the opening of canto I observing Marmion's arrival at Norham, Fitz-Eustace witnessing Marmion's departure for and return from the night-time encounter in canto III, Sir David Lindsay's eyewitness account of the visionary warning to the king at Linlithgow in canto IV, Marmion himself looking at Edinburgh in canto IV, the Scottish warriors looking at Marmion's English followers in canto V, Fitz-Eustace watching Clare on the battlements in canto VI, and so on. Scott possessed no talent with brush or pencil, but he had an almost obsessive fascination with angle of vision, needing to know where, when, and by whom a described scene was being viewed. The profusion of observers suggests a combination of an artistic with an almost judicial need for an eyewitness, a presence capable of locating each scene and incident and fixing its data as the raw material for subsequent narration. The insistence on witnessing creates narrative awkwardness when supernatural events are at issue, but its retention is indicative of Scott's desire for narrative accountability. The quest for narrative authority and authentication, made matter for aesthetic debate in the epistles, is also constantly in progress within the narrative itself.

The third of Scott's verse romances, *The Lady of the Lake* (1810), is metrically and structurally a more complex performance than either the *Lay* or *Marmion*. He was now moving with great flexibility and assurance in the romance form, creating quite deliberately a more elaborate and embroidered effect, deploying numerous set-piece elements – descriptions of scenery, separate lyrics and ballads, interpolated tales – within the basic narrative. Early in the gestation of this 'Highland poem' he had considered setting it as though told to Charles Edward during his wanderings after Culloden: 'Flora Macdonald, Kingburgh, Lochiel, the Kennedies, and many other characters of dramatic [interest] might be introduced' (*L* II, 37). But he abandoned such a formal historical framework, which would have harked back to the method of the *Lay*, in favour of introductory Spenserian stanzas at the head of each canto. These perform a more distinctively *poetic* role than the external frameworks of either the *Lay* or *Marmion*; they are deliberate exercises in technique, insisting upon the presence of the poet as creator of the whole work as aesthetic object. To initiated readers the opening invocation to the 'Harp of the North' not only asserts the poem's Scottishness and places it within a general tradition of tales of 'hopeless love' and 'Knighthood's dauntless deed'; it is also self-reflexive, matching the maker of this poem against the fictional minstrel of the *Lay*:

> O wake once more! how rude soe'er the hand
>   That ventures o'er thy magic maze to stray;
> O wake once more! though scarce my skill command
>   Some feeble echoing of thine earlier lay.[9]

The harp thus serves to connect this poem to a series of earlier poetic contexts, and the opening description of the instrument – 'that mouldering long hast hung / On the witch-elm that shades Saint Fillan's spring,' muffled by 'envious ivy' (3) – has just sufficient physical reality to function as poetic symbol. In the closing evocation of the twilight forest the harp and its elm continue to resist absorption into pure metaphor:

> Harp of the North, farewell! The hills grow dark,
>   On purple peaks a deeper shade descending;
> In twilight copse the glow-worm lights her spark,

The deer, half-seen, are to the covert wending.
Resume thy wizard elm! the fountain lending,
    And the wild breeze, thy wilder minstrelsy;
Thy numbers sweet with Nature's vespers blending,
    With distant echo from the fold and lea,
And herd-boy's evening pipe, and hum of housing bee.   (289)

This maintenance of the independent identity of vehicle and tenor, the coexistence of the physical and the metaphorical, is characteristic of the method of this poem and the working of Scott's imagination in general. When he returned from his Liddesdale raids with those curious notched sticks that one of his friends was persuaded were in some way the raw materials for the *Minstrelsy*, or when he filled Abbotsford with all kinds of mementos and antiquarian lumber, from Rob Roy's gun to a pair of spurs from Bannockburn, Scott was expressing an urgent need to objectify, to render into physical form the intangible stuff of memory, legend, and imagination. In his poems and novels connections have similarly to be established between the work as artefact and some external context, while the internal interplay of parallelisms and echoes – of actual minstrels and harps and their metaphoric counterparts, of Border winds and tempests and the forces of poetic inspiration – also insists upon a direct reciprocity between experience and expression.

In *The Lady of the Lake* this echoing interchange between framework and text serves to enhance the stylization of a work in which design everywhere preponderates over narrative process. The need to read the design, perceive the emblematic meaning in the arrangements of character and setting, interpret the metaphors, is continuously insisted upon. There is virtually no narrative suspense. That Ellen and Malcolm will be united, her father be freed from outlawry, Roderick Dhu find fulfilment in death, and Fitz-James be revealed in his true identity is clear from the very first. Prophecies will be brought to pass, identities revealed or confirmed, whether they be those of the king or the Douglas. The forces that belong inextricably to the disordered world of the forest – beautiful and beguiling though that world is – will not be able to come to terms with the forces of the court and the castle. Ellen and her father and Malcolm can come to Stirling, but Roderick Dhu cannot. The movement created is not that of narrative development or plot suspense but of patterns discerned and designs worked out: 'I never remember a narrative poem in which I felt the sense of Progress so languid' was Coleridge's understandable comment.[10]

The static qualities of *The Lady of the Lake* do, however, give it certain advantages over the more breathless *Marmion*. Occasional touches are almost novelistic – glimpses into the internal workings of a mind or into complexities in the relationships between particular characters. But Scott could not really exploit these without a greater range of action and a consequent blurring of the broad and simple outlines of his romance design. One of his problems with Malcolm Graeme, as he himself acknowledged, was his young hero's 'insignificance,' but 'the canvas was not broad enough to include him considering I had to groupe the King, Roderick, and Douglas' (*L* II, 464).[11] The good young men of the *Lay* and *Marmion* are equally forgettable, but the greater lifelikeness of the portraits of Ellen and the King makes Malcolm's pallid inactivity seem more noticeable.

Malcolm's predicament is one shared by many young men in Scott's poems and novels: he is deprived of his mistress and in danger of losing her for ever. Scott himself, of course, had suffered a wound that never really healed when, in the 1790s, he was rejected by the young heiress Williamina Belsches in favour of a richer and more obviously attractive suitor. A touch could always bring the old pain alive again,[12] and though Scott was unwilling or unable in *The Lady of the Lake* to give full fictional expression to his personal grief, he may be seen as in some sense keeping the wound fresh, recognizing subconsciously that the experience had generative power for his art. In January 1810 he wrote an unusually confessional letter to Lady Abercorn about his difficulty with Malcolm Graeme:

I have tried, according to promise, to make 'a knight of love who never broke a vow.' – But well-a-day though I have succeeded tolerably with the damsel my lover spite of my best exertions is like to turn out what the players call a *walking gentleman*. It is incredible the pains it has cost me to give him a little dignity. Notwithstanding this I have had in my time melancholy cause to paint from experience for I gained no advantage from three years constancy except the said experience and some advantage to my conversation and manners. Mrs. Scott's match and mine was of our own making and proceeded from the most sincere affection on both sides which has rather increased than diminished during twelve years' marriage. But it was something short of love in all its fervour which I suspect people only feel *once* in their lives. Folks who have been nearly drowned in bathing rarely venturing a second time out of their depth.   (*L* II, 286–7)

Transformed into the motif of the rejected lover, personal anguish could be drawn upon equally with the other powerful experiences and emotions that assumed an almost physical quality in Scott's memory. Certain places and buildings, particular legends and anecdotes, key historical figures and episodes – Scott returns over and over again to these special memories, employing them as elements in his narrative grammar. That the loss of the beloved or the failure of communication between father and son – two of Scott's most painful personal experiences – are also recurrent motifs in romance served to legitimize Scott's tapping of the emotional energy derived from the loss of Williamina or his sense of filial failure. Such materials could properly be made the stuff of fiction, transformed through narrative into something that had the meaning and order of art rather than the disturbing intractability of anguished memory. Sometimes the pain is not entirely accommodated by the fictional transposition – Scott's young heroes seem at times to be disabled by an anguish out of proportion to the experience they are actually undergoing – but the very existence of such 'uncontained' feelings demonstrates how important it was for Scott to be able to employ a form such as romance that allowed him to draw on his own experiences and yet assimilate them to literary tradition. It also suggests why he returned repeatedly to similar situations and plots.

Rokeby (1813), Scott's fourth long poem, has as its hero William Wycliff, a romantic dreamer whose portrait falls naturally into place alongside that of the young Edward Waverley in the as-yet-uncompleted novel. Both are suggestive of Scott's own younger self as evoked in the prefatory epistle to canto III of *Marmion* and, more specifically, in the fragment of autobiography he composed at Ashestiel in 1808 and other such fragments scattered through the introductions to the collected editions he prepared in his later years. From these, from the editions of the *Journal* and the *Letters*, and from Lockhart's biography – of which the Ashestiel fragment forms the opening chapter – readers have long been familiar with the story of Scott's childhood convalescence in the country and with his delight in ballads and romances and in 'the oft-repeated tale of narrative old age.'[13] A few years later he was absorbed in Spenser: 'Too young to trouble myself about the allegory, I considered all the knights and ladies and dragons and giants in their outward and exoteric sense and God only knows how delighted I was to find myself in such society.'[14]

Equally familiar, and from the same sources (even though Scott himself never mentions Williamina Belsches by name), is the romantic tale of how the penniless young law student found a beautiful young heiress fit for all his projective fantasies and dreamed of carrying her off to a future of private happiness. Rejection in favour of a wealthier suitor shattered the dream and left a lingering sadness, yet within a few years he was himself married, within ten famous, and within fifteen rich, the newly won fame and wealth deriving not from his labours as a lawyer, though these had been patiently and seriously pursued, but from his success as a poet. By 1812 the romantic fantasies had been made the stuff of literature; the dreaming boy had turned the dreams themselves to gold.

But while Scott himself establishes this whole pattern of transition and transmutation, his recollections rarely venture upon the confessional or analytical. Even in the privacy of his *Journal* Scott's impulse is always narrative rather than introspective, as in the following survey of his life, jotted down in 1825 at a moment when the whole edifice of his career seemed to be crumbling around him:

What a life mine has been. Half educated, almost wholly neglected or left to myself – stuffing my head with most nonsensical trash and undervalued in society for a time by most of my companions – getting forward and held a bold and clever fellow, contrary to the opinion of all who thought me a mere dreamer – Broken-hearted for two years – My heart handsomely pieced again – but the crack will remain till my dying day – Rich and poor four or five times – Once at the verge of ruin yet opend new sources of wealth almost overflowing – now taken in my pitch of pride and nearly winged (unless the good news hold) because London chuses to be in an uproar and in the tumult of bulls and bears a poor inoffensive lion like myself is pushd to the wall – And what is to be the end of it? God knows and so ends the chatechism.[15]

Thirteen years earlier, at what had then seemed the high point of his career, Scott was aware only of the upward swing of Fortune's wheel – the escape from the passivity of romantic dreaming into an active success measurable in public terms. Writing to a new correspondent of 1812, the poet George Crabbe, he recalled his old dreaming self as something left far behind, and yet there is little sign, at this time or later, of his having been able fully to grasp the significance and interconnection of the sequence of autobiographical events. Recollection left him always in a state of wonder, almost as if he viewed the process by which he had survived and become successful as analogous to waking from a disturbed sleep. Unable to come directly to terms with the transformation of his own life, Scott remained fascinated with the dreaming boy as literary subject – a figure, as James was later to put it, '*en disponibilité*' – as though seeking to resolve through narrative what had eluded him analytically, to discover in just what ways, and with what consequences, a romantic youth, inhabitant of the world of dreams, could become a man of the world of quotidian reality.

The correspondence with Crabbe, begun while *Rokeby* was in progress, makes clear how struck Scott had been by Crabbe's own variations on the theme of the dreaming boy. He mentions specifically his admiration for the tale entitled 'The Patron' in Crabbe's *Tales* of 1812, in which the hero, a 'Young Poet,' is removed to the country for his health and there sustains himself on a diet of romantic reading:

> Robbers at land and pirates on the main,
> Enchanters foil'd, spells broken, giants slain;
> Legends of love, with tales of halls and bowers,
> Choice of rare songs, and garlands of choice flowers,
> And all the hungry mind without a choice devours.[16]

It is easy to see the personal parallels Scott himself must have perceived – beginning with the removal of the sickly child from the town to the country – and he specifically acknowledged, in a letter of 21 October 1812, the way in which the poem had brought vividly to mind his own youth and the delight he had taken twenty years earlier in 'the description of the old Romancers' (*L* III, 182) encountered in an extract from Crabbe's *The Library* printed in the pages of Dodsley's *Annual Register*. But

Scott also clearly saw that it was necessary to get beyond the impasse dramatized by Crabbe in these poems, each of which presents as irreconcilable the opposition between the life of the imagination – as manifested in a youthful appetite for poetry and romance – and the life of reason and maturity: 'Enchantment bows to Wisdom's serious plan, / And pain and prudence make and mar the man.'[17] Scott in 1812 had apparently solved the problem pragmatically in terms of his own career, finding in the editorial stance of ballad collector a respectable bridge back into the world of fancy and moving with natural ease from the *Minstrelsy* to the *Lay*. But in reviewing that career he never probed for connection or causation beyond the simply sequential, and even in his literary exploration of the problem he seems not to have gone very far as yet beyond the position taken by Crabbe.

In *Rokeby* Scott certainly seems to have little to offer his dreaming hero. Wilfrid's greatest delight is in reading; he is an enthusiast who dreams 'on some wild fantastic theme, / Of faithful love, or ceaseless Spring.'[18] Himself something of a poet, he makes of his poems love offerings to the beautiful Matilda, who praises them but can return his passionate feelings only in sisterly terms, causing his life to wear away in fruitless emotion, 'though reason strove / For mastery in vain with love' (44). Scott draws the strict opposition between Fancy and Reason in terms which differ little from those invoked by Crabbe:

> Woe to the youth whom Fancy gains,
> Winning from Reason's hands the reins,
> Pity and woe! for such a mind
> Is soft, contemplative, and kind;
> And woe to those who train such youth,
> And spare to press the rights of truth,
> The mind to strengthen and anneal,
> While on the stithy glows the steel! (45–6)

The parallel between Wilfrid and Crabbe's young poets is by no means absolute, however. It is consistent with the shift from a realistic to a romantic mode that while Crabbe's hero in 'The Patron' learns his melancholy lesson by exposure to an arid world of politics and of great men too busy to spare time for the young poets in their anterooms – a world very different from the realm of fancy in which he has spent his youth – Wilfrid is caught up in an action which contains so many elements of romantic literature that he can truly be said to have entered the country of romance itself. He leaves the safety and monotony of his home in company with Bertram, the villainous ex-pirate, is attacked by outlaws hiding in the forest, enters a burning castle in an attempt to rescue his rival, and makes his final act of renunciation in an effort to save the father of his beloved from the scaffold. This is the stuff that dreams are made of, but it is also the stuff of Wilfrid's brief period of active life, and despite its tragic outcome the narrative reads more like a vindication of the dreams of his youth than an illustration of the 'Woe' which comes 'to the youth whom Fancy gains.' Wilfrid's dying actions achieve true nobility, and they have meaning and value for both his mistress and his rival.

That rival is the man-of-action hero of the poem, Redmond O'Neill: 'A form more active, light, and strong, / Ne'er shot the ranks of war along' (107). Part of the description of Redmond was often quoted by Erskine as 'an excellent portrait of the author himself,'[19] and since Scott was to confess in 1818 that Matilda had a special place among the heroines of his poems, 'in general mere shadows,' because 'she was attempted from the existing person and character of a lady who is now no more' (*L* v, 145) – presumably Williamina Belsches – it seems that in the free world of his poem Scott was able to find a compensatory satisfaction in drawing on different sides of his own character for the successful and unsuccessful claimants to the heroine's affections.[20] The young heroes share some common traits – Wilfrid has his moment of physical courage, Redmond has poetic sympathies – but in essentials the two remain strongly contrasted. Although they are capable of forming 'a compact of the mind' (213) in order to save Matilda, their paths are destined to be quite separate. One of them ends by rejecting his father, giving up his mistress, and meeting an untimely death, while the other survives to enjoy the new life of an identity recovered, a love returned, and a father found.

If Scott was to develop his use of the dreaming youth as protagonist, he had to find some way of combining the virtues of a Wilfred with those of a Redmond at a level more substantial than compacts of the mind. In creating Wilfrid and Redmond as, in a sense, two halves of a single character, he had already employed that twinning of the hero characteristic of romance and demonstrated his realization that any solution had to be more complex than the exposure of Wilfrid to a dose of reality sufficient to turn him into a Redmond. In order to establish a continuity between dreaming youth and successful maturity – rather than a division or an extension by proxy – he would have to work out the problem in terms of a single hero. The failure to resolve the problem of psychological depth undoubtedly weakened *Rokeby* itself but paradoxically enhanced its eventual usefulness to Scott the novelist. The poem served as a kind of negative experiment, an identification of a route not to be taken. The solution demanded, in fact, a change of genre. The romance in which Wilfrid figures is severely limited in its temporal and moral dimensions, and its apparatus seems excessively literary, the pirates, outlaws, and burning castles too obviously pasteboard. For all the local colour Scott was so careful to include in *Rokeby*,[21] its characters move in another and unreal world – you can't go there from here. But when – by accident or design, in a mood of casual experiment or out of deep creative impulse – Scott turned away from poetry to the novel he had begun several years earlier, he found an available hero already embarked on a romantic journey to quite a different kind of region.

3

Waverley:
Romance as Education

Waverley; or, 'Tis Sixty Years Since was begun in 1805, and some additions were probably made to the first volume in 1810; the remaining two volumes were only completed (after the rediscovery of the manuscript during the famous search for fishing tackle) in 1814 – by which date it is arguable that Scott understood the narrative situation of his hero far better than he had nine years earlier.[1] This is hard to establish absolutely since some of the basic elements of the final pattern are already present in the opening seven chapters that were composed in 1805, but it seems plain that Scott in 1813 was again ready to confront the problem of the maturation of the dreaming boy and that he now saw that maturation as involving not a rejection of romance but, on the contrary, a deeper immersion in the dangers, strangenesses, and shifts of identity character-istic of the romance experience.

Edward Waverley as presented in the opening chapters of the novel that was published on 7 July 1814 shares many features in common with the young poets of Crabbe's poems, with Scott's own youthful self, and with Wilfrid Wycliff of *Rokeby*. He reads indiscriminately, pursuing story rather than moral and favouring romantic authors; he delights in tales from his own family past which tell of heroic actions ending in tragedy; he loves the more solitary corners of the estate of Waverley Honour, especially the shores of Mirkwood Mere where he composes his own rather melancholy verses. To read Shakespeare, Milton, Spenser, Drayton, the Elizabethan and Jacobean dramatists, the more familiar classical texts, romances in English, French, and Spanish, and some examples of the 'earlier literature of the northern nations'[2] cannot in itself be bad: what the narrator deplores is the habit of reading solely for gratification, 'like the epicure who only deigned to take a single morsel from the sunny side of a peach' (I, 38). Because Edward's appetites are narrative, visual, unreflective, and undirected, he sails 'through the sea of books, like a vessel without a pilot or a rudder' (I, 37), with the result that 'knowing much that is known but to few, Edward Waverley might justly be considered as ignorant, since he knew little of what adds dignity to man, and qualifies him to support and adorn an elevated situation in society' (I, 40). To complete this fully developed case history of the dreaming boy, the narrator describes how shyness and sensitivity make solitude preferable to the company of other young men, so that Edward dwells more and more in his own 'ideal world' (I, 50) where fantasy replaces action: 'like a child amongst his toys, [he] culled and arranged, from the splendid yet useless imagery and emblems with which his imagination was stored, visions as brilliant and as fading as those of an evening sky' (I, 52–3).

In the course of the opening chapters a basic relationship between narrator, protagonist, and reader is established, but also partially undermined. The comic irony suggests that Edward is destined for an exposure to reality that will cure him of his youthful romanticism and transform dreaming boy into mature man of reason – bring him, that is, much closer to the narrator and the reader. The deliberate evocation of the manner of eighteenth-century fiction – those allusions to the *Spectator*, the semi-allegorical names, the Fieldingesque style – conjures up a world where satire of human folly takes precedence over particularities of time or place and where the reader's assent to the wise vision of the narrator can be taken for granted. Style and literary allusion are employed to make the experienced novel reader feel comfortably at home with this generalized English countryside at a moment in the past that is not very clearly specified. In such a world a young man may pursue a Cecily Stubbs or be exposed to sentimental Jacobitism without very much harm coming from either experience.

Yet for all his Fieldingesque manner the narrator is specifically identified as a man of the nineteenth century, the reader's contemporary rather than Edward's, and while this enhances rather than detracts from the bond of shared assumptions established between narrator and reader, it does require that the narrative perspective be registered as historical as

well as satirical. The political details – the rise to government favour of
Richard Waverley, the withdrawal from active political engagement of
Sir Everard, even the High Church views of Mr Rubrick – must be read
historically rather than as the local colour of an illusionary archaism, part
of an attempt to take the reader out of his own world into that of an
eighteenth-century novel. The ventriloquial skill of these opening chapters serves in fact to stress the importance of temporal distinctions at a
level more complex than that of simple dualities of the then-rather-than-
now, there-rather-than-here variety. 'Since' is the key word in Scott's
subtitle; it insists upon the necessity of distinguishing past from present
while yet connecting the two.[3] The author is in fact adopting his usual
crablike strategy of presenting innovation disguised as imitation.

The deliberate withholding of the date of the action, especially when
coupled with the retention of the 1805 deadline for the narrative
moment, compels the reader of 1814 (or of any subsequent year) to
engage in his own chronological calculations.[4] Once the crucial but
narratively unspoken date of 1745 has been generated, it is no longer
possible to think in terms of a generalized past, to see Edward's future
education as unaffected by temporal factors, or to regard the choice of
Scotland as his destination as in any sense casual. The distance between
now and then, between narrator and reader and the young man they
watch, has become historicized. The journey on which that young man
embarks is not timeless picaresque but one which will take him into the
realm of historical action.

Edward, however, as the account of his education has made clear, is
himself almost totally lacking in historical awareness, or, for that matter,
in any very adequate means for proceeding from the particular to a more
general understanding of what he observes. Possessed of 'powers of
apprehension ... uncommonly quick' (I, 32), 'brilliancy of fancy' (I, 33),
and 'power of imagination' (I, 36), he shows as he journeys into Scotland
an openness to experience, a responsiveness to everything that is new,
beautiful, or strange, that makes him seem at times like an Emersonian
transparent eyeball. But 'apprehension' is no substitute for comprehension. A repertoire of romantic motifs, that 'splendid and useless' imagery
of which the narrator speaks so dismissively, cannot supply the place of
the political information, moral awareness, and psychological insight
with which the narrator is careful to provide the reader. What is more,

the habit of haphazard association – this detail is like something in Spenser, that other recalls Ariosto or Tasso, this scene might come from a painting by Claude, that other from a Salvator Rosa – not only impedes Edward's ability to see Tully Veolan and Glennaquoich as they are; it also blinds him to those underlying patterns of significance that make the proper reading of romance an exercise in interpretation. Edward's lack of political wisdom is thus compounded by his lack of romance wisdom.

The change of scene from England to Scotland signals at one level Edward's emergence from the world of Waverley Honour into that of historical and regional actuality. The shift is made in stages – Tully Veolan, Glennaquoich, the Chevalier's court – and follows the ways of actual geography to Edinburgh, northeast to Dundee, on to the Perthshire Highlands, back to Edinburgh and the battlefield of Prestonpans. The narrator intervenes from time to time to offer information – historical, regional, social, or economic – and ironic commentary, but the narrative method also allows the reader to participate fully in Edward's vision of the countryside and its inhabitants. The alignment of perspective established in the opening chapters is thus further modified by this mobility on the part of the reader, his freedom to move closer to the protagonist without losing his privileged access to the narrator's commentary. The slight gap which thus opens up between reader and narrator allows for the recognition of the necessary restriction of the narrator's viewpoint – of the fact that his interpretations may be affected by the contingencies of time and place and the natural limitations of individual human sympathy. Despite his technical omniscience the narrator is himself a creature of history, fixed at a moment of time that even for the novel's earliest readers was already somewhat in the past.

One impulse behind the Scottish section of *Waverley* was the desire to depict an unfamiliar region and a distant period in such a way as to show what life was like in such places and times – to present to the reader a world accessible to him in much the same way as his own world, so that by listening and watching he could learn how things were. But the local also contains within it the potential for the microcosmic or emblematic, and the repeated emphasis on Edward's crossing of various boundaries, physical and geographical, demands recognition of the element of symbolic containment. The reader accompanies Edward Waverley into a Scotland of whose reality he is absolutely confident and is involved with him in events which are specifically datable and whose consequences for subsequent generations are known; but he also accompanies him into another country which has something in common with the land of Faerie roamed by Spenser's Redcrosse.

The irony of the narrator's tone and Edward's youthfulness and lack of military prowess notwithstanding, it seems that Scotland can be regarded both as North Britain, an actual place, and as that special kind of otherworld into which the romance hero journeys in order that his virtues may be tested in adventure. In this case, what Edward's romanticism requires is not so much eradication as transformation; he needs to understand the grammar of romance, not merely relish its lexical riches, if he is to employ it as a mode of explanation as well as of appreciation. The narrative that follows dramatizes the way in which Edward acquires the capacity for interpretation he so notably lacks at the outset; in the process his vision of the world is modified, expanded, and endowed with a moral as well as an aesthetic dimension. The narrator's view of the world, however, does not change. He is precisely as wise at the beginning as at the conclusion. It is upon the reader that the burden falls of drawing on the two perspectives, the one dynamic and changing, the other stable and fixed, so as himself to arrive at a more complex way of seeing and understanding.

This is to state the situation baldly and without proper regard for the gradualness of the reader's developing awareness of the need to draw on both narrator and protagonist. But it seems important to insist on this complexity at the outset of any discussion of *Waverley* since it is a much more sophisticated narrative exercise than many of its critics – including Scott himself – have given it credit for being. When the announcement is made that the narrative is moving off into a more romantic country, the reader would do well to take the statement seriously. If Edward has to be weaned from one kind of distortion and over-simplification, the reader has also to be taught a proper caution in accepting the narrator's view as the only way of seeing things correctly. It is not that the narrator is 'unreliable' but that in the historicized, relativistic universe into which *Waverley* takes its readers, the perspective of the narrator is necessarily limited and his satirical vision requires extension by the invocation of romance. *Waverley* is not merely the story of a young man who views the world romantically: it employs the devices of romance – paired figures, emblematic descriptions, mysterious journeys, pastoral interludes, and so on – to insist that the reader moralize the narrative and read its meaning through design as well as through plot and commentary. And Edward Waverley's abandonment of certain of the excesses of the dreaming boy in no way invalidates this larger use of the romance method.

Scott's apprenticeship to medieval and renaissance romance had been long and thorough. He was familiar, too, with the decline of the genre in the lengthy prose romances of the seventeenth century and its trivialization in those eighteenth-century Eastern and Gothic tales where the shift of location – once an essential element in the aesthetic and moral meaning of romance – had become largely a matter of décor. But he was also a devotee of the eighteenth-century novel as practised by Richardson, Fielding, Goldsmith, and Smollett, and recognized that rounded characterization, realistic dialogue, and detailed exploration of individual motivation or social interaction offered an alternative mode to romance. By extending the realistic novel's concern with concrete settings and specific times of day or year so as to comprehend that larger sense of place and time by which the specifically regional and historical could be distinguished, Scott restores to distancing and location-shift the organic function they possessed in renaissance romance. A new precision about time and place becomes the vehicle for imposing pattern on the realistic surface. Romance is not in competition with historical truth in *Waverley*; it is the medium through which that truth is expressed.

The picture of 'A Scottish Manor House Sixty Years Since' is drawn with loving detail. The exoticism of Tully Veolan is the product of regional and historical circumstance; every element in its outward appearance, its relation to the neighbouring village and adjoining countryside, affords potential material for the narrator's historical commentary. Yet the manor can also be read more abstractly, seen as one unit in a pattern of places that includes not only Waverley Honour and Glennaquoich but even Brerewood Lodge, Edward's Lake District retreat, and the palace of Holyrood. What is more, the four separate Tully Veolan episodes comprise a series each member of which requires to be interpreted in terms of all the others. It is no picaresque accident that Edward should come back to the house three times after his first visit. Each return helps define his progress into full imaginative understanding of himself and of the world outside himself – the movement from observation to insight.

The first visit is the most fully presented; the reader rides at Edward's side through the village with its scantily clad children, barking dogs, kailyards, and poorly built houses, along the tree-shaded avenue, between the bear-crowned gates, and on into the deserted courtyard. The vision is Edward's, each detail sharply perceived and quickly registered; his is the 'eye accustomed to the smiling neatness of English cottages' (1, 99) which is invoked to establish the contrast between these Scottish scenes and an English norm, but he is also the 'lover of the picturesque' prompt to recognize an affinity between the village girls and the figures in 'Italian forms of landscape' (1, 101). As an Englishman with proper respect for the '*comfortable*' he might wish 'the clothes less scanty, the feet and legs somewhat protected from the weather' (1, 102), but the romantic vision tends to screen out such mundane concerns once the gates of Tully Veolan have been passed:

The solitude and repose of the whole scene seemed almost monastic, and Waverley, who had given his horse to his servant on entering the first gate, walked slowly down the avenue, enjoying the grateful and cooling shade, and so much pleased with the placid ideas of rest and seclusion excited by this confined and quiet scene, that he forgot the misery and dirt of the hamlet he had left behind him.   (1, 107–8)

The 'monastic' illusion quickly gives place to the fancy that he has 'reached the castle of Orgoglio' (1, 112–13); later he notes, 'The scene, though pleasing, was not quite equal to the gardens of Alcina' (1, 115). His residual awareness of the incongruities involved in these kinds of analogy – the 'bare-legged damsels, each standing in a spacious tub, [who] performed with their feet the office of a patent washing-machine' and ran off crying 'Eh, sirs!' are somewhat removed from 'the maidens of Armida' (1, 115–16) – does not prevent the invocation of yet further comparisons. Davie Gellatley is 'not much unlike Shakespeare's roynish clowns' (1, 120), and the appearance of the butler-cum-gardener calls up a line from *Richard II*.

Edward's allusive imagination draws on art as well as literature; he catches 'those effects which a painter loves to represent' (1, 107), and the transforming power of his painterly vision can be observed in the paired descriptions of the Tully Veolan garden. The first dwells on the separate elements in the old-fashioned formal arrangement:

The garden, which seemed to be kept with great accuracy, and abounded in fruit trees, exhibited a profusion of flowers and evergreens, cut into grotesque forms. It was laid out in terraces, which descended rank by rank from the western wall to a large brook, which had a tranquil and smooth appearance where it served as a boundary to the garden. (I, 114–15)

Although his eye travels on to where the stream 'leaped in tumult over a strong dam,' he picks out not only the picturesque details of the 'octangular summer-house' and 'ruinous tower' but also the 'small washing-green' (I, 115) where the two girls are trampling the clothes. The second view is, however, more selective and extensive. It is taken from a higher perspective and after Edward has been more fully exposed to the pleasures of Tully Veolan and something of its history. The boundary of the garden is swiftly passed, its ordered detail reduced almost to nothing; the washing-green has been eliminated; the presence of a couple of cottages seems an element in the design rather than a reminder of the harsh realities of the village through which he has ridden a few days earlier:

The formal garden, with its high bounding walls, lay below, contracted, as it seemed, to a mere parterre; while the view extended beyond them down a wooded glen, where the river was sometimes visible, sometimes hidden in copse. The eye might be delayed by a desire to rest on the rocks, which here and there rose from the dell with massive or spiry fronts, or it might dwell on the noble, though ruined tower, which was here seen in all its dignity, frowning from a promontory over the river. To the left were seen two or three cottages, a part of the village; the brow of a hill concealed the others. The glen, or dell, was terminated by a sheet of water, called Loch Veolan, into which the brook discharged itself, and which now glistened in the western sun. The distant country seemed open and varied in surface, though not wooded; and there was nothing to interrupt the view until the scene was bounded by a ridge of distant and blue hills, which formed the southern boundary of the strath or valley. (I, 186–7)

This scene is, of course, not of Edward's making. Rose Bradwardine has selected this location for her private retreat: it is her glen as surely as that of Glennaquoich is Flora's. The description itself, however, with its built-in markers for the path to be followed by the trained observer of the picturesque, seems to speak more of Edward's heightened sensitivity than of Rose's. The scene has been subtly improved in the seeing, much in the same way that the text we are given of Rose's song has been 'somewhat corrected' (I, 188). The brief legend of the supernatural with which an unknown 'village poet' has intertwined the names of some of 'the race from which he sprung' (I, 188) has benefited from Edward's literary taste, and it is he who points out the similarities between the superstition it records and 'a rhyme quoted by Edgar in King Lear' (I, 187). Scene and song are assimilated to picturesque and literary models.

Quick to celebrate everything at Tully Veolan that chimes with his own fantasies, Edward makes of it a garden of delights, failing to appreciate the generations of loving domestication that have gone into the making of the actual garden, the gentle imposition of order that accommodates what might have been disrupting. He is far more attentive to the ruined tower than to the modulation from fortification into peaceful manor visible on the exterior of the house itself. He never pauses to think of his own situation and is irritated by reminders of political realities and his own military responsibilities. Much of what he sees before him he cannot properly recognize: Rose's growing love for himself, the Baron's expansive paternalism that embraces daughter, tenants, friends, and guest. Proceeding by projection rather than interpretation, Edward dramatizes the historical disquisitions of the Baron 'with the colouring of a warm and vivid imagination, which gives light and life to the actors and speakers in the drama of past ages' (I, 179–80), but he cannot focus the same kind of vivifying imaginative attentiveness on the father and daughter immediately before his eyes. He is puzzled by Rose's ability to speak coolly of scenes such 'as he had used to conjure up in his imagination, as only occurring in ancient times'; her story bears 'so much resemblance to one of his own day-dreams' (I, 226) that he finds it difficult to accept as an account of an actual event.

Edward's progress towards a more internalized perception of what he observes is most clearly articulated through the emblematic sequence of his three returns to Tully Veolan. On the first return his own selfhood seems almost to be in dissolution. Not only has he been humiliated at the hands of Gifted Gilfillan and physically injured in the rescue, but the immediately preceding interrogation by Major Melville has sapped his confidence in the talismanic power of his own name. To be Edward Waverley of Waverley Honour turns out to mean very little when you are accused of treason and treated as a dishonourable renegade. Enclosed in the tomb-like bed in old Janet's cottage, surrounded by strangers speaking a language he does not understand, his confusion and disorientation could scarcely be more complete. His impulse to observation is consistently thwarted – the side of the bed is nailed up, the spy hole he makes is discovered, and even when freed from the bed he is not allowed to pass beyond the doorway to take a wider view of his surroundings – so that he does not even realize he is at Tully Veolan. Since the reader is also left in the dark about the exact situation of the cottage, the ironic contrast between Edward's former arrival as welcome guest – offered free access to the entire estate, fed with a constant stream of anecdote, encouraged to feast his observing eye on everything within range – remains unexpressed, awaiting revelation and interpretation until Edward's next return. This delay not only maintains the reader's closeness to Edward in this central section of the narrative, thereby heightening the experience of confusion and alienation; it also requires that the narrative be decoded backwards as well as forwards once the revelation has been made. Mystery becomes a device for disrupting narrative sequence and obliging the reader to bring together all the Tully Veolan episodes for interpretation through superimposition.

Edward's helplessness and confusion are not so much the product of the restrictions placed upon him during this second visit as of his earlier response to Tully Veolan as picture observed. He has now been brought right into one of the scenes he so much admired at a Claudean distance, and he does not know where he is. Seen close up, the glen in which the cottage lies and the 'large and rough brook, which raged and foamed through a rocky channel' (II, 218) cannot be placed. Deprived of one kind of aesthetic distance, Edward nevertheless continues to grasp at picturesque formulations: the old woman who nurses him is perceived as an 'old Highland sybil' (II, 211); the young woman he glimpses must be some kind of romance heroine. These identifications hide rather than reveal, and prevent his recognizing old Janet Gellatley or Rose Bradwardine. Janet has been for Edward simply a creature of anecdote, the mother who figures in Rose's story of the two brothers, the one a gifted young poet who dies 'hopeless and broken-hearted' (I, 172), leaving only some fragments of song as legacy to his half-witted brother. She is also the old woman accused of witchcraft and rescued by the Baron's intervention in another of Rose's stories. The first anecdote had fascinated Edward as 'a tale bordering on the romantic' (I, 173); the second had provided the opportunity for an extended discussion of the supernatural. On each occasion he has missed the essential point – the Baron's active, protective tenderness for those 'born on his estate' (I, 192), belonging to his '*ground*' (I, 172). He has similarly paid little attention to the account of Davie Gellatley's saving Rose from attack by an angry bull. The ties that bind the community of Tully Veolan are those of affection and mutual concern strengthened by time; those that he has subsequently encountered at Glennaquoich are feudal loyalties deliberately revived and exploited in the service of political ambition. The master of Tully Veolan is mainly concerned to protect his people; the chief of Glennaquoich is ready to sacrifice his. Since Edward has abandoned and forgotten the men who followed him from Waverley Honour, it is hardly surprising that he fails to read the riddle of the Gellatleys. For him Janet and her family remain quasi-fictional figures in a romantic landscape.

The motif of entering the picture recurs on several occasions in the novel. Sometimes Edward's aesthetic expectations are disappointed – the cave of Donald Bean Lean does not house bandits appropriate in appearance to a Salvator Rosa painting. Sometimes they are more than fulfilled, as in the Poussinesque waterfall scene at Glennaquoich.[5] Each of these occasions confirms the basic thrust of the novel towards the penetration of romantic surface rather than the simplistic rejection of the romance vision. Edward and the reader are required to distinguish purely visual effects from those that, correctly interpreted, are eloquent of deeper meanings.

When Edward makes his third visit to the now-ravaged house of Tully Veolan, everything that had caught his eye on his first arrival has been insulted or mutilated. The bears are torn down, the fountain 'demolished' (III, 224), the great chestnuts mined, the borders 'overgrown with weeds, and the fruit-trees cut down or grubbed up' (III, 225). His own copy of Ariosto lies 'wasted by the wind and rain' (III, 226) and seems at first to be merely a memento of a way of seeing that has been lost forever.[6] As on the first occasion he is greeted by Davie, who now leads him 'towards the bottom of the garden,' along the bank of the stream which is its 'eastern boundary' (III, 229), over 'the ruins of the wall which once had divided it from the wooded glen,' past the old tower, and, as twilight falls, on down the stream and through 'the tangled copse-wood' to 'the door of a wretched hut' (III, 230). Edward has entered the picture once again, crossed over the boundary between formal garden and romantic landscape, but he can now recognize that the place where the Baron has found shelter and protection was earlier the place of his own succour. The only thing that remains intact at Tully Veolan is the bond of community and affection that had escaped his attention on his first visit. His own acknowledgment of old Janet is, however, postponed so as not to detract from the powerful recognition scene of his reunion with the Baron, the true father, always so determined to see his young guest 'scathless' (I, 154), who can only be properly repaid by receiving Tully Veolan back into his own hands.

The final return to Tully Veolan makes it clear that Edward's original romance delight in the house is not to be rejected but to be reinforced. In using the wealth of his own unfatherly father to return Baron Bradwardine to his proper place, Edward has been concerned to see restored all those external details which charmed him so much on his first encounter – even Davie Gellatley is 'bedizened fine enough to have served Touchstone himself' (III, 345). The salvaged Ariosto has reasserted its influence. But the loving care and generous tact with which the house and garden and the complete panoply of bears are returned to their master show that Edward's new appreciation of the 'pure-hearted and primitive Baron of Bradwardine' and his 'deep and tender' (III, 214) affection for Rose have made him a much more skilful reader of the values inherent in Tully Veolan. It is appropriate that so many friends should be present, that the celebration should be a communal affair in which the gifts of the children are placed in the hands of a parent whose immediate concern is how they can be passed on to the next generation. Unselfishness and reciprocity are two of the chief values embodied in Tully Veolan. The house is at peace with its own past and with its own place, and the master's concern for the weak and unprotected around him has ensured his own protection and survival. There is none of the museum feeling of Waverley Honour about Tully Veolan, nor of the self-conscious attempt to regenerate the feudal past that characterizes Glennaquoich.

The various entries and re-entries into the world of Tully Veolan thus offer the most fully developed paradigm of Edward's education. But this is a novel of many journeys and many places, and those other locations also have their part in the total design. The journey from Tully Veolan takes Edward northwards, in the opposite direction from the landscape seen from Rose's balcony and across the 'stupendous barrier' (1, 97) of the Perthshire Highlands that he had observed on his first approach to Tully Veolan. On this deeper penetration into the country of romance, beyond a boundary far more substantial than the walls and stream that mark off Tully Veolan, everything is intensified. He no longer rides along charted ways accompanied by his own servant but clambers at Evan Dhu's side through one of the 'tremendous passes,' along 'steep and rugged' paths (1, 240), across narrow glens, black bogs, by mazelike turnings of unknown streams, through thick woods by tracks hardly discernible in the murky darkness. There are no landmarks on this journey, and it can only be made under the guidance of strange men who speak an alien tongue. The humorous irony of the narrator continues to flicker over the description, but Edward himself is shown as deliberately suppressing the bathetic aspects of his quest for the Baron's milk cows so as to indulge to the full in what seems like an actualization of his most heated fancies.

When Glennaquoich is finally reached, a clear distinction is made between the relationship of house and surrounding country here and at Tully Veolan, while a more distant comparison with Waverley Honour is also implied:

Around the house, which stood on an eminence in the midst of a narrow Highland valley, there appeared none of that attention to convenience, far less to ornament and decoration, which usually surrounds a gentleman's habitation. An inclosure or two, divided by dry stone walls, were the only part of the domain that was fenced; as to the rest, the narrow slips of level ground which lay by the side of the brook exhibited a scanty crop of barley, liable to constant depredations from the herds of wild ponies and black cattle that grazed upon the adjacent hills ... At a little distance up the glen was a small and stunted wood of birch; the hills were high and heathy, but without any variety of surface; so that the whole view was wild and desolate, rather than grand and solitary.   (1, 299–300)

The bleakness of the immediate surroundings of the castle is in stark contrast to the glen up which Edward climbs for his meeting with Flora. Exaggeration temporarily takes over from irony as the overt controlling device, indicating that romantic vision is here reduplicated – that the setting to which Edward is reacting has already been appropriated by a sensibility whose reponsiveness to the sublime in landscape is even keener and more refined than his own. The glen 'seemed to open into the land of romance' (I, 335), and the terms 'romance' and 'romantic' keep recurring as each item in the repertoire of picturesque landscape is duly registered – the 'rapid and furious' brook 'issuing from between the precipices like a maniac from his confinement, all foam and uproar' (I, 334); the 'crag of huge size' whose 'gigantic bulk' seemed to block the path; the 'chasm' bridged by two pine trees forming a 'pass of peril' (I, 335); the 'broken cataract' and the 'second fall, which seemed to seek the very abyss' (I, 337). The stress on 'seeming' insists that natural wildness has been artificially enhanced. Flora has improved the materials she found, very much as an artist, accepting the licence permitted by Gilpin and other theorists, might adjust certain details to make the resulting picture more essentially picturesque.[7] There is an element of the theatrical in certain of the details: Flora and her attendant appear silhouetted on the narrow bridge 'like inhabitants of another region, propped, as it were, in mid air, upon this trembling structure' (I, 335–6); the borders of the 'romantic reservoir' are 'decorated with trees and shrubs, some of which had been planted under the direction of Flora, but so cautiously, that they added to the grace, without diminishing the romantic wildness of the scene' (I, 338). In this glen, scene has been translated into scenery; rocks, trees, waterfalls become a deliberately chosen backdrop for Flora's passionate performance of the verses celebrating the deeds of the Mac-Ivors and calling the Highland clans to arms.[8]

Counterpointed against Flora's rendering of the celebratory and stirring chant of the bard of the Mac-Ivors is the modest scene on Rose's balcony, where, amid carefully tended flowers, she has sung the ballad composed by some nameless 'village poet.' The shadowy form of Tully Veolan can, in fact, be discerned behind each moment of the Glennaquoich visit, establishing its own human norm against the hectic and histrionic world of the Mac-Ivors. The contrast between Rose – 'too frank, too confiding, too kind' (I, 207) to figure as a heroine – and Flora, so mysterious and unattainable, is obvious enough, but the pastimes of Tully Veolan, the reading, talking, modest hunting, and so on, also serve to throw into relief the assertive outlines of the military displays, the bardic chants, and the great hunting expedition at Glennaquoich. Flora appears to Edward 'like a fair enchantress of Boiardo or Ariosto, by whose nod the scenery around seemed to have been created, an Eden in the wilderness' (I, 339), but the danger of such an illusion, once it has been stripped of the comic overtones associated with similar comparisons at Tully Veolan, is all too clear. This transitory Eden created out of barren rocks and waterfalls by an enchantress who is a victim of her own idealizing imagination has nothing in common with the ancient garden of the house of Bradwardine. The artifice of Flora's landscaping is designed not so much to deceive as to heighten what she sees as the essential qualities of the scene; nevertheless the incantatory rituals she performs here create a kind of blindness both in herself and in Edward. In acting out her own fantasy she draws him further into the world of dream.

Fergus's interruption of his sister's performance goes right to the literary point. She is committed to the sublime, he to the anti-romance: 'A simple and unsublimed taste now, like my own, would prefer the jet d'eau at Versailles to this cascade' (I, 348). He is, with his own taste for the theatrical, taking advantage of the contrastive opportunity afforded by his sister's performance to come on stage in his own chosen role. The strangeness and specialness Edward registers at Glennaquoich are, in fact, not merely the products of history, geographical remoteness, and cultural difference; they have been deliberately fostered and even partly created by Fergus and Flora Mac-Ivor. He has set out to revive for his own political ends the old feudal world of the chief and his followers; she has subtly modified the natural surroundings so as to render the Scottish rocks and waterfalls conformable to a French painting of an imaginary Italian landscape. Glennaquoich is not simply a physical setting, nor just an element in the novel's romance patterning capable of being read as an emblematic second world in which the young hero is tested: it is also the artificial creation of characters within the fiction. In Fergus's case this is accompanied by a certain cynicism, in Flora's by idealism, but what counts is the active attempt to make life responsive to their wishes and ambitions, to force reality into the mould of a preconceived design. Where Edward hopes that life will be like a story-book, Fergus and Flora set out to make the story-book happen.

Edward views Fergus and Flora as figures out of romance. But their own proper mode is that of melodrama. They always have ready a dramatic response to the demands of the occasion, whether it be the carefully staged sequence at the waterfall or the approach to the scaffold – 'This is well GOT UP for a closing scene' (III, 326). They are always quick to react with the appropriate gesture – Fergus's striking Callum Beg to the ground after his treacherous attempt on Edward's life, Flora's response to her accidental wounding by a stray shot fired in celebration, or her gift of her jewels to Rose before her own departure for a convent. Even the final meeting between Edward and Flora shows an attention to detail on her part that derives from an instinct for self-presentation:

Her fine complexion was totally gone; her person considerably emaciated; and her face and hands, as white as the purest statuary marble, forming a strong contrast with her sable dress and jet-black hair. Yet, amid these marks of distress, there was nothing negligent or ill-arranged about her dress – even her hair, though totally without ornament, was disposed with her usual attention to neatness. The first words she uttered, were, 'Have you seen him?' (III, 307–8)

It is not a question here of sincerity or insincerity. The histrionic element in the words and actions of the Mac-Ivors is the direct expression of their vision of the world and their own role in it. When Flora insists that 'high and perilous enterprize is not Waverley's forte' (III, 71), she is making a statement as much about herself and Fergus as about Edward. Her subsequent characterization of Edward's appropriate role is too limited and condescending to be adequate,[9] and the reader would do well to treat it with some caution, but the pattern of the novel confirms the distinction between the style of the Mac-Ivors and that of Edward; he is carried off the main historical stage in a minor Cumbrian skirmish, while Fergus and Flora enjoy set-piece farewells and grand exits of almost operatic power. The fanaticism and absolutism that see the world in terms of black-and-white opposition find in melodrama their sufficiently appropriate expression. Edward's minor gift as reader and interpreter of Shakespeare is quite distinct from the kind of performance in which the Mac-Ivors engage; his role-playing, with its frequent changes of dress and even name, is the private acting out of *Bildung* rather than the public drama with many characters that Fergus is attempting to mount.

Edward's vulnerability at Glennaquoich is the product of romantic susceptibility, but also of political naïveté. Amid all this histrionic, and historic, activity, he does not know where he stands. Deprived of the information supplied by the narrator to the reader at the outset of the episode – a full account of Fergus's education at the French court, his father's involvement in the '15, and the political attitudes fostered by this background – Edward cannot process what he sees other than by disconnected analogies with his existing collection of 'imagery and emblems.' But even when due allowance has been made for Edward's situation, there remains a certain wilfulness about his deportment at this point. What he did not know about the Baron Bradwardine's politics had seemed unlikely to be harmful, though his failure to take account of the way his extended stay in a Jacobite family would strike his fellow officers was, in fact, damaging. His refusal to take full political account of what he observed on the journey and at Glennaquoich itself is, however, more culpable. The visit to Donald Bean Lean, the conversations with Evan Dhu, the sight of Fergus's armed followers, all tell their tale, and the point should not need to be driven home further by his close encounter with death at the great hunt, which is actually a revolution in the making.

By registering the paradoxical combination of poverty and extravagance at Glennaquoich – the tension between the sophistication of Fergus and Flora and the simplified outlines of the roles they adopt – but at the same time failing to organize his impressions into a form approximating to explanation, Edward is surrendering to a deliberate retreat from understanding much more dangerous than anything he had done or failed to do at Tully Veolan. The distance between narrator and protagonist is here at its most extreme, and the reader, while susceptible to the contagion of Edward's enthusiastic response to Flora as enchantress, retains a certain detachment. If Edward is to progress beyond the position of picturesque tourist, become actor as well as observer, he has to find some means of liberating himself from the visual intoxication to which he surrenders at Glennaquoich. The first step in that process requires that he begin to look at himself as well as at what lies in front of his eyes, and it is, indeed, with the impulse to 'clear his own character' (II, 87–8) foremost in his mind that he leaves Glennaquoich.

The interrogation by Major Melville that follows his arrest provides Edward with a harrowing exposure to that special privilege to which he has previously had very little access, that of seeing ourselves as others see us. It is not in the least remarkable that the consequence of this ordeal should be that total disorientation which makes of his second stay at Tully Veolan a dark mystery, nor that he should then surrender completely to the graciousness of the Chevalier at Holyrood. Suspected of treason, handed over to Gifted Gilfillan, rescued but again imprisoned by strangers in a place he does not recognize, it is no surprise that Edward should respond so positively to the prince who acknowledges him with such ready comprehensiveness: 'No master of ceremonies is necessary to present a Waverley to a Stuart' (II, 258).

But despite the attempt to take complete possession of Edward's heart, mind, and body symbolized in the prince's gift of his own sword and in Fergus's provision of Highland dress, a residual sense of his own identity and integrity – of the fact that he has a character to clear – continues to make itself felt. Reflection now accompanies observation, and the wavering that characterizes Edward's behaviour during the Edinburgh episodes and on the march into England is less the caprice of which he accuses himself than the hesitation contingent on an increased awareness of alternative perspectives.

Seen from afar, the Highlanders can supply a 'picturesque wildness' (II, 325) to the Chevalier's army as it moves south from Edinburgh, but 'A nearer view … rather diminished the effect' (II, 326): most of the troops at whose side Edward must fight are 'indifferently accoutred, and worse armed, half naked, stinted in growth, and miserable in aspect' (II, 327). As Edward enters the picture on this occasion, he can hear as well as see. He listens as the dying Houghton urges him 'not to fight with these wild petticoat-men against old England' (II, 341). No longer observer but observed, he recognizes his own false position. He sees 'the standard of the troop he had formerly commanded,' hears 'the well-known word given in the English dialect' by his former commander Colonel Gardiner, and then looks round him at 'the wild dress and appearance of his Highland associates' and hears 'their whispers in an uncouth and unknown language' (II, 351). His sudden sense of alienation makes him see himself as 'traitor' and 'renegade' (II, 352), and his self-revulsion is made complete as he watches, frozen by parricidal guilt, as Callum Beg takes aim at Colonel Gardiner. Having been too easily satisfied by the image of himself projected in his own youthful fantasies and reflected back in the admiration of his devoted family or the flatteries of Fergus, Edward has now no clear self-image to set against this extreme vision of himself as traitor and parricide. Readjustment of perspective must begin with compensatory action. It is crucial to Edward's survival that he rescue another father figure, Colonel Talbot, before being compelled to watch as Colonel Gardiner is mowed down by a Highlander's scythe.

The debates with Colonel Talbot that follow expand Edward's consciousness of the full implications of his own conduct, but they do not involve a simple exchange of perspective, the complete abandonment of his own vision in favour of Talbot's. Edward has travelled much further into the country of romance than his new adviser, and he can only come fully to terms with the meaning of that journey after a period of isolation and extended meditation, supplemented by a retracing of some of the crucial stages of the journey itself.

Although the episode of Edward's pastoral withdrawal in the Lake District is brief and its message ostensibly very simple, it reverberates with so many other elements in the novel that its effect is actually very complex. It offers an allusive recapitulation of much that has gone before and a preparation for the final stages to come. The play with the names Cicely and Edward takes us right back to Edward's infatuation with Miss Stubbs, the earliest phase of his romanticism, while the generosity of those who protect him calls to mind the many very different sheltering episodes in the novel – and throws into relief the exposed condition of Fergus, for whom no protection is possible. The enforced stay at the Ullswater farm falls into place beside those other occasions when Edward is afforded the opportunity to reconsider his own situation – after the Highland hunt, during his arrest by Major Melville, in Janet's hut. The news-from-England device, first used at Glennaquoich, recurs here, but in refusing to surrender to feelings of guilt about his father's death Edward demonstrates a much firmer sense of his own relationships and responsibilities. In passing for a young theological student Edward is on the surface simply adopting one of the many temporary identities he takes on in the course of the attempt to clear his own character, but by calling into the narrative again the memory of the dead young poet, Davie Gellatley's brother, this particular disguise evokes the dreaming boy in his tragic version and serves as a kind of final exorcism before Edward himself moves into the concluding stages of his own journey to survival.

Edward does not turn away during this sequence from the anguish of what he has experienced: he revisits the battlefield in search of Fergus's body and pays eloquent tribute to the friend he believes dead; he goes over in his mind the advice of Colonel Talbot, recalls the death of Colonel Gardiner, and imagines the desolation of Flora and Rose. In the course of meditating on these things 'he acquire[s] a more complete mastery of a spirit tamed by adversity, than his former experience had given him,' and feels himself 'entitled to say firmly, though perhaps with a sigh, that the romance of his life was ended, and that its real history had now commenced' (III, 179–80). This is what the narrator would have held out as the best hope for Edward at the outset of the narrative – that he should learn to put romance behind him, feeling only a gentle melancholy for its loss.[10] Yet this coincidence of Edward's position with the narrator's does not constitute a termination point in the novel, but rather a moment of exchange in which Edward begins to move beyond the narrator. He cannot simply awake from his long dream as though nothing had really happened. Experiences still lie in front of him that are more like nightmare than dream: the report of Culloden, the wanton destruction of Tully Veolan, the executions at Carlisle, the final meeting with Flora – these events belong to public history, not private fantasy, and so cannot be dismissed. As Edward travels in the coach southwards with Mrs Nosebag, the narrative method recalls that of the opening chapters, but it is impossible for the reader to accept such a deflationary return as an appropriate ending to Edward's journey into the country of history and of romance. The sheer fact that he must immediately turn around and travel north again ought to preclude too simple a reading of his assertion about the end of romance and the beginning of real history.

Edward's real history is not so much a matter of events as of interpretation. In so far as he is now capable of analysis as well as observation, comprehension as well as apprehension, he can be a better interpreter than the narrator. Throughout the main part of the narrative, the juxtaposition of the perspectives of narrator and protagonist have provided both an increased depth of field in the novel's portrayal of regional distinctions and historical circumstances and an opportunity to measure

Edward's progress in terms of the discrepancies between the two angles of vision. The divergence between Edward's limited, naïve, contemporary perspective and the informed, mature, historically privileged vision of the narrator gives to the narrative its effectual duality. But the narrator is not set up as an ideal that Edward would do well to emulate in every respect. In the ultimate range of his sympathies Edward is more generous than the narrator, and willing to take more risks; he is prepared to acknowledge his feelings without benefit of protective irony; he is ready to go to the end of the dark journey.

Edward, in fact, ultimately moves beyond his narrator-mentor, just as he moves beyond Colonel Gardiner, Major Melville, and Colonel Talbot. It is not just his responsiveness to romance excitement but his capacity for love, for giving himself away – in the deep bond with Fergus, in his unselfconscious affection for the Baron Bradwardine – that distinguishes him from those ostensibly much wiser than himself: the narrator would probably have been somewhat embarrassed to have the Baron for a father-in-law, and he would never have commissioned that portrait of Edward and Fergus in Highland dress. Edward comes in the end to a clear-sighted recognition of the gulf that separates him from the Mac-Ivors. But by his imaginative sympathy with what is fine in his lost friends he can eventually become a son of Ivor in his own way. The fact that this is imaged in the comic resolution by the Highland portrait does not undermine what has taken place but simply confirms it in a different mode. The mixing of modes in *Waverley* is usually confirmatory rather than ironic in effect. The novel begins with a comic and gently satirical presentation of youthful romanticism and posits at various moments, for the sake of its fictional argument, a simplified opposition between realism and romance. The eventual outcome of that argument involves not the rejection of youthful romanticism, but rather its transcendence.[11]

The demand for complex vision expressed through the insistence on alternating and changing perspectives falls on the reader as well as on the protagonist, and is most easily formulated in the currently somewhat overworked critical metaphors of reading and deciphering. Interpretation, however, demands action of Edward rather than simply a critical response. Whereas the reader can observe the way in which Edward's story contrasts with Fergus's, and can see it as shadowing forth the more fortunate patterns of later eighteenth-century British history as against

Fergus's adumbration of the tragic plot of Jacobite failure, Edward must himself make choices and adopt lines of action whose outcome he cannot foresee. That his choices are somewhat limited – as discussions of his role as passive hero have so frequently demonstrated[12] – should not distract us from their significance. In a text that employs the romance method of signification through design, gesture has its own value. The poignantly evoked return to the shattered Tully Veoland and reunion with the Baron Bradwardine, and the later journey to Carlisle–among the most powerful emotional moments in the novel – mark off Edward as educated both by romance and by history.

If this novel were simply the fairly straightforward dramatization of an awakening from youthful quixotism for which it is sometimes taken, then the final return journey to Scotland would hardly be necessary. Colonel Talbot's good offices would presumably have ensured reunion with Rose had Edward persisted in his strange preference for a Scottish bride. To read the novel as controlled by a simple ironic strategy, with the high points of delusion represented by the waterfall proposal scene and the moment of commitment to Charles Edward, and to see the completion of the pattern in disillusionment and awakening signalled by the affirmation that real history has taken over from romance – this is to truncate the design and miss its essential point. Proponents of such an interpretation give little weight to the journey to London and back north again to Scotland.[13] But Edward cannot rest in his homecoming to the familiar English world of the opening; he must take on yet other identities and go back for those final meetings with Fergus on the way to the scaffold and Flora on her way to a living death in a convent. History demands its price of Fergus Mac-Ivor, and Edward, though powerless to save him, can yet acknowledge their kinship in that parting visit.

It is imagination as a mode of vision which impels Edward Waverley, even while admiring Colonel Talbot and wishing to emulate him, to reject Talbot's narrowness of sympathy. The colonel is an interesting figure, not least because he is so clearly set in direct opposition to Flora Mac-Ivor. Flora's active romanticism, deliberately generated and constantly heightened, depends for its existence on a self-imposed quixotism which refuses to recognize probabilities and consequences until it is too late. Colonel Talbot speaks with the voice of a very down-to-earth but narrow reasonableness; he rejects everything Scottish or connected with the feudal past, sets his very unglamorous prince, the Duke of Cumberland, against the chivalric charms of Prince Charles, and puts himself in opposition to everything the Mac-Ivors represent. His refusal to see any good in these things comes not from distortion of the quixotic kind but from restriction of vision, the inability to respond imaginatively to what is alien. In the debate between romance and realism Colonel Talbot, for all his capacity for sentimental domestic affection, stands squarely for realism. And although it is to Colonel Talbot that Waverley owes his pardon and many of the practical arrangements involved in the restoration of Tully Veolan, the novel makes clear that something more is required than a switch of allegiance from Mac-Ivor to Talbot or a bringing of Edward's vision into line with Talbot's.

Waverley as completed in fact insists that, although in youth the power of imagination may find its outlet in dream, narcissistic fantasy, and escapism, in the mature individual it can express itself in different ways, can be indeed the very means of achieving that release from the prison of the self into full sympathy with other men which is the mark of maturity.[14] Scott could not dramatize this process fully within the conventions of verse narratives, in which the characters are fixed, the time-scales limited, the action a continuous series of high points with no free scenes. But given the more extended temporal and geographical frames of the novel, the introduction of the domestic as well as the heroic side of life, and above all the shift from a detached to an engaged form of presentation – so that the narrative does not simply look at the characters and meditate upon their situation but sees with them and dramatizes their lives in process – he could explore the tension between imagination and reason in a much more complex fashion. He had no philosophic interest in the problem and was incapable of any Coleridgean formulation of it, but in the movement from verse romance to prose fiction as embodied in the completed *Waverley* of 1814, Scott shifts from an initial romanticism of a very eighteenth-century kind to that much more nineteenth-century variety which perceives the imagination not as the enemy of knowledge and wisdom but as their very source.

4

Guy Mannering:
A Tale of Private Life

When *Waverley* was announced for publication in 1810, the year in which Scott first thought of completing it, no mention was made of the author's name. But when the book itself appeared anonymously in 1814, something altogether more deliberate and self-conscious was involved than the adoption of a common practice with respect to works of fiction. A remarkable instance of the exploitation of anonymity had already occurred in Scott's career early the previous year, when, very shortly after the publication of *Rokeby*, he hurried into print *The Bridal of Triermain* in the hope of deceiving the world in general, and Francis Jeffrey in particular, into believing that the anonymous poem was by some imitator, perhaps even Scott's close friend Erskine. Jeffrey failed in fact to rise to the bait, and neither he nor anyone else reviewed either *Triermain* or *Rokeby* itself in the pages of the *Edinburgh Review*, but that did not prevent Scott from finding the game-playing both enjoyable and instructive, so much so that in 1814 he prepared to publish a fresh combination of the acknowledged and the unacknowledged – the great Swift edition, on which he had been labouring since 1808, and the anonymous venture into prose fiction. The mechanics of anonymity had all been rehearsed during the production of *Triermain*, right down to the copying out of the manuscript by someone other than Scott himself, and nothing could be simpler than to put the same process into operation. For those of Scott's friends who were let into the *Waverley* secret, the only question was that of how long the jesting mystery would be kept up.

   Morritt certainly assumed that it would be only a short time before Scott admitted that he had written *Waverley*. In a letter of 14 July 1814, a week after the novel's appearance, he commented on the transparency of the authorial mask: 'You wear your disguises something after the manner of our friend Bottom the weaver.'[1] And when he had finished reading the entire novel, Morrit urged Scott to acknowledge authorship. He granted the obvious reason for the original decision – 'You could be supposed at first, from diffidence of success in a style of composition hitherto untried, to be unwilling to stake the fame you had acquired in a different branch of literature, on the event of a novel' – but went on to list the strong arguments for abandoning the disguise: first, 'the volumes we have just read would add to the fame of the best poet in our language'; secondly, Scott's name would procure readers who would not normally read novels; thirdly, Scott was commonly spoken of as the author in London as well as in Edinburgh; fourthly, further denial would be 'rather prejudicial than advantageous to your fame'[2] – meaning perhaps that it would look like affectation. In his reply of 28 July, Scott declared, 'I shall not plead guilty,' and reported that Jeffrey was reputed to be the author in some Edinburgh circles, a joke he knew Morritt would share. His profession now became the major excuse: 'In truth I am not sure it would be considered quite decorous for me as a Clerk of Session to write novels[.] Judges being monks clerks are a sort of lay-brethren from whom some solemnity of walk & conduct may be expected' (*L* III, 479).[3] The humorous note here suggests an element of evasion, but he returned to the more serious implications of Morritt's arguments in a postscript:

I dont see how my silence can be considerd as imposing on the public – if I gave my name to a book without writing it, unquestionably that would be a trick. But unless in the case of his averring facts which he may be calld upon to defend or justify I think an author may use his own discretion in giving or withholding his name. Harry Mackenzie never put his name in a title page till the last edition of his works and Swift only ownd one out of his thousand and one publications.

In point of emolument every body knows that I sacrifice much money by withholding my name and what should I gain by it that any human being has a right to consider as an unfair advantage – in fact only the freedom of writing trifles with less personal responsibility and perhaps more frequently than I otherwise might do. (*L* III, 480–1)

Clearly Morritt's suggestion that anonymity might be 'rather prejudicial than advantageous to your fame' had touched but failed to sway him. Morritt conceded defeat at this point – 'Your reasons for not owning *Waverley* are indeed cogent'[4] – and henceforth the topic became the subject of shared jokes rather than of argument between the two friends, Morritt perhaps sensing that behind the array of reasons and palliations lay something that Scott was not prepared to admit or even put into words.

In the years following the publication of *Waverley* Scott defended himself with considerable energy and verve against those who attempted to penetrate his disguise. His family and closest friends of course knew the secret from the first, and others were initiated later, but some friends and acquaintances remained in 'official' ignorance, and with them – for example, in his correspondence with Lady Abercorn – Scott was able to savour the fun of discussing the attributes and achievement of the mysterious Author as a mere fascinated onlooker. The teasing was given public projection and status in the early autumn of 1814 when Scott added to the third edition of *Waverley* a Preface in which 'the Author' left it

to the candour of the public to chuse among the many circumstances peculiar to different situations in life, such as may induce him to suppress his name on the present occasion. He may be a writer new to publication, and unwilling to avow a character to which he is unaccustomed; or he may be a hackneyed author, who is ashamed of too frequent appearance, and employs this mystery, as the heroine of the old comedy used her mask, to attract the attention of those to whom her face had become too familiar. He may be a man of grave profession, to whom the reputation of being a novel-writer may be prejudicial; or he may be a man of fashion, in whom writing of any kind might appear pedantic. He may be too young to assume the character of an author, or so old as makes it advisable to lay it aside.[5]

The riddle here propounded binds the Author and his audience together in the enactment of their separate but mutually dependent roles in the great game.

While Scott never had any intention of taking his secret beyond the grave like some Junius among novelists[6] – the manuscripts were preserved and his authorship could be instantly demonstrated – there is no indication that he contemplated a voluntary confession prior to the financial crash of 1826. After that disaster he commented on the anonymity issue on a number of occasions, most notably in the Introduction to *Chronicles of the Canongate* in 1827 and in the General Preface to the *magnum opus* edition in 1829. These retrospective accounts added little to the arguments and explanations invoked in the 1814 debate with Morritt, although he did now put greater stress on personal whim: 'it would be difficult to give any other reply,' he told his readers in 1827, 'save that of Corporal Nym – It was the humour or caprice of the time.'[7] Two years later the precedent cited was still Shakespearian but no longer comic: 'I can render little better reason for choosing to remain anonymous, than by saying with Shylock, that such was my humour' (*WN* I, xxii). By confessing to a lack of conscious motive and taking refuge in a formulaic allusion Scott absolved himself from exploring the deeper reasons for his actions. As he had written to James Ballantyne in 1814 apropos of the motivation of one of the characters in *The Lord of the Isles*, 'the ostensible reasons which we produce to ourselves as to others are very different from those which really influence our conduct' (*L* III, 541).

It was, of course, with the publication of his second novel, *Guy Mannering*, that the phrase 'By the Author of "Waverley"' first appeared on one of Scott's title-pages, and it was the writing of *Guy Mannering* that can properly be said to have made him a novelist: one novel might be deemed a mere sport, but a second signalled that at the age of forty-three he had embarked on yet another career. By the time the new book was published on 24 February 1815, moreover, Scott had acknowledged to himself and the few friends who were privy to the secret of the Author of *Waverley* that he saw his future as that of a novelist rather than a poet. It was a transition about which both too much and too little is known. The external justifications for the change are almost too numerous – the amazing success of *Waverley*, the emergence of Byron, the disappointing initial sales of *The Lord of the Isles*, the speed and ease with which he found he could write fiction, the availability of materials for the new novel. But there is no direct statement by Scott himself as to what the change meant in personal terms. As always, he preferred to submit himself to the flow of events rather than analyze his own motivation. It is therefore not easy to arrive at a coherent explanation that takes cognizance of all the surrounding circumstances, recognizes the underlying factors that made Scott ready for the change, and accounts satisfactorily for his determination to maintain the barrier of anonymity between his new career and its predecessors. And since the second novel differed in deliberate and significant ways from the first, it becomes necessary to ask just what kind of dialogue Scott was setting up between the various productions of the Author of *Waverley*.

When, on 29 July 1814, just three weeks after the publication of *Waverley*, Scott left Edinburgh on the Lighthouse Commissioners' yacht for a voyage round the Northern Isles, he was in pursuit of additional material for his new poem, *The Lord of the Isles*: 'I am stupid at drawing ideal scenery, and waited until I should have a good opportunity to visit or rather re-visit the Hebrides' (*L* III, 501). Originally planned before *Rokeby*, some early sections of the poem had already been composed, but most of the writing would have to await his return from the north. There was, however, no question of its being postponed in favour of a second novel – in the summer of 1814, the success of *Waverley* notwithstanding, poetry still had primacy over fiction. Six months later the situation was quite different. On 19 January 1815, ten days after the publication of *The Lord of the Isles*, Scott wrote to Morritt, 'It closes my poetic labours upon an extended scale [but] that I dare say I shall always be dabbling in rhime untill the Solve jam senescentem' (*L* IV, 12).

The simplest explanation of this shift in priorities is to assign it to disappointment with the reception of his poem and to attribute the starkness of the statement to the blow's being so recent. Lockhart insists that Scott had no sense of 'whether he had written well or ill'[8] until he had the verdict of the booksellers and the public. But remarks made by Scott during the composition of *The Lord of the Isles* suggest not only that he was finding the task much more burdensome than the writing of his earlier poems but that he was correspondingly defensive and doubtful about the likely results. Although always deprecatory about his own writing, Scott had been happy to show his friends sections of *Marmion* or *The Lady of the Lake* while they were being written and to provide cheerful reports on their progress. He had apparently recited some of the early verses of *The Lord of the Isles* to Morritt at the time of their composition, well before the northern journey of 1814.[9] But when engaged in writing the major part of the poem during the autumn of 1814, he sends no samples of his work in progress; his customary self-irony is much heavier, and the imagery of oppression and labour becomes hard to ignore. He has 'fallen under the tyrannical dominion of a certain Lord of the Isles,' he tells Terry on 19 November 1814, and can report that 'The *peine forte et dure* is ... nothing in comparison to being obliged to grind verses; and so devilish repulsive is my disposition, that I can never put my wheel into constant and regular motion, till Ballantyne's devil claps in his proofs' (*L* III, 514). Writing to Morritt a day or so later he uses much the same language about his 'literary tormentor ... a certain Lord of the Isles,' speaks of 'bothering some tales of him I have had long by me into a sort of romance,' and stresses his deliberate exploitation of exotic materials to heighten the effect on the Sassenachs: 'it is Scottified up to the teeth ... in a word the real highland fling' (*L* IV, 18–19).

It is hard to resist the conclusion that throughout the writing of *The Lord of the Isles* Scott felt he was completing a necessary task rather than giving free rein to his poetic gifts and narrative powers. As he struggled to write against the grain, out of duty rather than desire, a phase of his own existence was coming to an end. In October he had committed himself to Longman for a novel, and the prospect of this new undertaking, together with the sense of urgency produced by the financial crisis which he was currently experiencing in company with Constable and the Ballantynes, made the poem seem a kind of incubus of which he must rid himself before he could move forward. It was with genuine relief that he announced to Morritt on 19 January 1815: 'I am clear of the Lord of the Isles' (*L* IV, 12).

Even as he had set himself to work on 17 September 1814, Scott's note to Constable had been expressive of determination rather than of enthusiasm: 'I have made up my mind to do my best upon it' (*L* III, 499–500). In this letter, as so often in his remarks on the poem, his thoughts turn to the recent death of the Duchess of Buccleuch, the 'lovely chieftainess' who had presided over his first great triumph, *The Lay of the Last Minstrel*, and who was to have received the dedication of the new poem; he told Richard Polwhele, 'I thought to have inscribed to her the work at which I was labouring; but, alas! it will now only renew my sincere and peculiar share in a grief which is almost national' (*L* III, 502). It would be going too far to suggest that the news of her death, received when the Commissioners' yacht came into port in northern Ireland at the beginning of September, made all the difference to Scott's feeling about his own career as a poet, but there is no doubt that he was profoundly shocked and grieved. Many of his favourite delights suddenly seemed quite pointless: 'I am much out of love with vanity at this moment.'[10] He declined to go ashore to see the Giant's Causeway and fretted over the pain that would now be caused by the arrival of the humorous postscript to the verse epistle he had sent off to the Duke and Duchess from Shetland.

The conception of himself as the Duchess's minstrel had been at one level just a charming fancy, an available metaphor to deploy occasionally in their ordinary correspondence or at the opening of his verse epistle from Shetland:

> Health to the Chieftain from his clansman true
> From her true minstrel Health to fair Buccleuch   (L III, 481).

But it had also become inextricably involved in Scott's conception of himself as poet – a trope that allowed him to take his poetry both lightly and seriously by assimilating it to a traditional order quite different from the world of commercial publishing. His patroness lost, the new poem was reduced, in the words of its closing tribute, to 'one poor garland, twined to deck thy hair,' that must now be 'hung upon thy hearse, to droop and wither there!'[11] The two stanzas to the Duchess that conclude the poem form a deliberate farewell to his muse, a final lay from the minstrel.

Between the composition of these stanzas late in December 1814[12] and that letter to Morritt of 19 January 1815 announcing the end of his career as a poet, only three weeks or so elapse. Yet the tone of the letter is far from elegiac. The poem has been completed and published, the disappointment at its reception encountered, but what is far more important is that two volumes of the new novel are written and in print. There is no talk of grinding or torment with the novel as there had been with the poem. The miraculous speed of its composition must have seemed to Scott yet another of those fortunate outcomes that ratified courses of action taken but never analysed. 'Things must be as they are' – this was the kernel of Scott's philosophy of life. It was a stance based not on stoic endurance, nor on the histrionic heroism associated with the more extreme forms of making a virtue of necessity, but on the deliberate embracing of his own fate by taking up the hand he had been dealt and playing it for all he was worth.[13] Acquiescence was transformed into action as he freely took on the role he might not freely have chosen. It was essential to Scott's personal equanimity that he avoid recrimination and regret and that he engage in the kind of self-accounting that is expressed in the terms of personal narration rather than in those of introspective reflection.

As he entered on this fresh phase of his existence, he immediately began to lay out for Morritt the shape of his new career. The novel in progress was distinguished not so much from the poem published ten days previously as from the novel of six months earlier:

I want to shake myself free of Waverley and accordingly have made a considerable exertion to finish an odd little tale within such time as will mistify the public I trust unless they suppose me to be Briareus. Two volumes are already printed and the only persons in my confidence W. Erskine and Ballantyne are of opinion it is much more interesting than Waverley. It is a tale of private life and only varied by the perilous exploits of smugglers and excisemen. (*L* IV, 12–13)

This is the only comment of Scott's we have on *Guy Mannering* during its composition, and every phrase is worth weighing. There is the usual humorous irony at his own expense in the exaggeration of 'perilous exploits,' but the remarks are clearly those of someone pleased with, and confident in, what he is doing. The refusal to be type-cast by *Waverley* is strongly expressed, amounting to rather more than the usual determination to do something different characteristic of novelists embarking on a second book: identifying the element of public history as *Waverley*'s hallmark, he now determines to try his hand at 'a tale of private life.' The Briareus reference clearly pertains to the poetry as well as the fiction: the six-month gap allowed a feasible amount of time for a fluent novelist to produce a second work, and it was only if Walter Scott the author of *The Lord of the Isles* was also the author of the novels that the issue of hundred-headedness really arose. Yet Scott's invocation of such an allusion anticipates, consciously or otherwise, that passion for multiplicity and variety which was to be unleashed by his amazing success in the new literary form.

Scott's early career had been remarkable for the range of his achievements as editor, biographer, and poet, but in the half-dozen years that followed the publication of *Waverley* he seems to have been seized by an almost uncontrollable impulse to try new things, make fresh gambles for increasingly higher stakes. As he emerged into his new identity he was throwing off the restrictions associated with his previous avatars as lawyer and poet. Anonymity was an essential requirement for this new enterprise, an inexhaustible game in which he could exploit all the facets of his own personality, experience, reading, and fantasies, while engaging directly with his readers through the challenge thrown out to them to pin down the author, pick out the characteristics that would tie him to some known individual beyond the boundaries of his fiction. The full realization of these possibilities did not, of course, come as early as the composition of *Guy Mannering*, but by December 1814 Scott had allowed Ballantyne to insert in the *Scots Magazine* an advertisement that brought poet and novelist into tantalizing juxtaposition. The first item in the 'Literary Intelligence' section informed readers that 'Mr Scott's poem of the "Lord of the Isles," will appear very early in January.' The fourth item noted: 'The author of Waverley is about to amuse the public with a new novel, in three volumes, entitled "Guy Mannering."'[14] At first it had seemed to Scott that simultaneous production of both poetry and fiction was necessary to the anonymity game initiated by *Waverley*, but he quickly recognized that his fame as a poet could still be kept in play even after he had abandoned any thought of further major poems. By keeping Scott the poet distinct from the Author of *Waverley* he transformed his poetry into a separate literary corpus, ostensibly discontinuous with the new prose texts but remaining none the less available for purposes of contrast or allusion.

Guy Mannering; or, The Astrologer is indeed 'a tale of private life.' Though it opens some sixty years since, at the end of the 1750s, and has its main action at the beginning of the 1780s, it makes hardly any reference to public history. Certain Indian battles are mentioned to give colour to the account of Colonel Mannering's military career; a passing allusion is made to the wearisome nature of the war with the American colonies, but its pages include no figure like Charles Edward, nor any historical event such as Prestonpans. It is the exclusion of this kind of material that Scott clearly has in mind when he speaks of shaking himself free of *Waverley*. But this does not mean that the concerns and methods of his second novel differ at every point from those of his first. The setting has moved from the fringes of the eastern Highlands to the southwest Borders, but it is still Scottish; there is a continued emphasis on regional mores; the perspective of the travelling Englishman is once more brought into play; and for all the absence of public history there is an underlying emphasis on the workings of time. The regional distinctiveness of Dinmont's Liddesdale and Pleydell's Edinburgh are fully recognized by Bertram and Mannering, as is the specialness with which the pastoral and legal mysteries practised through centuries of evolving tradition and ritual have endowed those self-contained worlds. But the narrative insistence on the changes that have taken place both in the Borders and in the capital in the intervening years adds a further dimension to their portrayal. *Mannering*, like *Waverley*, concerns itself not only to present the life of earlier times and distant places but to invoke the dimension implicit in the connective 'since' – the process by which then becomes now. It represents, in fact, a deliberate attempt to extend the possibilities of regional and historical fiction as adumbrated in that first novel.

The most striking structural features of the new novel are its use of two heroes and of a two-generation plot with a sixteen-year time-gap at its centre. The doubling of the hero and the break in continuity are accompanied by an echoing relationship between apparently disparate situations and characters: Mannering is counterpointed against both the Bertrams, father and son; Mannering's return to Ellangowan is set off against both his own first visit twenty years earlier and the entry of Harry Bertram into the lost place of his childhood; Pleydell's inconclusive first investigation of the murder and abduction prepares the way for his second successful attempt to unravel the mystery; the actual and potential father figures are mutually defining; Mannering as astrologer is linked to Meg as sibyl; Glossin the bad lawyer contrasts with Pleydell the good; and so it goes on. It becomes quite natural, and indeed necessary, to read minor as well as major features of the novel in terms of the answering echoes, contrasts, and variations to be found elsewhere in the text.

As in many Scott novels, the motif of the journey connects episodes together, while the traveller himself also functions as perspective device. But *Guy Mannering* is about the condition of strangeness, isolation, and exile in a more fundamental way: the introductory sequence in which the young Mannering attempts to find his way along difficult roads in the twilight, with little assistance from a suspicious peasantry, reverberates throughout the remainder of the text. This opening may seem like some kind of false start once attention has shifted to young Harry Bertram[15] and his fate: here, as so often, Scott was his own worst critical enemy with his open admission, in the Introduction he attached to the novel in 1829, of his shift of interest away from the astrologer plot. But the figure of Mannering as the wanderer for whom no simple resolution or home-coming to happiness is possible continues to haunt the narrative and modify its final effect, remaining unexorcised by the story of Harry Bertram, the lost heir re-established in his proper place.

In Bertram's case the wanderer motif is easily translatable into the pattern of the quest. He has, after all, returned from India in pursuit of his mistress. But he is also engaged in a second and more important quest about which he initially remains unclear; its movement is not forward in search of the beloved but backward in search of his own origins and identity. The physical goal of both journeys is Scotland, and only by confirming that Ellangowan is his rightful place can he in fact be sure of securing the lady. The dynamic of the novel inheres, in fact, not in whether Bertram will win Julia Mannering but in how his identity will be established. It thus requires the combination of legal process, personal proving by ordeal, and an elaborate action arranged by Meg Merrilies, one of the two seers present at his birth, with the assistance of (among others) Guy Mannering, the second seer. In the process the bad father of the Indian duel is transformed into the good father whose wealth will make possible restoration of the inherited lands, though it is in keeping with Mannering's equivocal attitude to his own prophetic powers that he is off-stage in the climactic scenes of this sequence.

Before the final elements in a whole series of recognitions fall into place, Bertram's worth has been tested by the 'adventure' of the combat on Bewcastle Moss and his subsequent stay in the Dinmont world of Charlieshope. The episode at the Liddesdale farm is both conventional pastoral interlude and vivid portrayal of regional life in all its physical detail. It requires, however, to be read in conjunction with the false pastoral of the Lake District interlude that precedes it, an episode which permits Bertram to meditate a good deal on his own situation but advances him very little either in his attempt to gain possession of his mistress or in his desire to find his own proper place in the world.

The Lake District is presented first of all in the extracts from Julia Mannering's correspondence with her bosom friend Matilda Marchmont. Julia is humorously aware of the extravagance of her own enthusiasm for romantic scenery but nevertheless determined to indulge it to the fullest extent as appropriate backdrop to the savouring of her love affair with Bertram. That Matilda's side of the correspondence remains unrepresented is no accident; what Julia requires is not so much a friend as an audience. She is making her own life into a fiction, and in choosing the epistolary mode for her novelizing she places a premium on sentiment and sensation. Like Waverley's all her perceptions are coloured by art or literature: the mountains and lakes are seen through the eyes of Claude or Salvator Rosa; the balcony scene with her lover is preceded by a reading of Lorenzo and Jessica's moonlight scene from *The Merchant of Venice*.

The making of fictions is here an inherited trait. Mrs Mannering was 'a misjudging mother, who called her husband in her heart a tyrant until she feared him as such, and read romances until she became so enamoured of the complicated intrigues which they contain, as to assume the management of a little family novel of her own, and constitute her daughter, a girl of sixteen, the principal heroine.'[16] Colonel Mannering has fashioned a much darker drama in which he casts himself in the role of Othello. Whether as novel hero or as Cassio, Bertram's enlistment in these family fictions has not been entirely voluntary, and though he is willing to enter into Julia's fantasies to the extent of himself suggesting the romantic signal of the Hindu tune, he is fully aware of the extent to which her literary imaginings depart from reality: 'if she thinks of love and a farm, it is a *ferme ornée*, such as is only to be found in poetic description, or in the park of a gentleman of twelve thousand a-year' (I, 334). In the Lake District, however, his only defence against inclusion in other people's cast-lists is the creation of a more powerful fiction of his own.

Like Julia – or Mannering himself in his correspondence with Mervyn – Bertram chooses the genre of letters-to-a-friend. Though less elaborately artificial than Julia's, his correspondence is by no means free from its own kind of posturing – as Scott signals by the employment of literary stereotypes somewhat closer to those of 1815 than of 1780. Though some of Bertram's reactions to the scenery are perfectly appropriate to the picturesque conventions of the earlier decade, he is faintly Byronic in his talk about the estrangement of foreigners and the sensations of exile and quite Wordsworthian when it comes to mountains and streams: 'a blue hill to me is as a friend, and a roaring torrent like the sound of a domestic song that has soothed my infancy' (I, 337). These responses, though educated, are by no means entirely second-hand, deriving in part from Bertram's haunting memories of the country of his childhood. But the translation of memory into metaphor that characterizes his Lake District meditations in no way assists him to re-establish connection between past and present. Indeed, he seems almost to luxuriate in the impossibility of such an endeavour, delighting in his deracinated condition and allowing the pursuit of Julia to distract him from his more urgent quest. Once Bertram actually lands on the shores of Ellangowan, Scott, with characteristic artistic panache, will transform the metaphor of 'domestic song' into actuality, as the young man hears the girl singing the half-remembered verses he has been unable to complete for himself. But in the suspension of the Lake District Bertram runs the grave risk of conforming to one version of the stereotype Mervyn irritatedly describes: 'walking gentlemen of all descriptions, poets, players, painters, musicians, who come to rave, and recite, and madden, about this picturesque land of ours' (I, 263). Since he cannot draw like his friend Dudley – or like Mannering, who both draws and writes poetry – Bertram's only outlet, apart from his performances on the flageolet, is through the self-dramatization of his letters.

The description of Bertram's departure from the lakes brings the air of actual rather than literary mountains into the novel. The injunction, 'Let the reader conceive to himself a clear frosty November morning, the scene an open heath' (II, 3), signals a new relationship between the reader and the action. In what follows the reader is at Bertram's side, sharing his sensations and experiences. The mountains are no longer generalized scenery; they have names – Skiddaw and Saddleback – and a meditation on the Roman Wall and the fall of ancient civilizations quickly gives way to the promptings of hunger that lead Bertram into a 'small public-house' (II, 8). He has adopted the simplest of dress and carries the minimum of belongings; the only tribute to his literary tastes is surely permissible, a 'volume of Shakespeare in one pocket' (II, 4). He whistles as he walks along, his scampering terrier Wasp at his side, and he has 'a kind greeting or a good-humoured jest' for everyone he meets, eliciting in response: 'That's a kind heart, God bless un' (II, 5).

The contrast between this and the twilight journey of Mannering that opens the novel could not be more marked – though Bertram has in fact ahead of him an even more dangerous journey over the very terrain traversed by Mannering on that occasion. What at first seems paramount in this particular transition is the emergence of the young hero from a narcissistic contemplativeness into a more active encounter with nature. But at the very moment when Bertram's need to free himself from the habit of registering his experience in literary terms is being stressed, the text demands that the reader bring to the interpretation of the episode a keen awareness of literary convention. Bertram's change of dress and scene, his association with simpler folk, the recognition he receives – all signal an entry into a pastoral world, the initiation of the ritual of 'proving' traditionally dramatized in the pastoral interlude. In making the point it is hard not to sound crude and schematic where Scott is deft and undoctrinaire. From the moment when Bertram first encounters Dandy Dinmont at Mumps Ha' to the departure from Charlieshope, Scott's tact in combining the emblematic with the realistic is faultless. He even supplies a new instance of the classic pastoral debate about nature and nurture in Dinmont's breeding of generations of terriers all called Pepper and Mustard – 'a fancy of my ain to mark the breed' (II, 11) – and his lament over Bertram's failure to train his own terrier to go after vermin – 'beast or body, education should aye be minded' (II, 10).

The remote world of Liddesdale is as alien to the experience of the urban reader as Arcadia itself, but it possesses the additional fascination of the geographically locatable. The crossing of Bewcastle Moss and the defence of Dandy from the robbers who attack him can be read as a version of the perilous journey of romance, but it is the actual rather than the ideal that is attested to by the sharply drawn physical features of the landscape, the reminders of the region's past history in the scattered remnants of Border fortresses, and the highly individualized figure and speech of Dinmont himself. Scott's conquest for the novel of this special combination of the regional and the pastoral made possible some of the finest things in his own later fiction, while also preparing the way for *Adam Bede* and *Far from the Madding Crowd*.

The description of Charlieshope as Bertram and Dinmont approach it after their journey across the barren waste is both pastoral and, in its concluding allusion, deliberately biblical:

Night was now falling, when they came in sight of a pretty river winding its way through a pastoral country. The hills were greener and more abrupt than those which Brown [i.e. Bertram] had lately passed, sinking their grassy sides at once upon the river. They had no pretensions to magnificence of height or to romantic shapes, nor did their smooth swelling slopes exhibit either rocks or woods. Yet the view was wild, solitary, and pleasingly rural. No inclosures, no roads, almost no tillage – it seemed a land which a patriarch would have chosen to feed his flocks and herds.   (II, 33–4)

The emphasis on 'smoothness' indicates that this is a very different scene from the Gilpinesque roughness and wildness Bertram has been admiring in the country through which he has recently passed.[17] The values associated with this world are human and moral rather than aesthetic, and Bertram enters it as one who has already fought in defence of his host – a status quite different from that of tourist and connoisseur which, like the young Mannering of the novel's opening, he has formerly enjoyed.

Bertram participates in the hunting, feasting, and dancing that are the familiar rituals of Charlieshope, but he is, like the traditional hero in pastoral interludes, only a temporary member of this world, never losing his separateness. The testing, reductive process embodied in such sequences involves the shedding of certain superficial attributes, a willingness to be measured in new terms, a chance to reorder one's own values, but it does not require a change of identity. The hero does not become a simple shepherd; Bertram remains the Captain. His otherness is never lost sight of or glossed over: he prefers to place a little aesthetic distance between himself and the gorier aspects of the salmon-spearing; it is at his suggestion that a particularly resolute old badger is spared; and he declines to have Wasp entered against the vermin after all.

Dinmont's world embodies full love and trust openly expressed between husband and wife, parents and children, hosts and guest. It is very different from the Mannering world in India, or from Bertram's childhood experience after his kidnapping from Ellangowan. The young man's acceptance by this world is complete – 'Captain, come back,' urges the six-year-old as she kisses him goodbye, 'and I'll be your wife my ain sell' (II, 73–4) – but Dandy's last and finest gesture of trust is to offer money to help him in that other world where he actually belongs: 'I have heard that you army gentlemen can sometimes buy yoursells up a step, and if a hundred or twa would help ye on such an occasion, the bit scrape o' your pen would be as good to me as the siller, and ye might just take ye're ain time of settling it – it wad be a great convenience to me' (II, 78). The tact matches that which Bertram had himself exhibited in asking Ailie for a plaid like Dandy's, and though he declines Dandy's offer, the bond of mutual trust is sealed by his leaving Wasp behind, safe despite the whole tribe of Pepper and Mustard. Bertram's ability to function harmoniously with nature in the simpler society of Charlieshope has confirmed his worth and endorsed the recognition of his 'kind heart' expressed by the market girl that first November morning when he started on the road for Scotland.

For all its pastoral attributes, however, Charlieshope does not belong to that golden age whose relationship to the present is expressed simply in terms of contrast. The golden age is a first age with no prehistory; the pastoral world of Charlieshope, like everything else in Scott, is fully historicized. It has a prehistory memorialized in ballads and attested to by the ruined peel towers. Time moves on in Liddesdale as elsewhere, its presence marked not so much by the customary pastoral acknowledgment of death – *et in arcadia ego* – as in the developmental change that constitutes history. The narrator-as-historian makes the point in his own slightly pedantic way when he insists upon the differences between the farmers of the region in his own day and in Dinmont's. But the point is also made in Dandy's turning outwards to the legal world of Edinburgh for redress in his dispute with Jock o' Dawston Cleugh after the traditional process of resolution – combat by a singlestick – has been tried three times and failed.

In the analogical structure of *Guy Mannering* the visit to Edinburgh is to Mannering something of what the stay at Charlieshope is to Bertram. He proves himself worthy of his own role in the final drama – that of wise subordinate agent rather than protagonist – and he establishes a bond of trust with a crucial ally. The reappearance of Dinmont on the steps of

Pleydell's tenement when Mannering first arrives confirms the legitimacy of the parallel. The entire Edinburgh episode, indeed, becomes for
Mannering a kind of city pastoral, in which he samples delights that
parallel the badger-hunting and salmon-spearing of Charlieshope. Hearing Erskine preach in Greyfriar's Church, attending an old-fashioned
funeral and will-reading, enjoying a venison dinner with Pleydell and
other Edinburgh figures, making good use of introductions to the literati
of the Athens of the North – David Hume, Adam Smith, John Home,
Adam Ferguson, Lord Kames, John Clerk of Eldin, and others – Mannering shows all the adaptive powers Bertram displayed in Liddesdale,
finding easy admission to 'a circle never closed against strangers of sense
and information' (II, 329) but also proving himself an adept at the kind of
'playing' that takes place in Clerihugh's drinking parlour on Saturday
nights.[18]

Mannering makes his way to Clerihugh's in the wake of the sturdy
Dinmont, pursuing a parodic version of the perilous journey – up the
High Street, down a dark alley, up an unlit and noisome staircase, past 'a
sort of Pandaemonium, where men and women, half undressed, were
busied in baking, broiling, roasting oysters, and preparing devils on the
gridiron' (II, 263) – to that inner world within the urban pastoral realm of
Edinburgh where the game of High Jinks is in full swing, with Pleydell as
leading participant. The lawyer, whose normal dress is 'a well-brushed
black suit, with very clean shoes and gold buckles,' and whose customary
manner is 'rather reserved and formal than intrusive' (II, 282), is now
found coatless, his wig on one side, 'his head crowned with a bottle-
slider' (II, 265), as he acts out the part of a medieval Scottish monarch
surrounded by a boisterous court. The greatest forfeits extracted in the
game are for breaking the illusion or for introducing some reference to
the weekday world of the law – being 'professional.' We have here an
almost perfect small-scale example of Harry Berger's definition of the
'second world' of renaissance literature:

The second world is the playground, laboratory, theater or battlefield of the
mind, a model or construct which the mind creates, a time or place which it
clears, in order to withdraw from the actual environment. It may be the
world of play or poem or treatise, the world inside a picture frame, the world
of pastoral simplification, the controlled conditions of scientific experiment.

Its essential quality is that it is an explicitly fictional, artificial or hypothetical world. It presents itself to us as a game which, like all games, is to be taken with dead seriousness while it is going on. In pointing to itself as serious play, it affirms both its limits and its power in a single gesture. Separating itself from the casual and confused region of everyday existence, it promises a clarified image of the world it replaces.[19]

High Jinks differs, however, from the usual run of such second worlds in that it is not a single episode – like Bertram's stay at Charlieshope or Mannering's Edinburgh visit – but a recurrent ritual. 'In civilized society, law is the chimney through which all that smoke discharges itself that used to circulate through the whole house, and put every one's eyes out' (II, 326), Pleydell tells Mannering, and it is in order to prevent himself becoming too hard and cynical, begrimed with the soot, that he needs the cleansing saturnalia at Clerihugh's.

In the daytime world of the law Pleydell does not allow himself the luxury of role-playing; his old man's flirtation with Julia at the supper-table in a later episode constitutes merely a brief excursion into High Jinks in a toned-down and domesticated form. Like the rituals of power in the monarchy game at Clerihugh's, the flirtation ritual hints at aspects of the self deliberately suppressed – in this case the yearning for a fuller expression of the life of the affections. In this portrait of the complex, divided self, the distinction drawn by Scott between *homo ludens* and *homo laborans* is quite Dickensian. He does not fail to underline his point by setting Pleydell off against the simple figure of the whole man, Dandy Dinmont, whose response to High Jinks is, 'Deil hae me, if they are na a' mad thegither' (II, 268).

Like Mannering, the man of arms, the man of law suffers from a restriction of part of his personality. He is by no means inhumane – he well knows what burdens the slow workings of the law place upon individual men and women – but as the servant of Themis he dare not allow such awareness too loud a voice or it would inhibit his ability to function.[20] Neither Pleydell nor Mannering can enjoy the direct involvement in the final rescue of Bertram that is allowed to Dinmont. Though Pleydell tells Bertram, 'Since you have wanted a father so long, I wish from my heart I could claim the paternity myself' (III, 219), this cannot be – and the tragedy is Pleydell's rather than Bertram's. In the absence of

his real father Bertram can draw on the strengths of the various surrogate fathers who stand in the wings at his rebirth, but the existence of an
available heir does not necessarily transform into genuine fathers those
with wealth or wisdom to transfer.

Like all of Scott's novels, *Guy Mannering* is full of Shakespearian allusions.
Many of these seem quite adventitious – a phrase from the Falstaff-Hal
scenes of *Henry IV* used by Pleydell, an epigraph chosen for the apposite-
ness of a couple of words – but even such apparently casual references re-
pay attention, since Scott's memory was of that reverberative kind which
cannot call up an isolated fragment without simultaneously evoking the
echoing presence of the entire work. Two kinds of more extended Shakespearian references seem to demand particular attention in *Guy Mannering*.
The first occurs when an individual character draws self-conscious parallels
between his own situation and that of a dramatic character – Mannering's
allusion to Othello, for example – while the second pertains to the employment as a deliberate narrative device of structural and thematic elements
derived from Shakespeare's plays, especially the late romances.

There is a certain rough parallelism between the final phase of
Mannering's marriage and the plot of *Othello*, Lieutenant Archer even
supplying a feeble version of the Iago figure. But the confusion of mother
with daughter, the foolish inadequacy of Sophia when compared with
Desdemona, the fact that haughtiness and withdrawal do the work
originally assigned to pride and racial isolation – these push Mannering's family disaster in the direction of tragic farce rather than of high
tragedy. Mannering is himself capable of perceiving the incongruity of
the parallel – he speaks of his 'silly jealousy' (1, 203) – and yet he clings to
it as a means of endowing his personal anguish with a dignity that makes
it both more bearable and more remote. Like other self-dramatizing
characters in Scott – Flora Mac-Ivor, for example, with the 'busy devil at
[her] heart' (*Waverley* III, 309) – Mannering cannot entirely suppress his
awareness of the particular mistakes and personal failures that render his
situation individual rather than archetypal. The invocation of *Othello* is
not an aid to self-understanding but a defense against self-analysis: 'If you
read over – what I never dare open – the play of Othello, you will have
some idea of what followed – I mean of my motives – my actions, thank
God! were less reprehensible' (1, 201).

When at the end of the novel Mannering disclaims any intention of repairing to Donagild's tower 'for the nocturnal contemplation of the celestial bodies' and insists 'Here ends THE ASTROLOGER' (III, 358), there is a suggestion of staff-breaking and book-drowning that calls up, in the figure of Prospero, another available alter ego. In describing the young Mannering's disturbance at the coincidence in his astrological predictions about the new-born Harry Bertram and Sophia, the narrator has already made this parallel explicit:

> The result of his calculations in these two instances left so unpleasing an impression upon his mind, that, like Prospero, he mentally relinquished his art, and resolved, neither in jest nor earnest, again to practise judicial astrology. (I, 57)

At the point at which this occurs in the text, Mannering's youthfulness makes the comparison seem somewhat incongruous, the product merely of a single point of contact between two very different men and situations. The discomfort Mannering feels as man of reason when faced with the inexplicable leads him to treat with ironic mockery his own 'prophetic' powers, and his combination of scepticism about astrology with skill in its mechanics puts him, apparently, at a considerable distance from Prospero as magus. But as so often in Scott, what begins as ironic allusion sheds its distancing incongruities as the action proceeds, and becomes tellingly appropriate. The older Mannering does not find irony a very complete defence against the profound uneasiness he feels not simply with his apparent ability to predict the future but with his power in the immediate world of action. As surely as Prospero, Mannering the great soldier deals in matters of life and death, and he wields those responsibilities in the private as well as the public sphere. He blames himself for his wife's death; he almost kills Harry Bertram in the duel, and he does kill the man whose name Bertram has shared, the smuggler Vanbeest Brown. It is, in fact, the power of death that Mannering possesses, without any compensatory power over life. He cannot prevent his wife falling into a decline and dying; he cannot regenerate the relationship with his daughter; though his killing of the smuggler may be read as the signal for the freeing of Bertram from his false identity, Mannering himself remains unaware of the connection between the two men and continues to believe Bertram to be dead long after Julia knows him to be alive. It is significant that it is Dinmont who comes to comfort Bertram in jail, and that it is Meg, not Mannering, who presides over the rebirth ritual in the cave. Her investment in her own prophetic powers is the very opposite of Mannering's; she insists on seeing the positive prophecy come to pass, while Mannering remains obsessed with the negative aspects of his own predictions.

Whereas the young Captain Vanbeest Brown can be transformed into Harry Bertram and the connection re-established with the child he once was, no such rebonding is possible for the broken halves of Mannering's own life. The young tourist of picturesque taste who figures in the novel's opening sequence seems very far removed from the stern victor of numerous Indian battles who returns to Ellangowan twenty years later. In youth he dreamed of retirement with his beloved Sophia in a place like Ellangowan, possessed of just the right combination of 'striking remnants of ancient grandeur' with 'modern elegance and comfort' to allow life to 'glide on' (I, 61), but he has actually transported Sophia to the exotic and violent world of India. In the process he has made a radical break with his immediate antecedents, rejecting the paths recommended by his uncle the bishop and his uncle the merchant, and deliberately attempted to reincarnate one of his medieval ancestors famed for his skill in arms. It is no accident that Pleydell immediately assigns to Mannering the role of this ancestor in the High Jinks scene. Pleydell, whose weekly equilibrium depends upon the indulgence of fantasies on Saturday-at-e'en, is quick to sense the fantasist in Mannering. In severing his ties with his uncles – 'I slipped my neck out of both nooses' (I, 198) – Mannering has sought to free himself by an act of the romantic will. He goes, however, far beyond the 'lover's day-dream' (I, 61) of a Scottish exile with Sophia, and in endeavouring to live out his ancestral fantasy cuts himself off not merely from the worlds of commerce and the church but from his wife and from his own younger self.

Commitment to the dream of military glory also makes Mannering a stranger to his daughter Julia. When she laments, 'O Matilda, I hope none of your ancestors ever fought at Poictiers or Agincourt' (I, 283), something more than comic satire of family pride is at issue. While the reader is aware of the anguish Mannering suffers at the loss of his wife and the probable death of Bertram, it is one of the novel's saddest ironies that Julia believes that her father is quite comfortable with the idea of death. In seeking to justify her failure to inform him of Bertram's survival she too has recourse to *Othello*: 'A soldier, that "in the trade of war has oft slain men," feels probably no uneasiness at reflecting upon the supposed catastrophe, which almost turned me into stone' (I, 269). The parallel Mannering has himself employed to elevate his jealousy points here to a more fundamental source of his unhappiness and estrangement – the subsuming of the man of feeling within the man of arms.

To the reader who comes to *Guy Mannering* after *Waverley*, the variations on the motif of the travelling Englishman seem at first sight unimportant, but on closer inspection they take on considerable significance. Mannering enters the novel as an unknown figure, not as the heir of Waverley Honour. He is a stranger with no permanent home of his own, and though he may dream of living at Ellangowan and even attempt to buy the estate on his return from India, it can no more properly belong to him than to the usurper Glossin, who longs in vain to receive the territorial appellation 'Ellangowan.' The plot of reclamation belongs in fact to another returning stranger. Unlike Mannering, whom no one in the village remembers, the rightful heir is quickly recognized, and his future is assured by the presence of Julia, waiting to be his bride. Mannering can assist with his wealth in the restoration process, but he cannot enjoy it in his own right. When the young people go off to plan the rebuilding of Meg's cottage at Derncleugh, Mannering is left alone to plan his Bungalow. This persistence of the dark figure of the returned stranger who carries the condition of exile with him thus weaves into the main plot of the lost heir the theme of the severed life.

What look at first like awkwardnesses in the novel's plotting – the two heroes and the sixteen-year time-gap – are in fact essential to both the story of the returned heir and that of the severed life. The epigraph from Time as Chorus in *The Winter's Tale*[21] that signals the break in the action simultaneously invites the reader to extend the repertoire of Shakespearian allusion and compare the cases of Bertram and Mannering with the lost children and lonely father-figures of all the late romances. For Mannering the magical resolutions and rebindings of the world of Shakespearian romance are not available in their most complete form. He never really 'finds' his daughter; the scene that should mark a new confidence and openness in their relationship is only partially achieved;

the relationship remains one of felt vacancy rather than the strong bond of Prospero and Miranda or Leontes' magical recovery of Perdita.[22] Mannering's inability to speak fully and openly to Julia creates an undertow of unexpressed emotion throughout the later scenes. He can do more for Godfrey Bertram's daughter than for his own, be franker and kinder with the stranger's child. Julia, for her part, is more at ease with Pleydell than with Mannering: the gap of mistrust is never fully closed, and she finds her Ferdinand almost in spite of her father rather than because of him. For this Leontes the tragedy of jealousy remains unredeemed; unlike Hermione, Sophia cannot be miraculously restored. To marry a foolish woman, carry her into a society that makes extreme demands upon her, and pay little subsequent attention to her or to their child – these constitute a sequence of errors in the realm of everyday conduct that add up to something quite distinct from the single right-angled turn that marks Leontes' loss of faith in his wife.

The tangible presence of *The Tempest* and *The Winter's Tale* in the latter part of the novel, together with earlier invocation of patterns and motifs from Shakespearian comedy and romance, serves to define not merely the continuities between Scott's fiction and its pastoral and romance predecessors but also what is essentially different about his transposition of the stylized patterns and timeless themes of romance into the realistic and time-bound world of the novel. Mary Lascelles says of Shakespeare's pastoral romance that it 'is, and must always remain, *elsewhere* and *some other time*,' and she goes on to define its essential detachment from the world of everyday existence:

Its happy endings are not flattering fantasies, but tokens of fulfilment to be imagined only, not hoped for. In this fulfilment, the partial and piecemeal returns and renewals which life grants us are capable of completion; not only does the future stretch before us, with its assured rhythm of the seasons and the generations – the past itself is no longer irretrievably lost.[23]

So it seems to be at first glance with the patterned structure of *Guy Mannering*, where every element of that final sequence fits so splendidly together with the earlier piecing-out of the abduction in Pleydell's inquiry, where each father is defined against a whole series of other fathers, where Edinburgh can fit with Liddesdale as another version of pastoral, and so on through a whole network of echoing details. But that structure partakes in fact of the incompleteness of realistic fiction as well as of the completeness of romance, and the tension between the two modes makes the felt loss all the more moving. The happy ending for the children cannot obliterate awareness of those workings of time that preclude the recovery of the losses of the fathers. This is a story about mistakes and their sometimes irreversible consequences, and Mannering never for one moment shares Dominie Sampson's illusion that the sixteen-year time-gap can be obliterated.[24]

The novelistic insistence on incompleteness that characterizes the Mannering plot is deliberately set off against the perfect exemplification of the romance plot of the lost heir embodied in the Bertram story. The ritual over which Meg Merrilies presides in the final stages of the novel is a rebonding of past and present, not only connecting the separated parts of Harry Bertram's life but also affirming the links between the young man and his ancestors and his community. He is recognized both as the abducted child – through the survival of the astrological prediction round his neck – and as his father's son: 'the resemblance was too striking to be denied' (III, 302). His power to bring about a future very different from the disaster his father has made of his inheritance, or the barren and limited use to which Margaret Bertram of Singleside has put hers, is affirmed by the absence of his actual father and the presence instead of so many wiser surrogates. His personal worth has already been amply confirmed by the plot of proving, in which his physical and spiritual courage have been fully tested.

The time-shift which initially looks so disruptive thus becomes the central dynamic of the final stages of the novel. Any suspense about the identity of Captain Brown is dissipated very early in the tale, and the impulse towards connecting past and present becomes the strongest force in the narrative – embodied as it is in Bertram's need to establish his identity, Pleydell's anxiety to find the solution that eluded his original inquiry, and Meg's insistence on a re-enactment that will carry Harry Bertram back over the ground of his childhood abduction until he is face to face in the cave with the man who broke his life into separate fragments. But this very drive towards completion underlines the poignancy of Mannering's situation as witness rather than protagonist.

Nothing essentially changes for Mannering from that morning when he first revisits Ellangowan after his return from India and is overwhelmed by his awareness of the workings of time:

The landscape was the same; but how changed the feelings, hopes, and views, of the spectator! Then, life and love were new, and all the prospect was gilded by their rays. And now, disappointed in affection, sated with fame, and what the world calls success, his mind goaded by bitter and repentent recollection, his best hope was to find a retirement in which he might nurse the melancholy that was to accompany him to his grave. (I, 211)

The histrionic element in this preface to a meditation on the fall of ancient houses has softened by the end of the novel into the self-mockery of his plans for a Bungalow in which to be 'separate and sulky' (III, 358) when he pleases, but the new stance is a modification rather than a transformation of his essentially solitary and grieving condition, and he is still using self-dramatization as a protective strategy.

To place so much emphasis at the conclusion of a discussion of *Guy Mannering* on Mannering's story rather than Bertram's is undoubtedly to push the novel somewhat out of shape by drawing out the implicit at the expense of the explicit aspects of its meaning. And it would be disingenuous to appeal to the title for justification, since Scott delighted to be oblique in such matters. Nevertheless, it seems by no means inappropriate to lay special emphasis on the sub-plot of the middle-aged hero, since this was to remain such an important element in Scott's fiction – not surprisingly, perhaps, in view of his having completed his first novel when himself entering middle age. He never abandoned the conventional love plot with its young hero and heroine and marriage as its goal, but by melding with it the two-generation plot of consequences he could amply accommodate his other concerns – although the potential of the novel with a middle-aged hero would have to wait till the later fiction of Henry James for its fullest exploration. The double structure also went largely unnoticed by Scott's immediate successors. But not entirely so: when *Wuthering Heights* is set against *Guy Mannering*, or even *Redgauntlet*, or the combination of *The Monastery* and *The Abbot*, its structure looks a good deal less idiosyncratic than critics might have us believe. And the brooding figure of the middle-aged Heathcliff has certain affinities both with Mannering and with Hugh Redgauntlet.

So far as Scott himself was concerned, the patterns and techniques of *Guy Mannering*, as considered in their own right and in relation to those of *Waverley*, were crucial for the shaping of his future career. By excluding the most obviously innovative feature of *Waverley* – its introduction of major historical events – Scott tests both the range of his subject-matter and the validity of his method. *Waverley*'s fairly even and continuous employment of the dual perspective of narrator and naïve protagonist is now diversified by the variant perspectives afforded by the excursions into the epistolary mode, but the narrator-as-historian is retained as a controlling device. His vision is distinguished from that of Bertram and Mannering by its ability to place the idiosyncratically local in temporal as well as in geographical and sociological terms, and the presence of such an overarching view facilitates the invocation of earlier literary conventions designed to locate the particular within a larger scheme of meaning. This concern with an individual region at a datable moment in its history does not, however, preclude the deployment of pastoral conventions to set off Charlieshope or the legal landscape of the old town of Edinburgh as intact realms able to function distinctively within the fictional design so that the realistic surface becomes capable of moralization. It was this combination of historical, regional, and romance elements that was to remain quintessential to the Waverley method.

Scott had good reason to be satisfied with the result of 'the work of six weeks at a Christmas.'[25] The writing of *Guy Mannering* not only exorcised the burdened feelings associated with the completion of *The Lord of the Isles* but gave him renewed appetite for further fictional experimentation. By ascribing it on the title-page to 'the Author of "Waverley"' he was simultaneously making a declaration of independence from his earlier self and projecting an active future for the novelist he had now so securely become.

5

The Antiquary:
Reading the Text of the Past

The gestation of *The Antiquary* belongs to one of the busiest years in Scott's life. To read his letters from the early spring of 1815 to the spring of 1816 is to be overwhelmed by a sense of constant public activity, unremitting energy, and sheer comprehensive appetite. Whether he was playing the anonymity game with the Prince Regent, trading compliments with Byron, hob-nobbing with Wellington and the Czar of Russia, engaging in detailed legal arrangements about a young friend's marriage settlement, or putting in bids for more land around Abbotsford, no effort was spared and all possibilities seemed open. Since the visit he made to London in the spring of 1815 was his first in six years, Scott was able to draw upon considerable accumulated credit as a literary lion, and he repeated the experience in Brussels and Paris later in the summer. Scarcely less intoxicating than the public occupations of sightseeing, court presentations, and dining with the great and famous were the hectic commercial dealings being conducted through the Ballantynes – arrangements for the renewal of bills, schemes to sell dead stock along with the rights to yet-unwritten works, devices for keeping Constable, Longman, Murray, and Blackwood constantly in play. The two aspects of Scott's life – on the one hand that of gentleman, lawyer, and poet, on the other that of speculator in literary commodities – remained on the surface quite distinct, but there was always the danger of collision, and anonymity seemed essential to the maintenance of a safe separation.

To the end of his life Scott was always quick to insist that his financial independence and status as gentleman were fully established long before the appearance of *Waverley*. Indeed, one factor at least in the early stages of the anonymity game was his sense that to write fiction was to practise a trade, to engage in activities not quite becoming a gentleman. But by employing the wealth derived from the novels in the purchase of more and more land and by failing to make a sharp distinction between raising money for the printing house and borrowing to buy property, the life of the laird of Abbotsford became increasingly inextricable from that of the business partner. The Scott of the early Waverley years seems at times to resemble some hero of fairy-tale equipped with a magical power to generate wealth in illimitable amounts. But the new wealth had to be immediately transformed into something tangible that would not vanish – land, books for the library, trophies for the wall, all the furnishings of the second life that overlay the first and secret life. The special kind of excitement which secrecy created was enhanced by the sense of involvement in something forbidden or illicit – the comparison Scott himself invoked was with coining.[1]

The ethics of Scott's unpublicized participation in the multifarious joint enterprises with the Ballantynes can certainly be called into question, but at the time Scott himself treated the issue purely as a matter of decorum: the poet who dined with the Prince Regent, Castlereagh, and Wellington did not choose to make public his commercial involvements. Any general uneasiness about his behind-the-scenes business activities was subsumed within that more specific but less discomforting anxiety as to whether novel-writing was a proper way for a gentleman to make a living. The weight of the commercial secret was thus transferred to the secret he was prepared to live with, exploit, and even enjoy – that of the identity of the Author of *Waverley*.

The heavy incidence of minor works completed during this period can no longer be attributed to a lack of creative direction on Scott's part, and it seems necessary to posit a sheer excess of literary energy, a protean fury that compelled him into multiplicity. He even engaged in parodic variations on the game of the Great Unknown: *Paul's Letters to His Kinsfolk*, the poems and articles for the *Edinburgh Annual Register*, the reviews for the *Quarterly* of the *Culloden Papers* and of *Emma*, the poem *Harold the Dauntless* – all were anonymous products of the twelve months surrounding the publication of *The Antiquary*. Since the disguise was in each instance of the thinnest, the secret of authorship widely shared, these served simultaneously to attract attention to the Great Unknown and, by their very number and variety, to deflect it away again.

The restless, unresting Scott of this period has in fact all the appearance of a man possessed, supremely confident in his own powers but seized with the self-contradictory and potentially self-destructive impulse both to protect himself and to give himself away, as if the magic would work only so long as secrets were both kept and deliberately endangered. In the quasi-confessional Introduction to *The Chronicles of the Canongate* of 1827 Scott invoked the metaphor of the actor playing Harlequin for whom 'the mask was essential to the performance of the character' (I, ii). But the mask of the Author of *Waverley* did more than release Scott's powers as a novelist; it created a double to run the risks of fame – those dangers to 'peace of mind and tranquillity' (I, xxiv) he was unwilling to encounter continuously in his own person – while at the same time allowing him to explore through the displacements of fiction some of the inmost concerns of Walter Scott of Abbotsford. In particular, a good deal of Walter Scott went into the character of Jonathan Oldbuck, antiquary of Monkbarns, and when he built into the new novel the fable of Martin Waldeck destroyed by magical new wealth or included the brilliant depiction of Sir Arthur Wardour's unbalanced reaction both to the discovery of the silver that might save him and to the inescapable signs of ruin, Scott was touching on fears that currently underlay his personal thoughts and anxieties.

The Antiquary was written, like its two predecessors, with amazing speed. But it had been simmering in Scott's brain for the previous nine months – its title was already settled when he left for London in March 1815 – and he was impatient to get *Paul's Letters* out of the way so as to be able to start. As he told Morritt on 22 December 1815:

I shall then set myself seriously to the Antiquary of which I have only a very general sketch at present. But when once I get my pen to the paper it will walk fast enough. I am sometimes tempted to leave it alone and try whether it will not write as well without the assistance of my head as with it – a hopeful prospect for the reader. (*L* IV, 145)

This sense that the narrative could virtually write itself was clearly grounded in the vividness with which the figure of Oldbuck was already present in his imagination. On 29 December he wrote to Ballantyne:

> Dear James – I'm done, thank God, with the long yarns
> Of the most prosy of Apostles – Paul;
> And now advance, sweet Heathen of Monkbarns!
> Step out, old quizz, as fast as I can scrawl.   (*L* IV, 147)

Although Scott preferred not to dwell upon those aspects of his own experience and subconscious fears that went into the creation of his forlorn young hero, Lovel, and the foolishly sanguine Sir Arthur, he delighted in exaggerating some of his personal foibles in the figure of Oldbuck, making fun of his own antiquarianism and predilection for anonymity in Oldbuck's grand scheme for a 'Caledoniad.' As Oldbuck expounds it, the 'plan of the story' and annotation will be his, the poetry – 'the mere mechanical department'[2] – Lovel's. His own name will not appear, though his assistance will be indirectly acknowledged. His published notes have all come out over pseudonyms such as *Scrutator* or *Indagator*, and he will now discharge his 'shafts,' designed to 'annihilate Ossian, Macpherson, and Mac-Cribb' (1, 309), from 'behind the shield of [his] ally' (1, 307). Scott's humorous identification with Oldbuck extended beyond the finished novel: in May 1816 he refers to the 'author of a late popular novel' as having bought 'the Kaime of Kinprunes' (*L* IV, 235); six years later he writes to cheer up Constable by promising they will share in 'many an old-fashiond Scotch tale and story such as would have pleased Mr. Oldbuck of Monkbarns' (*L* VII, 66–7); in March 1825 he compares himself to Oldbuck when writing to his daughter-in-law (*L* IX, 34); and in October 1831 he tells Basil Hall, who had just bought the manuscript of *The Antiquary*, that he 'had a particular partiality' for the novel 'from its connection wt. the early scenes of my life' (*L* XII, 36–7). Lockhart comments on the affinities between Scott and Oldbuck and reports that 'the founder of the Abbotsford Museum' compiled a 'Descriptive Catalogue of that collection, which he began towards the close of his life, but, alas! never finished ... entitled "*Reliquiae Trottcosianae – or the Gabions of the late Jonathan Oldbuck, Esq.*"'[3] The Introduction to *The Chronicles of the Canongate* speaks of *The Antiquary* as having nearly given the author's identity away by drawing so freely upon the traits of George Constable the antiquary, an old friend of Scott's youth. But this was in its way a final smoke-screen; although the Introduction contained Scott's public avowal that he was indeed the Author of *Waverley*, he still preferred to preserve for his own enjoyment his closeness to Jonathan Oldbuck.

The imaginative energy and exhilaration that went into the portrait of Oldbuck emerge strongly and distinctly from the text itself, and the natural instinct of most readers to concentrate on the middle-aged protagonist rather than the young lovers is perfectly sound. Any discussion of the novel's structure – so often criticized – must take account of Oldbuck's centrality, and since it is his avocation rather than his name that supplies the title, due attention must be paid to the function and significance of those activities of collecting, investigating, and interpreting that are proper to the antiquarian calling. For once a Scott title bears an obvious appropriateness to the text it prefaces, the signalled concern with delving into the past having clear relevance for everything that follows.

Like its immediate predecessor, *The Antiquary* turns upon the establishment of a connection between two sets of occurrences separated by a gulf of many years. But in *Guy Mannering* the earlier events are depicted at the outset, forming a kind of prologue to the later action, and are formally set off from that action by a deliberate insistence on the sixteen-year time-shift and the exotic Indian location of the intervening events. The apparent disconnection of the two dramatized sequences, both centring on Ellangowan, is thus thrown into sharper relief. Pleydell has once attempted to discover a satisfactory explanation for Frank Kennedy's death and the disappearance of Harry Bertram, but without success; inquiry and hypothesis have not sufficed, and when he takes up the search a second time, not only new pieces of information and additional or more co-operative witnesses but also the participation of the central figure in the mystery are required before past and present can be connected to form a single whole. Investigation, speculation, and explanation must combine with new action before the disjunction is resolved, the gulf bridged, and a new future life made available to Harry Bertram. The differences between the two inquiries are firmly insisted upon: in the first Pleydell is simply the diligent, intelligent, but unnamed local official; in the second he is the sharply individualized and involved participant whose own affections and interests sharpen his eagerness to get at the truth. The break of continuity is fundamental to the narrative structure of *Guy Mannering*, and it is essential that the second set of events should require a fresh going-over of the ground of the first set, with much more now at stake for all the participants – and for the reader.

The same need to connect past and present is felt in *The Antiquary*, but much less direct action is involved and the concern is far more with making correct sense of the past than with making possible some potential future. The events of a generation earlier are not now dramatized to provide the opening section of the novel but are recalled within the later action, emerging as the stuff of memory and narrative rather than as presented event. The gulf between past and present is not signalled by anything so emphatic as the sixteen-year break that marks the structural division of *Guy Mannering* but rather by the treatment of past events in a different literary mode. Whereas the Monkbarns world of the present is handled with comic realism, the Glenallan material is presented largely in Gothic terms. It lies with Jonathan Oldbuck to establish some kind of connection between the two, but not by those methods of legal inquiry which, like Sheriff Pleydell, he has pursued in vain at the time of the earlier tragedy. Since on the surface it does not appear that more is at stake for Oldbuck on the second occasion than on the first – when he had, after all, been investigating the death of the woman he loved – the question of why he succeeds at the second attempt assumes major importance. Like Pleydell, he has available a great deal of new information – the lost heir, too, has reappeared – but the stress seems to fall on the enhanced receptivity that enables Oldbuck to make use of the new materials not merely to resolve the mystery but also to redeem some of his own past mistakes and, hence, endue his life with new meaning. Oldbuck's piecing together of the tragedy (like Pleydell's) ensures the future happiness of the young heir, but Lovel's absence from the scene during the crucial revelatory stages ensures that the emphasis falls at least as much on what it all means for the investigator himself. If Lovel and Isabella Wardour are much paler figures than Harry Bertram and Julia Mannering, and Lovel's role far more passive, that is not because there has been some failure of imaginative energy on Scott's part but because the focus of attention is different in this third novel from what it was in the second.

Three different modes of truth-seeking are distinguished in *The Anti-quary*. The first two, the legal and the antiquarian, are activist, involving the deliberate initiation and pursuit of inquiries. The third mode is more passive; it depends upon listening rather than questioning, and though it may employ skills particular to the lawyer or the antiquary, these are controlled by human sympathy for the men and women whose fate depends upon the establishment of the truth. Legal inquiry – the develop-ing of a case that would hold up in court, convict the guilty, and protect the innocent – was of little avail twenty years earlier,[4] and within the main narrative the quasi-legal interrogation of old Elspeth by Oldbuck in his capacity as Justice of the Peace – or, more humorously, of Edie Ochiltree by Bailie Littlejohn – serves further to establish the limitations of this approach. Elspeth has already confessed to the man she has injured, and now insists 'it's but sitting silent when they examine me' (III, 233). Edie will not confide in Oldbuck as a magistrate with pen in hand (III, 187), but he will trust him as friend. The pedantic inquiries of the antiquarian are also shown to have their limitations, either because they involve a concern for trivial detail which continually distracts attention from the main matter at hand or because they are undertaken for the sake of defending a theory already adopted, or confirming knowledge already possessed, rather than for arriving at new understanding – as when Oldbuck self-absorbedly pursues his preferred hypothesis about Lovel instead of observing the young man and striving to come at the real cause of his unhappiness. The famous demolition of Oldbuck's Roman-camp theory at the Kaim of Kinprunes – 'Praetorian here, Praetorian there, I mind the bigging o't' (I, 77) – provides a model for the many minor examples afforded by Oldbuck and his fellow antiquaries later in the novel.

Oldbuck defends the usefulness of the legal profession, for which he was himself originally trained: 'I will vouch for many, who unite integrity with skill and attention, and walk honourably upright where there are so many pit-falls and stumbling-blocks, for those of a different character' (III, 303). And he makes resounding claims for the applicability of antiquarian skills to inquiries of great moment:

If you want an affair of consequence properly managed, put it into the hands of an antiquary; for, as they are eternally exercising their genius and research upon trifles, it is impossible they can be baffled in affairs of importance – use makes perfect; and the corps that is most frequently drilled upon the parade will be most prompt in its exercise upon the day of battle.   (III, 136)

But the action of the novel demonstrates that the delight in such skills for their own sake – detectable in the exulting note that creeps into this speech – can easily vitiate their usefulness. It is only in the later stages of the action, when Oldbuck becomes listener and observer rather than interrogator and theorist, that he acquires the power to bring out the truths that will restore happiness or peace of mind to Lovel, Lord Glenallen, the Wardours, and himself. He can employ his legal and antiquarian skills in the service of this new receptivity and attentiveness, as when he reassures Lord Glenallan about the probable reliability of Elspeth's narrative: 'Her confession was voluntary, disinterested, distinct, consistent with itself, and with all the other known circumstances of the case' (III, 149). But it is 'sympathy with [Lord Glenallan's] sorrows, and detestation at the frauds which have so long been practised upon [him]' (III, 151) that supply the driving force behind his new search for the truth.

Central to *The Antiquary*, in fact, is a profound concern with the fullness of individual lives and with the achievement of right relationships among men and women. In one way or another all the major characters are in danger both of diminishing their own humanity and of denying themselves fellowship with the rest of the community. Old loyalties, griefs, mistakes, and losses severely impede their full life in the present. Partially blinded by private obsessions or false pride, they run the risk of egocentric isolation. Hector MacIntyre, Sir Arthur Wardour, and the Countess of Glenallan are victims of a genealogical vanity that may take ostensibly comic or tragic forms but is in either case capable of violent results; Lovel and Lord Glenallan fall prey to a personal despair, originally caused by external forces but subsequently embraced with a self-destructive fervour; old Elspeth, perhaps the clearest example of self-isolation, is totally cut off from her children and grandchildren, reduced to silence and the mindless twirling of her spindle.[5]

Even Jonathan Oldbuck is to some extent his own prisoner, but he has successfully displaced some of the anguish of the past by his obsessive dedication to antiquarianism, finding in the activity of investigating, collecting, classifying, annotating, and so on a model for the formalization of the past, a way of reducing it to something orderly and non-threatening. The stability he enjoys is more precarious than he would like to believe – hence the elaborate game of misogyny, for domestic tyranny, like antiquarianism, is an anodyne, though not a cure, for the personal griefs that have so long resisted comfortable assimilation. The loss of Eveline Neville and his own consequent childlessness have made him solitary, and though he chooses to treat his bachelor state as a special kind of freedom to do what he likes, the yearning towards Lovel, endorsed by the offer of a home and perhaps even an inheritance to this young stranger, tells a sharply different story.

Oldbuck has established a kind of truce with his own past, and the quixotism he displays in riding his antiquarian hobby-horse is relatively harmless, kept in check by a saving capacity for self-irony. He thus suffers no permanent impairment of his acuity and can respond shrewdly when more vital matters are at stake. He is able to move beyond solipsism to recognize the needs of those around him, though the wary defensiveness of a burnt child near the fire makes difficult the full expression of the concern and sympathy he feels. His comic unwillingness to continue making loans to Sir Arthur has something to do with a fear of personal commitment as well as with financial caution, and the hesitation that accompanies his offers to Lovel, though more touching, expresses the same mistrust of involvement. And the very fact that Oldbuck's attempts at assistance usually emerge (however reluctantly) as proffers of money is a further sign of his instinct to translate the obligations of affection into debts of a more concrete and therefore controllable kind – even in dealing with his nephew and niece his talk is all of financial benefits to be given or withheld. The activity of managing his wealth is, like his antiquarianism, a diversionary occupation, capable of salving, if not curing, the old wounds to his feelings; as such it is a source of power, to be talked about but only rarely used.

Oldbuck's initial inability to act is counterbalanced by the partnership he shares with the novel's other elderly bachelor, the old beggar Edie Ochiltree. These two childless old men are in their different ways the guardians and transmitters of the past of Fairport; by linking the present to the past they ensure continuity on into the future. That Isabella and Lovel are the only ones who properly value what their elders have to teach perhaps constitutes a more substantial validation of their claims to heirship in the novel than all the apparatus of the Glenallan inheritance and the rescue of the Wardour fortunes from the machinations of Dousterswivel. Both Edie and Oldbuck are givers rather than takers – despite the fact that one of them is a beggar and the other enjoys the reputation of being tight-fisted. Oldbuck's reluctance to part with large sums finds an inverted echo in Edie's refusal to accept donations of gold, as opposed to coins of lesser value; but both are compelled to deviate on numerous occasions from their stated policies. The opening encounter at the Kaim of Kinprunes establishes the antiphonal relationship between the two, as Edie undercuts the more extreme flights of Oldbuck's antiquarian fancy. A romantic delight in hypothesis for its own sake is always capable of deflecting Oldbuck; to Edie belongs the gift of bringing speculation sharply back to earth. At a time when Oldbuck is busy theorizing as to whether Lovel is an actor or a poet, Edie recognizes that the young man's main problem is Isabella's rejection of his suit. On a later occasion Oldbuck pauses at the door in the hope that old Elspeth will complete her ballad: 'a genuine and undoubted fragment of minstrelsy! – Percy would admire its simplicity – Ritson could not impugn its authenticity' (III, 222). He longs to hear more, but Edie reminds him: 'had ye not better proceed to the business that brought us a' here? I'se engage to get ye the sang ony time' (III, 227).[6]

Despite his unsentimentality in this and other instances, Edie has his own respect for the local traditions and customs of which he is the repository. As Oldbuck points out, Edie has constituted himself the 'oracle of the district through which he travels – their genealogist, their newsman, their master of the revels, their doctor at a pinch, or their divine' (III, 160–1). The news Edie brings is distinguished by its reliability from the idle rumours that otherwise fill the Fairport air; his role as keeper of the lore of the countryside is quite distinct from that of Caxon, who purveys gossip without grasping its implications – it is Caxon, characteristically, who misinterprets the burning mine machinery and lights his bonfire to set off the false alarm of invasion. Oldbuck and Edie are both great sticklers for the text, respecters of the old forms and of the exact words and details of ancient traditions and rituals. They are clearly differentiated from those who distort, corrupt, or misapply the texts of the past for selfish ends. When Oldbuck is compelled to abandon a theory, he has injured nothing but his self-esteem; Sir Arthur, however, is almost destroyed by the necromantic mumbo-jumbo and manipulation of local traditions that is Dousterswivel's stock-in-trade, while the Countess of Glenallan's tampering with the evidence of family relationships separates her forever from one son, ruins the life of the other, and kills her niece.

In the early part of the novel it is Edie who acts; Oldbuck's interventions come too late or remain ineffectual.[7] It is Edie who is down on the cliff-face with Isabella and her father, who appears at the scene of the duel and rescues Lovel, who plants the treasure designed to save Sir Arthur from ruin, and who takes on Dousterswivel. He accepts responsibility for himself – always having about him the cost of his burial – but he also takes responsibility for others. Enjoying a perfect fit between his habits of life and his personal desires, he could easily have closed himself off within the security of his own happiness; he chooses instead to observe, interpret, and intervene. The risks Edie runs are the concomitants of intervention; the delight in his own powers becomes a kind of hubris that carries him away in the attack on Dousterswivel and results in the temporary loss of what he most treasures, his personal freedom – that freedom which Oldbuck claims to possess but cannot readily enjoy.

Oldbuck and Edie are both sharply distinguished from those whose paralysing inability to connect past and present keeps them trapped within their own solipsistic universe. For these prisoners, external intervention is needed. Lovel's predicament, like that of other lost heirs of romance, requires past and present to be brought together so that his two identities can merge and he can enter on his proper role. But the process by which this is achieved requires very little action on his own part, little disturbance of his essential passivity. A similar passivity is displayed by the other victims: the solution to the mystery of Lord Glenallan's tragic past is initiated not by the Earl himself but by Elspeth, with Edie and Oldbuck as her agents; Sir Arthur Wardour's rescue is orchestrated by Edie with funds supplied by Lovel. What we have here is not just a novel with a passive hero, but one in which many of the key figures are strangely powerless. In *Guy Mannering* the hour and the man must coincide, but in *The Antiquary* it seems rather that it is the pieces of the tale itself that must be brought together: the blank incommunicativeness of the past must be shattered and the fragments rearranged into a new order.

The central problem in *The Antiquary* is ultimately resolved not through deliberate inquiry but through receptivity, that discovery of meaning which depends upon a heart open both to other people and to one's own former self. What is required is not so much investigation or action as utterance. Lips formerly sealed begin to speak when the due hour and the right listener have arrived. As trained lawyer and practising antiquary, Oldbuck possesses certain truth-seeking skills, but they serve him well only when subordinated to directly human concerns. His inferiority to Edie as an effective intervener in the early part of the action is an indication that he needs to give voice to his own true feelings before he can act as articulator of the final story. Once he has recognized, and hence been released by, his affection for Lovel, Oldbuck's standard preoccupations – with the particular and the local, with the traces left by the past on the present, and with the organization of individual details so as to arrive at larger explanations – ideally equip him to become the conduit for the emergence of new meaning.

The thrust of *The Antiquary*, for all its stretches of apparently static verbal skirmishing, is thus essentially narrative, directed towards the creation of a story rather than the establishment of a legal case or the verification of a theory. The novel is full of story-tellers, and sometimes the impulse to tell is so strong upon characters that it sets up a positive 'strife of narrators' (II, 95), as in the comic interlude during the St Mary's Abbey visit which sees the three rival antiquaries, Oldbuck, Wardour, and Blattergowl, vying with each other for the audience's attention. But the result of such competition is an 'indistinguishable string of confusion' (II, 95); only those stories count in which the narrator and listener act in complementary association. Oldbuck's habitual lack of concern as to whether or not anyone is listening to his lectures, his failure to recognize the effect, or lack of effect, of his stories on his audience, is one of the clearest symptoms of the quixotic withdrawal which hampers his full participation in the life of the community. Conversely, one of the clearest signs that Lovel and Isabella are rightful heirs consists in one of them being an excellent listener and the other a gifted story-teller.[8]

The network of references within the novel to documentary and oral texts and their treatment or mistreatment serves to articulate, with considerable richness and complexity, a simultaneous concern with everything that impedes the sense-making power of story – secrecy, deception, fraud, and silence – and with whatever facilitates it – openness, honesty, fair-dealing, and utterance. The first episode in the novel, Lovel's encounter with Oldbuck and their journey to Fairport, acts as a sort of prologue for what follows. Lovel is the observer and listener, Oldbuck the actor and talker, and it is no accident that Oldbuck arrives on the scene fresh from the conclusion of an honest bargain and equipped with his own emblem, an old book for his collection of bibliographic rarities. His confrontation with the appropriately named Mrs Macleucher takes the form of an attack upon her for being party to false claims made about the coach's departure time, supplemented by the charge that she is probably cheating the customer she is serving in her shop. There is, of course, an element of excess in the performance Oldbuck puts on – Lovel detects the old man in 'laughing at his own vehemence' (1, 13) – but this initial comic establishment of the themes of truthfulness, honest dealing, and the verification of texts in no way undermines their significance for the narrative that is to follow. Oldbuck's quick recognition that the name Lovel is probably false – 'Lovel or Belville are just the names which youngsters are apt to assume on such occasions' (1, 38) – leads him to guess that the young man has taken up the profession of acting, and while the conjecture turns out to be technically incorrect, the instinctive recognition of the element of self-dramatization in Lovel's conduct is sound enough. The attempt to 'read' Lovel and hypothesize about him implies a responsiveness to others that takes on increased value as the narrative proceeds.

Much play is made in the novel with right and wrong readings, beginning with Oldbuck's explanation of the undulations at the Kaim of Kinprunes and continuing at the comic level with such details as Lovel's suggestion that the illegible carving over the Monkbarns door might be a mitre, or the interpretation Edie Ochiltree persuades Dousterswivel to give to the inscription 'Search I' on the box containing the silver. Other more extended examples of the need for interpretation are provided by Lovel's dream and, at a much more crucial level, by the fragments of the

Glenallan story that come from old Elspeth and other sources. Every story told in the novel demands comment or explanation, and the expository or interpretative role usually falls to Oldbuck or Edie.

No doubt an elaborate semiotic decoding of all the many texts in this novel could be developed. The stories proper range from Oldbuck's favourite tale of the Abbot's apple and Miss Griselda's account of the haunted chamber to the Gothic elaboration of the Glenallan tragedy, and there are, in addition, numerous instances of details requiring interpretation and of characters engaging, singly or in groups, in the divination of mysteries of various kinds. But it seems less useful to lay out the entire system of meanings that emerges from this network of stories and signs than to emphasize, more simply, their contribution to the stress on Oldbuck's function as 'reader,' to the high valuation placed on warm-hearted as opposed to self-indulgent curiosity, and to the controlling impulse to put pieces together until they make a coherent narrative fit. We are told very early that Lovel is a text 'of whom the *town* ... could make nothing' (1, 90). It is Jonathan Oldbuck's capacity to read the riddle and make something of Lovel that establishes him as the centre of the novel's design and the major focus of the values it embodies. But in arriving at such a reading Oldbuck must first allow himself to be a good listener and observer; he must confine his attention to the text before him rather than go off into a creative narration of his own.[9]

The movement from observer to actor, from theorizer to involved participant, is initiated by the outflow of affection towards Lovel and then developed and tested in terms of Oldbuck's other relationships within the novel. Shocked by his nephew Hector's wounding, he comes much closer to the young soldier. Even though pride and a mistrust of openly expressed emotion ensure that their conversations continue to be characterized by a teasing and (one might say) hectoring tone, they nevertheless arrive at a more direct communication. When Hector first comes on the scene, he and his sister engage in an almost conspiratorial conversation in which she tries to prevent him from giving his uncle offence and so losing his inheritance. But by the final pages of the novel Oldbuck's concern for his nephew can find open expression. Though the manner has not changed – jokes are still made at the expense of Hector's martial ambitions and pride of ancestry – there is a genuine tenderness in the uncle's inquiries about his nephew's feelings for Isabella. Hector has clearly little in common either with his uncle's younger self or with Lovel, but callow and limited though he may be, there is now no danger of his being disinherited. Domestic affection has assumed new value in the course of Oldbuck's reading of the Glenallan family tragedy.

Perhaps the most vivid demonstration of Oldbuck's new willingness to show feeling openly comes in the Mucklebackit strand of the novel. Though frequently celebrated for its realistic power, the depiction of Steenie's funeral has sometimes been regarded as an excrescence with little direct connection to the central narrative. It is, however, a perfect example of Scott's favourite method of proceeding by parallel and analogy. By showing Oldbuck's sensitive response to the family's grief, by incorporating Saunders Mucklebackit into the pattern of bereft fathers, Scott is able to demonstrate Oldbuck's renewed humanity, his coming into full life, his assumption of parental stature.[10]

When Oldbuck sets out for the Mucklebackit funeral, his avowed motivation is the antithesis of sympathy and fellow feeling – 'as to this custom of the landlord attending the body of the peasant, I approve it, Caxon' (III, 6) – and he hopes to use the occasion to demonstrate to his unappreciative nephew 'the resemblances ... betwixt popular customs on such occasions and those of the ancients' (III, 17). Once launched on this train of thought he amplifies and embroiders it with a mini-lecture on the feudal system, sprinkled with Anglo-Saxon and Latin terms and replete with the mandatory reference to his predecessor, John of the Girnell. But as soon as he arrives at the home of the stricken family, all these arguments and precedents are forgotten in the outflow of fellow feeling: his 'heart bled to witness' (III, 44) old Elspeth's inappropriate animation, and he sees the need to prompt the clergyman into action and proceed quickly with the ceremony. When the dead boy's father cannot be persuaded to take his proper place at the head of the coffin, Oldbuck 'interfered between the distressed father and his well-meaning tormen-tors' (III, 46), finally resolving matters by taking the head of the coffin himself. He informs the mourners that 'he himself, as landlord and master to the deceased, "would carry his head to the grave" ' (III, 46), but the ac-tion represents a complete transformation of the spirit of his earlier medita-tion on the feudal system by the instinctive recognition of what needs to be done to ease the suffering of the grieving father. The ceremony can now proceed, serving its ritual purpose of formalizing the pain of death.

The same sympathetic tact marks Oldbuck's later conversation with Saunders Mucklebackit as the fisherman attempts to mend the boat in which his son has died. The promise to send the carpenter to finish the task and to see that there is food to supply the needs of the family until the fishing can begin again could be taken as a further illustration of Oldbuck's quixotic attempt to maintain an anachronistic feudalism within a thoroughly commercial world. But Mucklebackit's response makes it clear that he reads the true meaning: 'Ye were aye kind and neighbourly, whatever folk says o' your being near and close ... And, Monkbarns, when ye laid [Steenie's] head in the grave, (and mony thanks for the respect,) ye saw the mouls laid on an honest lad that likeit you weel, though he made little phrase about it' (III, 95). This expression of thanks, from a man who himself usually makes 'little phrase' about anything, beats down Oldbuck 'from the pride of his affected cynicism' (III, 95), and the two men weep openly together for the lost son.

It is at just this point that Lord Glenallan appears with his appeal for compassion from the man he had scorned and tormented twenty years earlier. Oldbuck's response could not be cooler: 'My compassion? Lord Glenallan cannot need *my* compassion – if Lord Glenallan could need it, I think he would hardly ask it' (III, 96–7). But the Earl will not be put off. He pursues Oldbuck, recalling their old rivalry over Eveline Neville as a way of insisting upon the existence of a bond between them. His penitence and anguish break through Oldbuck's pride, and as the two men come to a full mutual explanation, more than twenty years of silence, misunderstanding, and unvoiced recrimination are set aside. What the narrative ordering makes clear is that without the new openness of heart articulated in Oldbuck's changed relationship to his own family and that of his tenants, the Earl's plea 'for advice, for sympathy, for support' might have gone unheard and the 'wisdom and intelligence' (III, 108) of Oldbuck as interpreter have been withheld. When Oldbuck later rejoices with Glenallan over the son that is found, the moment of his weeping with Mucklebackit over the son that was lost is implicitly echoed and recalled. The Mucklebackit strand, that is to say, is in fact bound into the fabric of the novel by something far tougher than the somewhat tenuous plot device that makes old Elspeth the sole surviving witness of the Countess's wrongdoing.

Oldbuck thus presides over the entire narrative exercise, the putting together of the Glenallan story that will supply Lovel with the name he is lacking at the outset and make possible a true reading of the Lovel text. Thwarted in his attempt twenty years earlier to find out the truth about Eveline Neville's death, Oldbuck is now able to piece out the story that connects the earlier mystery to the later. But he cannot himself provide the final confirmation. In the classic scene of recognition that establishes Lovel's new identity – the perception of his resemblance to the dead Eveline – the participation of the actual father is required to supplement the vision of the adoptive one who has already done so much for the young stranger. Oldbuck and Glenallan both loved Eveline and never forgot her, but the antiquary's recognition of the resemblance between her and Lovel remains unarticulated until prompted by Glenallan's. Oldbuck orchestrates the final stages of the story first hinted at in servants' gossip, then developed by Elspeth's and Glenallan's confessional recollections, and now concluded in a quasi-judicial cross-examination of Lovel himself. But the effect of all this is quite different from that created by Pleydell's conferring of legality on the Bertram story at the end of *Guy Mannering*. When Oldbuck finishes by taking 'the pleasure of introducing a son to a father' (III, 352), the reader is left with the question of why only the actual father could proclaim the identification that Oldbuck had registered but not understood. The answer seems to lie in Glenallan's absolute need of a son. Caught up in his own personal tragedy, this is all the redemption he can hope for – a flesh-and-blood descendant. Oldbuck, though childless and a self-professed misogynist, has shown himself truly paternal – not only to Lovel but also to his MacIntyre niece and nephew, to Isabella, and to his tenants the Mucklebackits. Unlike the self-absorbed Sir Arthur, towards whom his daughter must act with quasi-parental protectiveness, or the tyrannical Countess Glenallan, Oldbuck takes under his protection various children, gives of himself not for the sake of personal power or pride of lineage but out of that intrinsic generosity of heart which had enabled him to appreciate Lovel for himself – calling him his '*rara avis*,' his 'black swan,' his 'phoenix' (I, 180) long before there was any hint of his being the son of the lost beloved.[11]

The presence in the novel of the comically melodramatic Wardour strand and the darkly Gothic Glenallan strand helps to establish a right reading of the Oldbuck plot. One old man, Sir Arthur, is utterly powerless, dependent for rescue absolutely on others, too foolish and stubborn to change. The other, Lord Glenallan, is so incapacitated by remorse that he can never return to life but only recognize his son and then wait for death. Edie, the third old man with an important role in the novel, survives his punishment for overreaching and emerges from imprisonment to continue his essential function of binding the community together. Oldbuck's own reintegration into that community can only be partial – Edie acts as his agent in his subsequent dealings with the Mucklebackits – and he still lacks that full friendship with a circle of equals that would temper his excess of self-esteem. The sadly funny stay of Lord Glenallan at Monkbarns, replete with misreadings of the Earl by the antiquary, clearly demonstrates that the latter's years of self-protective withdrawal have blunted his sensitivity in ways that cannot now be fully repaired. Lovel is dedicated to a future happiness that belongs to Isabella; there will be a place for Oldbuck in their new world, but not at the centre of it. What Oldbuck lost as a young man remains, therefore, a loss. Although possessed of the interpreter's power essential to the resolution of the oppositions that pattern the novel – withdrawal and involvement, passivity and activism, silence and utterance – and gifted with the talents of the good father and the willingness to use them, Oldbuck remains the childless one. He is not, after all, Lovel's father, and central to the whole experience of reading *The Antiquary* is the poignancy of that moment when he must stand aside while Lord Glenallan claims his son.

Lovel's importance in the novel is, quite simply, that he is lovable. A recognition – indeed, an affectionate exaggeration – of Lovel's qualities has opened up for Oldbuck the possibility not only of loving a stranger but of loving his neighbours, and himself as well. The lost-heir plot and the conventional romance structure ending in marriage are thus exploited in *The Antiquary* not for their own sakes but as ways of dramatizing the steps by which Oldbuck comes to terms with the past and opens himself up to the future. As so often in Scott, the reader's interpretation of the central matter of the novel is guided by parallel and related elements in the structure.[12] To recognize the downplaying of the romance plot implicit in Lovel's pallidness and his absence from crucial episodes is to be directed towards the necessity of focusing attention on Oldbuck. Even at the end of the novel the reader has no great investment in the question of what Lovel will make of his new identity: the Glenallan estate is clearly in quite flourishing condition and not in need of the kind of restoration that was required at Ellangowan; the important future does not consist in the many years of happiness ahead of Lovel and Isabella but in the few still left to the antiquary; he and Edie, indeed, and not the young hero and heroine, are to be the agents of the reconciliation and social restoration traditionally associated with the conclusion of a romance.

Despite the novel's comic mode, the focus on the middle-aged hero is quite Jamesian in its seriousness. Scott appreciated as clearly as his American successor the thickened texture afforded by such a protagonist when compared with the shallower possibilities of the still-youthful hero. And, like James again, his concern was with the development of perception and with the effect on the central figure of a gradual process of recognition and understanding. *The Antiquary* does not, of course, concern itself with the kind of heightened self-awareness that provided James with the germ of *The Ambassadors*. Oldbuck is totally without any taste or talent for analysing his own condition – indeed, his stability and happiness have been maintained precisely by his avoiding introspection and translating personal anguish into an obsessive concern for antiquarian trivia – and what is valued in Scott's novel is the kind of perceptivity that manifests itself as an unselfconscious ability to see other people clearly and recognize their qualities and needs. For Oldbuck, seeing and understanding open the door to loving; or rather, loving makes seeing and understanding possible.

Complaints about the unsatisfactoriness of the structure of *The Antiquary* and the weakness of some of its characters, notably Lovel and Isabella, arise in the main from a failure to understand what Scott was attempting. The most fascinating characters in his early novels are generally acknowledged to be such middle-aged men as Baron Bradwardine, Pleydell, Oldbuck, Edie, Rob Roy, and Nicol Jarvie. Scott's impulse to focus on such figures was obviously powerful, but he chose to indulge it without abandoning the kind of conventional plotting which required the presence of a young hero and heroine ostensibly at centre-stage. He moved, indeed, with some caution and obliquity towards the full exposition of his central imaginative preoccupations, and the first three novels can be seen in terms of a staged sequence. Important though the various father-figures in *Waverley* undoubtedly are, the main emphasis remains upon Edward and his experiences. *Guy Mannering*, as its title announces, exhibits a much greater concern with the personal disaster the middle-aged Mannering has made of his life and with the unhealed wounds whose pain all the resources of personal stoicism cannot quite deaden. But Mannering is not at centre-stage in the latter part of the novel, and there is no real exploration of what comfort, if any, he gains from the restoration of Ellangowan's heir and the marriage of his daughter to that heir. His initial astrologer role establishes him as a foreteller of disasters he is powerless to avert, and, like Prospero, he has no future once his wand is broken. The subsidiary father-figures, Pleydell and Dominie Sampson, can, like Mannering, participate in the final process of revelation, but the focus is never on what it means for them. The real father, Godfrey Bertram, is dead before his son returns to Ellangowan. In *The Antiquary* this concern with the effect of the sins of the fathers on the second generation is downplayed in order that the reader's attention may be directed back to the fathers themselves. Lord Glenallan, unlike Godfrey Bertram, lives to see his son restored, winning in the process a minimal peace with his own past. But what is far more crucial is that the figure of Oldbuck occupies a central position denied to any of his predecessors and that the novel sets out quite deliberately and consistently to record the stages of his re-emergence as a man of feeling, not just a man of old books.

The Antiquary, coming at the climax of the first great phase of the anonymity game, was in fact used by Scott for a self-indulgent transformation of concealment into a form of self-revelation that for the time being he could not afford to push any further. On completing the novel he signalled privately to himself, and publicly to his readers, that it marked some kind of an ending and that a fresh beginning would now be necessary. On the last page of the manuscript he wrote: 'Finis is is is.'[13] And in April 1816, when most of the novel had gone through the press, he composed a preliminary Advertisement in which the Author of *Waverley*, observing that the three novels, *Waverley*, *Guy Mannering*, and *The Antiquary*, constituted a completed series, formally bade his readers farewell. He further signalled the completion of a series by supplying a glossary of Scottish words used in the three novels. When negotiations for the next novel began, as they did almost immediately, the Ballantynes were empowered to seek a new set of publishers, and when the book appeared, the Author of *Waverley* was replaced on the title-page by Jedediah Cleishbotham. It seems almost as though a new phase of the game and a new authorial persona were demanded by Scott's sense that too much of himself had gone into what claimed to be the Author of *Waverley*'s concluding work.

6

The Black Dwarf and *Old Mortality*: Ending Right

The absence from the title-page of *Tales of My Landlord* of any reference to the Author of *Waverley* was no accident. In authorizing the Ballantynes to find him new publishers[1] – who were not to be let into the Waverley secret – Scott took the anonymity game one stage further, creating for the new series of narratives their own special authorial apparatus. He gleefully reported the new twist to his actor friend Daniel Terry:

To give the go-by to the public, I have doubled and leaped into my form, like a hare in snow: that is, I have changed my publisher, and come forth like a maiden knight's white shield (there is a conceit!) without any adhesion to fame gained in former adventures (another!) or, in other words, with a virgin title-page (another!). (*L* IV, 288)

The shift allowed Scott to draw back from the barely disguised personal involvement that had characterized *The Antiquary*. Having put perhaps too much of himself into the figure of Jonathan Oldbuck, he now created, in Jedediah Cleishbotham, a much less gifted middle-aged annotator and confined him safely to the framework. By teaming Cleishbotham with Peter Pattieson he allowed for the metaphoric expression of questions about external control and authority that derived from his fascination and uneasiness with the whole idea of authorship.

The interplay within the Gandercleuch framework between the romantically self-conscious Pattieson, the inditer of the tales, and the assertively egotistical Cleishbotham, their publicist and occasional annotator, revives in more extreme form the arrangement Oldbuck proposed to Lovel in *The Antiquary* for the composition of the projected 'Caledo-niad.' Like Oldbuck, Cleishbotham is not shy of proclaiming his own talents; at the same time he is just as anxious as Oldbuck to escape authorial responsibility:

Now, therefore, the world may see the injustice that charges me with inca-pacity to write these narratives, seeing, that though I have proved that I could have written them if I would, yet, not having done so, the censure will deservedly fall, if at all due, upon the memory of Mr Peter Pattieson.[2]

Cleishbotham, as a dogmatic literalist, has not taken it upon himself to make any changes in Pattieson's text – apart from the expansion of a few references to himself – but he remains distrustful of the freedom with which Pattieson has handled his source materials:

I have only further to intimate, that Mr Peter Pattieson, in arranging these Tales for the press, hath more consulted his own fancy than the accuracy of the narrative; nay, that he hath sometimes blended two or three together for the mere grace of his plots.   (1, 19–20)

Pattieson's own claims make no reference to such manipulations but speak rather of the care he has taken to rid his materials of superstitious distortion and to clarify the sequence of events:

After my usual manner, I made farther enquiries of other persons connected with the wild and pastoral district in which the scene of the following narra-tive is placed, and I was fortunate enough to recover many links of the story, not generally known, and which account, at least in some degree, for the circumstances of exaggerated marvel with which superstition has attired it in the more vulgar traditions.   (1, 33–4)

Despite the ostensible antiquarian scrupulosity, the stress on recovering 'links of the story' suggests an activity novelistic as well as investigative, the pursuit of an enhanced coherence that may derive not only from inquiries thoroughly and conscientiously pursued but also from the shaping power of the 'fancy' as it engages narratively with the materials

– the very activity, in short, castigated by Cleishbotham as blending 'two or three together for the mere grace of his plots.'

But if Pattieson is the artist figure here, the comic tone of the framework indicates that it would be a mistake to see him as an authorial ideal, set off against the pedestrian editorial figure who merely oversees publication. He is too easily satisfied with his own achievements, while his somewhat effete romanticism suggests other kinds of inadequacy. He is a dreaming poet gone to an early grave, an observer rather than an actor, and it becomes increasingly difficult to rest completely satisfied with his talk of stripping vulgar traditions of their circumstances of exaggerated marvel. There may be a kind of truth about Canny Elshie, or about Claverhouse or John Balfour of Burley for that matter, that eludes the workings of enlightened inquiry. What the framing fable seems to be suggesting by its stress on the limitations of all those involved in the narrative process – from Pattieson and Cleishbotham to subordinate narrators like Bauldie and Old Mortality – is that the authority of a narrative may depend on something other than the conscious efforts of the author. Concentration on freeing truth from falsifying coloration may be in its own way an evasion of responsibility, a deflection of concern in the direction of external verification and away from the inner dynamics of the narrative itself.

The Waverley Novels are full of incidents that stress the unreliability of narrators, the distortions, deliberate or accidental, that creep in once speech and action are translated into the stuff of anecdote and legend. The varied accounts of his own first appearance at Ellangowan that Mannering overhears on his return more than twenty years later offer an obvious example, and within the framework of the *Tales* themselves we learn of the 'hantle queer things' (I, 28) that used to be told about the Black Dwarf. But while Pattieson the collector, sifter, and arranger would make a distinction between the efforts of the sophisticated, truth-seeking investigator and the naïve anecdotalist, he fails to take account of that narrative momentum which makes stories true to themselves. In his two previous novels Scott had assigned the interpretative and narrative activities – the attempt to make sense of a story and to develop a story that makes sense – first to a gifted lawyer and secondly to a dedicated antiquary. In his new work he introduces the most privileged practitioner of the sense-making power of narration, an actual author.

Pattieson's reluctance, however, to make any large claims for himself as maker rather than as collector and arranger throws the emphasis back on the stories themselves. And that curious title – *Tales of My Landlord* rather than, say, 'Tales of the Schoolmaster' – serves further to undermine the idea of authorial control.[3]

The Gandercleuch framework allows Scott the privilege of a dialogue with himself about authorship without requiring that he come down on any one side of the argument. During the writing of the *Tales* he had adopted a number of the positions here dramatized, on the one hand refusing to alter the completed *Black Dwarf* – though he himself recognized its weakness – and, on the other, indicating a willingness to tailor the ending of the almost completed, and much finer, *Old Mortality* to suit the preferences of James Ballantyne. The apparent contradiction can, on the face of it, be resolved by seeing Scott's relationship to his completed text as editorial and that to the text still in progress as authorial – although the ending actually imposed upon *Old Mortality* may suggest that such a formulation is too neat.

The first of the new tales, *The Black Dwarf*, failed to please Scott's new publishers and has found little favour with subsequent readers. Despite his intransigence about altering it – 'I belong to the Death-head Hussars of literature who neither *take* nor *give* criticism ... Nor would I cancel a leaf to please all the critics of Edinburgh & London' (*L* IV, 276) – Scott's letters of 1816 clearly indicate his own dissatisfaction with the story. His comments can, however, be somewhat misleading. His stress on having 'bungled up a conclusion' (*L* IV, 293) when he got bored with going over 'the ground I had trode so often' (*L* IV, 292) can lead, when taken in conjunction with his talk of having planned four tales about the different regions of Scotland and ended up with only two, to the conclusion that the main problem with *The Black Dwarf* was one of proportion. But it seems to have been the case that *Old Mortality* expanded under his hand rather than that there was anything awkwardly compacted about the first tale, which was always intended to be of one-volume length. The ending may have seemed to Scott 'bungled,' but it is not really rushed. No more plot material is covered in the final quarter than in each of the three preceding, and the narrative pace remains remarkably even throughout.

Although the tale opens with Hobbie Elliot and Earnscliff, the matter of the dwarf comes increasingly to the fore. The melodramatic soliloquies by which his disturbed mind seeks to authenticate and fix his vision of the world provide the most striking set pieces of the narrative and affect its balance accordingly. Scott is, as always, acutely sensitive to those characters who, like Meg Merrilies, deliberately work themselves up by verbal rituals into a state of heightened consciousness that allows them to dominate those around them, excluding other voices and alternative perspectives. Elshie seeks to compel utterance and experience into conformity. His favourite trope is personification, and he turns to allegorical generalization as a means of escaping human particularity. Willie Graeme of Westburnflat is for him 'rapine and murder once more on horseback' (1, 121), but Willie's own much more vividly physical metaphor – 'this is nae great matter, after a'; just to cut the comb of a young cock that has been crawing a little ower crousely' (1, 123) – quickly drives Elshie away from abstraction and back to names: 'Not young Earnscliff?' (1, 123) he asks, and a little later, of Hobbie Elliot, 'What harm has the lad done you?' (1, 124) The soliloquy that follows embodies the dwarf's attempt to regain the security of misanthropic isolation. 'Let Destiny drive forth her scythed car through the overwhelmed and trembling mass of humanity!' he cries out when the verbal spell is almost complete, but human feeling again breaks through: 'And yet this Elliot – this Hobbie, so young and gallant, so frank, so – I will think of it no longer' (1, 126–7). A few pages later the contrast between allegory and human individuality becomes even starker as Elshie, grieved at the killing of his favourite goat, drives Hobbie away with mysterious threats: 'If I go not with you myself, see if you can escape what my attendants, Wrath and Misery, have brought to thy threshold before thee' (1, 136). Hobbie's reply goes right to the stylistic point: 'I wish ye wadna speak that gate' (1, 136).

The melodramatic excess which characterizes Elshie's utterance is symptomatic of mental disturbance and, as such, dramatically effective, the contrast with the concrete specificity of Hobbie's speech establishing an ironic grid that enables the reader to keep his rhetorical bearings. But when the melodramatic colouring leaches out from the dwarf's speeches into the surrounding text, the effect is one of stylistic crudity, an undiscriminating recourse to the somewhat shop-worn conventions of second-rate Gothic fiction:

> The sun setting red, and among seas of rolling clouds, threw a gloomy lustre over the moor, and gave a deeper purple to the broad outline of heathy mountains which surrounded this desolate spot. The Dwarf sate watching the clouds as they lowered above each other in masses of conglomerated vapours, and, as a strong lurid beam of the sinking luminary darted full on his solitary and uncouth figure, he might well have seemed the demon of the storm which was gathering, or some gnome summoned forth from the recesses of the earth by the subterranean signals of its approach. (I, 119–20)

Descriptions associated with Isabella Vere are particularly subject to this kind of stylistic slippage:

> Within these narrow precincts Isabella now found herself enclosed with a being whose history had nothing to reassure her, and the fearful conformation of whose hideous countenance inspired an almost superstitious terror. He occupied the seat opposite to her, and dropping his huge and shaggy eyebrows over his piercing black eyes, gazed at her in silence, as if agitated by a variety of contending feelings. On the other side sate Isabella, pale as death, her long hair uncurled by the evening damps, and falling over her shoulders and breast, as the wet streamers droop from the mast when the storm has passed away, and left the vessel stranded on the beach. (I, 317)

Isabella's own speech shares certain features with that of the dwarf. She talks in abstractions that are paler echoes of those habitually employed by Elshie: 'All ... that need aid, have right to ask it of their fellow-mortals' (I, 320) she tells him, and when he asks her specifically if she is afraid, she replies that 'Misery ... is superior to fear' (I, 321). It might be argued that she is seeking in this scene to appease him by 'talking his own language,' but there is a histrionic quality about her words and actions throughout the novel that belies such a naturalistic interpretation. Isabella belongs, like Elshie, to the polarized world of melodrama. She embodies the innocence that the tale finally vindicates. The scene of the interrupted marriage is mounted not as a means of restoring her to Earnscliff and providing a romance resolution in their union but as a dramatization – as

Elshie orchestrates it, an emblematization – of the quality of innate goodness she shares with the dead mother by whose monument she kneels.

The stylization of the portrayal of Isabella Vere is clearly not the central problem in *The Black Dwarf*, and it would be pointless to attempt to defend her presentation against a charge of lifeless formality – as one might the depiction of another Isabella in *The Antiquary*. She is given only one free scene in which to act at less than full heroic stretch – the conversation with her cousin Lucy Ilderton – and this is not only much feebler than similar scenes in the other novels, its invocation of fictional parallels heavy-handed rather than witty, but it blurs the clarity of the melodramatic method employed elsewhere in her portrayal. Scott had created his own problem: he needed one kind of heroine for the black and white of Elshie's story and another for the social-restoration theme he had attempted to articulate through the story of Earnscliff.

The assimilation of Isabella to the dwarf's story does little to bring coherence to the other elements of *The Black Dwarf*. The book remains part attempted exorcism and part preliminary exercise. The mode of Gothic melodrama, expressive of the subconscious world of nightmare, allows Scott to touch on some of his own deepest concerns – the potential effect of crippling deformity, the wounds of disappointed love – but the translation of his personal anxieties into terms so grotesque prevents their really troubling his equanimity and vitiates their effectiveness as expressions of the otherwise inexpressible. There is a correspondingly perfunctory quality about the accompanying anthology of favourite motifs. Some details that Scott had already used are taken to parodic extremes, while others that he was to take up later are deployed without being allowed full articulation. The motif of the father dependent on a daughter, with its associated theme of exploitation, had occurred in each of the first three novels and is here pushed even further. Both Mannering and Oldbuck had tendencies towards misanthropy, but Elshie is its very personification. The treatment of the Border clans recalls both the *Minstrelsy* and the Dinmont section of *Guy Mannering*. Isabella Vere is in part a preliminary sketch for Diana Vernon. The 'thoughtless humour' (I, 331) of the young bridesman at the forced marriage looks forward to the conduct of Lucy's brother in *The Bride of Lammermoor*. The final dismissal of the Jacobite plotters – 'we'll no hurt a hair o' your heads, if ye like to

gang hame quietly' (1, 340) – anticipates in comic terms the justly celebrated climax of *Redgauntlet*. The examples could be extended further,
but what is striking about these elements as they appear in *The Black
Dwarf* is the breadth of the pen strokes and the brevity of the treatment
each motif receives – as though Scott was ranging them before him,
testing their potential but restraining himself from active imaginative
engagement.

The Black Dwarf remains in the end a work composed of separate
strands that fail to mesh together: the comic realism of the Hobbie Elliot
plot, the melodrama of the dwarf and Isabella, the quieter account of
Earnscliff as a man of moderation caught up in violent events. Coherence
might have been achieved by allowing the melodrama full play, but Scott
shares with Hobbie Elliot a reluctance to allow extended verbal expression to an extremist vision of the world. Though his novels were to be
simplified into the scenarios for melodramas and operas, he was himself
reluctant to surrender an entire work to such a mode. The other
solution – the registering of the cost and value to Earnscliff of each phase
of the action – is never really attempted. It was, however, precisely by
holding the focus consistently on the hero that Scott gave the second of
his new *Tales* the coherence the first had lacked: in *Old Mortality* Henry
Morton is compelled to confront the nightmare polarizing vision of
absolutists and fanatics, and the significance for him of every turn in
events is given full weight.

In the Advertisement to *The Antiquary*, Scott (as the Author of *Waverley*)
had told his readers:

I have been more solicitous to describe manners minutely, than to arrange in
any case an artificial and combined narration, and have but to regret that I felt
myself unable to unite these two requisites of a good Novel.   (1, vii)

Encountered at the outset of *The Antiquary* this has to be read as an
apology for structural weaknesses in the novel that follows, but considered as a remark set down by the author on *completion* of that novel it
begins to look like a deliberate self-challenge. Over-eagerness to take it
up may, indeed, have played a part in the comparative failure of *The Black
Dwarf*, but the composition of the second of the new *Tales* was at once

more deliberate and more successful. Scott's own delight in *Old Mortality* echoes through the letters that followed its completion: 'In the next tale I have succeeded better'; 'the last is, I think, the best I have yet been able to execute'; 'the long one which occupies three volumes is a most extraordinary production'; 'the second is exceedingly good indeed'; 'the second opens new ground ... and possesses great power of humour and pathos' (*L* IV, 293, 296, 307, 324, 331). That most of these statements were prefaced by negative remarks on *The Black Dwarf* may have released Scott from his customary self-deprecation – a habit he kept up even while maintaining the mask of anonymity. Even so, these comments on *Old Mortality* remain remarkable for their positiveness.

The pattern established in the letters is repeated in the famous review of *Tales of My Landlord* which Scott, with some assistance from Erskine, produced for the *Quarterly* and which combines severe criticism of *The Black Dwarf* with praise for *Old Mortality*. Discussion of both the new *Tales* is preceded by comments on the first three Waverley Novels, and since quotation from this section of the review has tended to distort discussion of Scott's attitude to *Old Mortality*, it is important to discriminate between remarks applied to *Waverley*, *Guy Mannering*, and *The Antiquary* and those reserved for the new work. It is in fact the earlier novels that are castigated for their plotting – 'slightly constructed' and showing 'slovenly indifference' to the requirements of 'a clear and continued narrative' – and for their heroes – 'very amiable and very insipid sort of young men ... never actors, but always acted upon by the spur of circumstances.'[4] These criticisms are then extended to *The Black Dwarf*, described as 'even more than usually deficient in the requisites of a luminous and interesting narrative'[5] and as containing a hero cast in the same passive mould as his three predecessors. But *Old Mortality* is not associated with these criticisms: 'The story which occupies the next three volumes is of much deeper interest'[6]; its protagonist is praised for 'having, as is incumbent on him as the hero of the tale, done prodigious things to turn the scale of fortune ...'[7] Despite the lightly ironic reviewer's tone, the intention is clearly to distinguish the second of the new *Tales* from the previous productions of the Author of *Waverley*.

A clue to Scott's highest ambitions as a novelist can be found in some of the critical comments on Richardson and Fielding contained in the prefaces he wrote in the early 1820s for the volumes of *Ballantyne's*

Novelist's Library. He praised *Pamela* for the 'return to truth and nature' it represented when contrasted with the seventeenth-century prose romances, those 'huge folios of inanity, over which our ancestors yawned themselves to sleep,'[8] and he celebrated *Tom Jones* as a kind of structural ideal: 'The felicitous contrivance, and happy extrication of the story, where every incident tells upon, and advances the catastrophe, while, at the same time, it illustrates the characters of those interested in its approach, cannot too often be mentioned with the highest approbation.'[9] In *Old Mortality*, his fourth full-scale novel, Scott seems to have embarked on a conscious and sustained attempt to combine realistic power with structural control, to draw upon the strongest elements of his earlier works while engaging more deliberately than hitherto with questions of narrative organization. In the review the 'deeper interest' of *Old Mortality* is in part attributed to 'its connexion with historical facts and personages,'[10] which had been one of the strengths of *Waverley*, while its portrayal of the royalists and Covenanters continues that concern with the depiction of 'manners' which Scott had singled out in his comments on *The Antiquary*. But it is, in fact, in its deployment of the kind of 'artificial and combined narrative' found lacking in *The Antiquary* that the novel most clearly marks a new departure.[11] Though much has been written about the historical power and authenticity of *Old Mortality* – a tradition established by the amplitude of historical and anecdotal illustration in Scott's own review – far less attention has been paid to its narrative strength.

Scott recognized that his earlier novels had been characterized by a heavy reliance on dramatized scenes as opposed to narrative analysis, noting in the *Quarterly* article that the Author of *Waverley* had 'avoided the common language of narrative, and thrown his story, as much as possible, into a dramatic shape.'[12] This had 'added greatly to the effect, by keeping both the actors and action continually before the reader,' thus compelling him 'to think of the personages of the novel and not the writer'; on the other hand, this method was 'a principal cause of the flimsiness and incoherent texture of which his greatest admirers are compelled to complain.'[13] Scott had no intention of abandoning the dramatic method in his new novel – its preaching and testifying episodes contain some of his most elaborate set-piece scenes[14] – but he did embark upon it with a heightened sensitivity to the distinction between telling and showing, a concern that was to remain with him throughout the first three series of the *Tales* and be formally articulated in the debate between Peter Pattieson the writer and Dick Tinto the painter in the introductory chapter of *The Bride of Lammermoor*. In *Old Mortality*, 'telling,' the quintessential authorial act, takes the form not of narrative amplification but of structural control. The presence of the teller is felt in the design rather than in any displacement of the dramatic method by the expository.

The seventeenth-century prose romances to which Scott scornfully referred when praising Richardson are invoked in both *The Black Dwarf* and *Old Mortality*, ostensibly as touches of period colour but clearly with the intention of drawing attention to what distinguishes Scott's narrative from its ponderous and non-realistic predecessors. In *The Black Dwarf* the trick does not quite come off. Lucy Ilderton tells Isabella Vere: 'You laugh at my skill in romance; but, I assure you, should your history be written, like that of many a less distressed and less deserving heroine, the well-judging reader would set you down for the lady and the love of Earnscliff, from the very obstacle which you suppose so insurmountable' (I, 116–17). This slightly heavy-handed invitation to the reader to employ his familiarity with literary conventions both to connect Isabella with the heroines of the folios she loves and to discriminate her from them fails in its intention because *The Black Dwarf* cannot rise above melodrama, and the pallid Isabella is assimilated to her romance precursors. But Scott was not therefore deterred from advancing a similar comparison in *Old Mortality*. He makes the point jokingly but firmly, setting off his own novel – 'the little cock-boat in which the gentle reader has deigned to embark' – against 'the laborious and long-winded romances of Calprenede and Scuderi, the mirrors in which the youth of that age delighted to dress themselves' (II, 47). When Edith Bellenden requests her uncle to send her the second volume of the *Grand Cyrus*, a deliberate contrast is being set up between her very human concern for her endangered lover, for which this request serves as camouflage, and the stylized rituals of prose romance. Major Bellenden's scorn of 'the fellows that write such nonsense,' his feeling that they should be 'brought to the picquet' (III, 274) for telling lies, serves as an indirect claim for the greater truthfulness of *Old Mortality* itself.

Scott's aim is a narrative made convincing by its historical and regional truth, by the realistic power of its characterization, and by the special kind of 'rightness' that derives from the expression of historical and psychological inevitability in terms of narrative pattern. In pursuit of this goal he reaches back beyond the late prose romances to those medieval and renaissance romances whose narrative designs were directed specifically towards the endorsement of aesthetic and moral significance. As the reader of *Old Mortality* acquiesces in the necessary outcome not only of the public events whose course has been settled by the passage of historical time but also of the private action, as he acknowledges that these characters in combination would be likely to act in this way and that these social, economic, religious, and political forces would have this kind of effect, so he finds his judgment supported by the way in which the various narrative pieces fall steadily into place. Scott had achieved something of this effect in *Waverley*, but in the less directly historical novels that followed he had relaxed his narrative grip slightly in the interests of achieving greater detail in his portrayal of regional mores and personal idiosyncrasies. Now he returned to the *Waverley* method and employed it with a new deliberateness and sophistication. In *Old Mortality* there is scarcely a speech, incident, or description that does not find an echoing response elsewhere in the story; nothing is surplus to the requirements of narrative coherence.

The pattern of *Old Mortality* must thus be read both as aesthetic structure and as moral design, creating satisfaction by its shapeliness but also directing judgment by the connections it establishes. Henry Morton sets out on a quest for a moderate individual freedom that does not depend upon any denial of the reasonable freedom of others – a goal as difficult of attainment as anything undertaken by a knight of romance. He is an isolated figure determined to act wisely and with judgment in a world where violence and fanaticism, the abandonment of private reason to public dogma, have reduced personal freedom almost to non-existence.[15] Some men retreat behind locked doors or into private rooms, like his uncle or Neil Blane the piper, while others, like Burley and Claverhouse, see themselves as the agents of providence or the pawns of destiny. The loudest voices cry prophecies, or proclaim that everything is determined for them by God, or higher laws, or history, or inherited duty, or simply fate. Events assume a pattern that appears unalterable – the journey back to Milnwood recapitulates the voyage out: the staging points at the inn, the crossroads, Milnwood itself, are the same. But Henry Morton, the mortal Everyman of this drama, must still make choices, act as a free man, refuse the evasions and seductions of unreasoning commitment to cause, or faith, or individual. His freedom of action is severely restricted; he cannot change the historical circumstances, his own familial heritage, or the attitudes of those with whom he must contend. But narrowness of choice increases rather than diminishes moral responsibility, and his voice must be raised no matter how deaf the ears on which his testimony falls. He is denied the passivity of his Waverley predecessors; the inactivity he might have preferred is glimpsed and then lost in that brief moment when his uncle's miserliness seems to allow him the luxury of remaining near Edith rather than seeking his fortune abroad. Like so many Scott characters he is sought out by history, and he responds with reasoned action.

The first step, the decision to attend the wappenschaw, has already been taken when the narrative opens and seems casual enough – the easiest course for a man of moderation, subscriber to an indulged minister. Success in the shooting contest distinguishes him from his fellows; henceforward he is both marksman and marked man. His defence of the rights of ordinary Scotsmen to be free of military harassment attracts the attention of the soldiers, and when he refuses to allow an instinctive shrinking from Burley to deter him from granting him protection on the road from the inn, he takes a further step on the path towards the repeated encounters with death that will pattern his future. But Henry Morton does not simply acquiesce, abandon himself to the tide of events; he acknowledges each turn in the journey, either by an act of conscious choice or at least by a clear recognition of what is at issue. It is the interaction between Morton's stubborn commitment to a belief in personal freedom, in both the political and the metaphysical sense, and a situation that denies the possibility of such freedom and destroys those who proclaim it that makes the experience of reading *Old Mortality* so strenuous and painful. What is more, the very structure of the narrative can be read as denying what we admire the hero for continuing to affirm.

The opening scene at the wappenschaw serves as a kind of dumb show adumbrating the outlines of what will follow. The social, religious, and political divisions which become apparent in the support given to the different contenders at the shooting of the popinjay will take much more violent and bloody form at Loudon Hill and Bothwell Bridge. Morton competes against his aristocratic alter ego, Lord Evandale the Tory moderate, and his parodic counterpart, the ploughman Cuddie Headrigg. The pattern of the novel later invites us to compare the conduct of Morton and Evandale both in victory and defeat, to observe their reactions to captivity and sentence of death, their bravery and generosity. The parallels between Cuddie and Morton are even more continuously registered, requiring the reader to transpose from the comic to the tragic a whole series of demands that weigh very lightly on Cuddie but prove anguishingly burdensome to Morton. Cuddie's non-compliance, at his mother's behest, with the commands of Lady Margaret Bellenden points towards Morton's resistance against illegitimate authority, and the ploughman's feelings about the maid Jenny Dennison offer a comic commentary on those of Morton for her mistress Edith Bellenden.[16]

Cuddie is able to escape most of the painful consequences of being 'son of that precious woman, Mause Headrigg' (IV, 72), but Morton has to struggle continuously with the duties implicit in being 'the son of the famous Silas Morton' (III, 92). 'What has your father's son to do with such profane mummeries?' (II, 89) demands Burley, who will not be satisfied with Morton's moderate justification of his attendance at the wappenschaw. When Burley challenges him to make up his mind whether to abandon or protect the man who had saved his father's life, the decision, though quickly made, is a genuine choice rather than an instinctive reaction, taken with due recognition of the possible consequences for himself and his uncle. Burley clearly hopes for an automatic response to the naming of the father, but though Morton 'idolized' (II, 98) his memory, it is no unthinking loyalist he reveres but the man of independent judgment who showed himself capable of separating himself from the extremists among his former comrades in the final stages of the Civil War. Claverhouse has something of the father's true measure – though he assimilates him to the fanatics and does not give due weight to his separation of himself from Burley: 'His father was positively the most dangerous man in all Scotland, cool, resolute, soldierly, and inflexible in his cursed principles. His son seems his very model' (II, 334). To be truly his father's son, Morton must be his own man.

Commentary on Morton's conduct is afforded not merely by the parallels between him and Lord Evandale or Cuddie, or by the more distant reverberations to be registered in the violent conduct of Sergeant

Bothwell, another man obsessed with his father and his father's father. Each episode in Morton's career has to be read as part of a sequence. This is particularly true of the various armed conflicts in which he is involved and of the trial episodes in which his principles are challenged and his life or liberty placed at risk. When questioned by Sergeant Bothwell at Milnwood he begins by demanding by what authority the soldier interrogates him at all, but later reflects that he is exposing his family to 'useless risk' (II, 184) and agrees to answer. He takes full responsibility for hiding Burley and seeks to exonerate his uncle. The pattern repeats itself in intensified form when he is interrogated by Claverhouse in front of his friends, Major Bellenden and Edith, at Tillietudlem: 'By what right is it that these soldiers have dragged me from my family, and put fetters on the limbs of a free man?' (II, 328) And this time he does not retreat, since no one is endangered but himself: 'I will die like the son of a brave man' (II, 330). His calmness under sentence impresses Claverhouse: 'he is tottering on the verge between time and eternity, a situation more appalling than the most hideous certainty; yet his is the only cheek unblenched, the only eye that is calm, the only heart that keeps its usual time, the only nerves that are not quivering' (II, 336).

When held captive by the extreme Covenanters, Morton's conduct is equally courageous and forthright. He will not deny his own beliefs or actions, but though he remains for a time remarkably calm in the hands of these 'pale-eyed and ferocious zealots,' his complete isolation – 'without a friend to speak a kindly word, or give a look either of sympathy or encouragement' (IV, 82) – makes the ordeal far more severe than its predecessors. He has entered a nightmare realm where his 'destined executioners ... seemed to alter their forms and features, like the spectres in a feverish dream,' and far from his heart keeping 'its usual time,' as at Tillietudlem, 'the light tick of the clock thrilled on his ear with such loud, painful distinctness, as if each sound were the prick of a bodkin inflicted on the naked nerve of the organ' (IV, 82–3). Afraid of losing himself completely, he reaches out instinctively for familiar phrases of support and comfort from the Book of Common Prayer, but in a world where religion divides and language separates, his murmured words serve as a final provocation to his fanatical opponents. Rescue does not mean release but a return to the hands of his former captor and judge, Claverhouse. And when his life is spared, no acknowledgment of the justice of his public conduct is involved, merely the repayment of his own earlier generosity to Evandale. The pattern of indebtedness that weaves together the lives of Morton, Burley, Evandale, Claverhouse, and, by extension, Silas Morton and Claverhouse's nephew Cornet Grahame appears to place a high valuation on particular humane acts, and yet its very insistence on pattern seems to detract from individual freedom by transforming such acts of private conscience into elements in a reciprocal design.

Morton's third trial, before the Privy Council, is ostensibly a simple formality, his pardon made certain by the surety of Claverhouse and Evandale. But he is compelled first of all to watch the procession of the men he has led into battle as it winds through the streets of Edinburgh preceded by 'two heads borne upon pikes; and before each bloody head ... the hands of the dismembered sufferers' (IV, 115). Having himself accepted the King's mercy at the price of exile, Morton must witness two very different interrogations that can only increase his painful awareness of the difficulty of justifying his own commitment to moderation and principled action and of discriminating that commitment from, on the one hand, expediency and, on the other, fanatical obduracy: while Cuddie moves from prevarication to blithe acceptance of any terms whatsoever so long as they are accompanied by a pardon, the young preacher Macbriar endures the most agonizing torture without breaking and goes to his execution sure of soon finding himself in 'the company of angels and the spirits of the just' (IV, 138). Morton's severest testing is this time indirect. He is in the presence of properly constituted legal authority, as he has been demanding since his first interrogation by Sergeant Bothwell, but he finds the highest council in the land disgusting in its brutality and levity, far more cruel and arbitrary than even Claverhouse and his soldiers had been. As he measures his own situation against that of the nameless prisoners stumbling along 'like over-driven oxen, lost to every thing but their present sense of wretchedness, and without having any distinct idea whether they were driven to the shambles or to the pasture' (IV, 118), or that of the delighted Cuddie, who would gladly drink the king's health 'when the ale's gude' (IV, 129), or that of the 'radiant' Macbriar meeting death with 'enthusiastic firmness' (IV, 139), Morton's efforts on behalf of his countrymen's rights seem to have had little value or effect. Sailing into exile he watches the features of his native land become 'undistinguishable' (IV, 147). And the next news his friends receive is that he has been lost at sea in the sinking of the ironically named 'Vryheid' (IV, 213).

The movement of history that brings about the accession of William and Mary makes possible Morton's return. The new sovereigns are committed to the ideals of moderation and tolerance Morton has espoused, and the forces of resistance clustered around Claverhouse cannot be expected to prevail. But since Morton himself has played little part in bringing about the change of situation, he has the appearance of a mere pawn in the game of history. Sadly transformed by his exile, he seems drained of life. Edith takes him for a spectre, and old Alison comments: 'ye're sair altered, hinny, your face is turned pale, and your e'en are sunken, and your bonny red-and-white cheeks is turned a' dark and sunburned' (IV, 239). Though he may resume his old dress and retrace the crucial stages of the journey that commenced with his first encounter with Burley – 'The scene was another, and yet the same' (IV, 258) – he claims his beloved only when she is herself a mere shadow of the beautiful girl at the wappenschaw; moreover, as she hovers over the dying Evandale, she remains 'unconscious even of the presence of Morton' (IV, 335). The narrator's comments on their reunion could be viewed as the bitterest of ironies: 'nor was she aware that fate, who was removing one faithful lover, had restored another as if from the grave' (IV, 335).

Read in this way, the narrative pattern of the novel gives the better of the argument to Morton's opponents, all those who believe in predestination in one form or another. Interpreted in even its most favourable aspect his own story seems to tell against him – the original victor over Evandale at the wappenschaw wins the greatest prize in the end and lives to fulfil old Alison's prophecy that he will inherit Milnwood and marry the woman of his choice. All that he has maintained in the heroic phase of the action seems to be denied. But such a reading fails to recognize that the pattern reflects the action rather than controls it. Morton's own deeds and choices are what make possible his survival, just as surely as Evandale's point towards death.

At the sinking of the ship on the way to Holland Morton had 'leaped' from the deck into the boat launched by two seamen 'and unexpectedly, as well as contrary to their inclination, made himself partner of their voyage and of their safety' (IV, 242). Fording the river after seeing Edith for what he believes must be the last time, he is saved from drowning by 'the instinct of self-preservation' and is 'obliged to the danger in which he was placed for complete recovery of his self-possession' (IV, 224–5). Though he yearns briefly for oblivion, wishing the dark waters had closed over him and obliterated his 'recollection of that which was, and that which is,' his faith in Providence (as distinguished from Fate) and the memory of how his life has 'been preserved through ... almost incessant perils' (IV, 225–6) both serve to arouse him. Rejecting passivity, Morton acts in order to survive. With Lord Evandale, on the other hand, excessive activity is presented as a choice of death rather than life: without waiting for orders he rides 'furiously' (III, 55) into combat to avenge the death of Cornet Grahame, and at the end, 'determined to face a danger which his high spirit undervalued' (IV, 328), he leads his servants into the mortal encounter with Burley and his troop.

Before Morton is released into reunion with Edith, his moral and physical courage has received its most severe test in the fourth of his sequence of trials, his own final confrontation with Burley. He testifies once more to his own beliefs, acknowledges his past actions and future intentions, and refuses either to be bought off or deterred from the right course by Burley's ritual invocation of the name of Silas Morton. Brought to the point of actual physical combat with Burley, Morton stays true to the decision he originally made in protecting Burley from the soldiers: 'I will not fight with the man that preserved my father's life' (IV, 312). But neither will he yield: 'exerting that youthful agility of which he possessed an uncommon share, [he] leaped clear across the fearful chasm which divided the mouth of the cave from the projecting rock on the opposite side, and stood there safe and free from his incensed enemy' (IV, 313). By repeatedly making the leap for life rather than allowing himself to drown or fall into the chasm of forgetfulness and oblivion, Morton makes possible the 'happy' ending. Narrative design confirms what character in action brings to pass – or, to put it in terms appropriate to the moral drama of this novel, the pattern is to be read providentially rather than fatalistically.

For the ending is part of the debate between Morton and Burley and Morton and Claverhouse about Fate and Providence and the value and

meaning of human life. To Burley and his comrades these are synony-
mous terms: 'the casual rencounter' that delivered Archbishop Sharpe into
their hands is for them 'a providential interference' (II, 88). They impose
a closed shape, as of a story already told, on a situation that is in fact open
to choice. In portraying Burley from the outset as a man troubled by an
alternative vision, his sleep tormented, Macbeth-like, by the memory of
the slain man's grey hairs, the novel makes clear the degree to which
Burley's position is a wilful one, deliberately adopted and dependent
upon the suppression of other possibilities. When Burley tries obliquely
to justify the murder as the result of a call 'to execute the righteous
judgments of Heaven' (II, 115), Morton retorts, 'I should strongly doubt
the origin of any inspiration which seemed to dictate a line of conduct
contrary to those feelings of natural humanity, which Heaven has
assigned to us as the general law of our conduct' (II, 116). For Burley 'the
moral law' (II, 117) here enunciated by Morton has no force for those
bound by a higher law that enjoins them 'to smite the ungodly, though he
be our neighbour' (II, 117–18). In thus rejecting the New Commandment
he clearly marks out the gulf separating him from Morton, subsequently
making repeated attempts to draw Morton across that gulf, call him back
into an Old Testament world where the imperative of vengeance leaves
no room for love and forgiveness. The chasm on whose edge they have
their final meeting emblematizes the risk of personal destruction that
Morton runs either in opposing Burley or in surrendering to him. For
Morton men's actions are not compelled; Providence creates opportunities for action, but choice is still required. He argues to Major Bellenden,
'Providence, through the violence of the oppressors themselves, seems
now to have opened a way of deliverance from this intolerable tyranny'
(III, 245–6), but claims that he has taken his own decision to act 'in honour
and good faith, and with the full avowal of my own conscience' (III, 245).
In the violent debates that rack the Covenanting army before the Battle
of Bothwell Bridge, he similarly insists: 'they blaspheme who pretend to
expect miracles and neglect the use of the human means with which
Providence has blessed them' (IV, 14).

Burley is paired in the pattern of the novel with Claverhouse, an
affinity Claverhouse himself is willing in part to acknowledge: 'we are
both fanatics; but there is some distinction between the fanaticism of

honour and that of dark and sullen superstition' (IV, 103). Both 'shed blood without mercy or remorse' (IV, 103), and their inhumanity makes them as careless of their own lives and neglectful of their own feelings as they are of those of others. In Burley the struggle of the divided self expresses itself in his nightmare conflicts with doubt and pity; in Claverhouse it is presented in the contrast between the cultured manner, the 'gentleness and gaiety of expression' (II, 287) that characterizes his private conduct, and the violence of his language and action when engaged in his mission of destruction. The terrified Edith witnesses it almost as a physical transformation – as his brow becomes 'darker and more severe, and his features, though still retaining the expression of the most perfect polite-ness, assumed ... a harsh and inexorable character' (II, 298–9). A void seems to divide Claverhouse's present self from some past self. He has suppressed the 'aversion to seeing blood spilt' he felt at the beginning of his career – 'it seemed to me to be wrung from my own heart' (IV, 94) – and can say on the death of his nephew, 'I will not yield to my own feelings a deeper sympathy than I have given to those of others' (III, 139). In time of battle he is never (unlike Evandale) drawn by emotion into rash actions, and it is, of course, Morton's disciplined courage that he admires. But Claverhouse's own control is that of the 'hawk perched on a rock, and eyeing the time to pounce on its prey' (IV, 60); once he swoops down at Bothwell Bridge, his cry is 'Kill, kill – no quarter – think on Richard Grahame,' and the swords of his troop 'drank deep of slaughter among the resisting fugitives' (IV, 62).[17]

When Claverhouse asks 'why should we care so much for death?' (IV, 94) he speaks as one who cares nothing for any life, not even his own. Civility has replaced morality; the gentlemanly cultivation of his public manners is the obverse of the abandonment to violence he displays at Bothwell Bridge. The only thing that gives meaning to his life is death: 'the hope of pressing one day some well-fought and hard-won field of battle, and dying with the shout of victory in my ear – *that* would be worth dying for, and more, it would be worth having lived for!' (IV, 95) When the gory figure of the dying Mucklewrath rises up and prophesies to an 'unmoved' (IV, 98) Claverhouse that 'the wish of thy heart shall be granted to thy loss, and the hope of thine own pride shall destroy thee' (IV, 97), his words contain as much of shrewd psychological insight as of the supernatural power attributed to them by the superstitious Cuddie.[18]

The presentation both of Burley and of Claverhouse insists on the degree to which the wilfulness of the egotist finds expression in a fatalism that seems on the surface to deny individual volition[19]: each man imposes a pattern upon events and then reads it back as an imperative. Burley and Claverhouse embrace vengeance and bloodshed and find the death they seek. That it is the death for which they are designed in moral as well as in narrative terms confirms rather than detracts from the rightness of what happens to Morton. He never surrenders his beliefs to their tyranny; he repeatedly makes the leap for life; he concerns himself with the fate of others – urging Cuddie's case and confronting Burley in order to try to rescue Edith's inheritance for her and Evandale to enjoy. By refusing to sacrifice personal morality to the cause he serves, he remains free to return and take up the threads of his old life. Though the life he resumes has a far more sombre colouring than it had at its outset, he has not been cut off, like Claverhouse, from the man he once was.

The cost is certainly heavy. If Morton lives, his surrogates perish: Evandale and Edith's other former suitor, Basil Olifant, are slain; Burley carries to death with him beneath the waters of the river where Morton almost perished another man from Holland, the nameless Dutch soldier round whose neck his hands are so tightly clenched they have to be buried in a single grave. Nothing could make clearer the point that Morton barely escapes with his life and that the happiness he and Edith may enjoy will always be shadowed by the anguish and violence that preceded it. As their hands are joined by the dying Evandale, it seems almost as though Morton's journey through the underworld presided over by Burley has won him only a spectral bride.[20]

Scott is here articulating his own version of the fate–versus–free-will debate. He presents in Morton a figure who insists, no matter what the opposition, on acting like a free man. To surrender the belief in freedom of action and in the necessity of taking responsibility for one's actions is to lose full humanity. It is a surrender Morton refuses to make, and his values are ultimately endorsed by the narrative. Burley and Claverhouse die violent deaths; he survives. The happiness of Cuddie and Jenny and old Alison indicates that the rights of his fellow countrymen were worth fighting for. His own reward is a pale shadow of the dreams of his youth, but it is, nevertheless, the reward he would himself have chosen.

Very late in the novel's composition Scott himself appears to have been in some doubt as to just how it ought to conclude. On 27 October 1816 he wrote to James Ballantyne:

I wishd much to see you here to consult you about the tales as well as to settle our accompts. I can end my story either tragically or otherwise – the last is the most commonplace but the most pleasing – on this I had wishd your advice particularly. (*L* I, 508)

There is little doubt that Ballantyne opted for the 'commonplace' and 'pleasing,' but it is hardly likely that Scott would have concurred had he thought there was any danger of seriously damaging the narrative design over which he had laboured with such care. By asking Ballantyne to strike, as on so many other occasions in their long partnership, the commonplace note that would find echo in every reader looking for a comforting and comfortable conclusion, Scott was in fact seeking to identify as plainly as possible one of the poles between which he proposed to find his way to a conclusion less extreme but more complex than either. He ends with reunion rather than separation, but the coming together of Morton and Edith is not only set in a very minor key; it is not allowed to stand as the last word in their story.

The addition of a closing chapter in which Peter Pattieson and Miss Martha Buskbody, the Gandercleuch mantua-maker who has read 'through the whole stock of three circulating libraries' (IV, 337), converse about endings in general and this ending in particular is unashamedly deconstructive.[21] Authorial responsibility has become so splintered – shared among Patterson who preserves the legends as he does the gravestones, Pattieson who collects, assembles, and shapes, Cleishbotham who edits, Buskbody who criticizes – that the characters from within the main narrative seem finally to be out of control, escaping out of the realm of fiction and back into that of historical record: 'I am not quite positive as to the fate of Goose-Gibbie, but am inclined to think him the same with one Gilbert Dudden, alias Calf-Gibbie, who was whipped through Hamilton for stealing poultry' (IV, 344–5). Though some of Scott's first readers, Jeffrey among them, found this an abrasive conclusion to so moving a tale, it represented something more than thoughtless high spirits on Scott's part. It was not simply an attempt to have it both ways, to end pleasingly while appearing to deny responsibility for opting for the commonplace solution. Scott wanted precisely to create discomfort and uncertainty in the reader as a way of drawing authorship itself into the debate about freedom of choice and action embodied in the main narrative.

The Gandercleuch framework of the *Tales* constitutes Scott's characteristically dramatized (rather than analytical) confrontation of fundamental questions about narrative truth and about his own authorial responsibility towards material variously derived from history, from tradition, and from his own creative imagination. The reader may wish to evade this debate, ignore the framing passages, and remain comfortable within the boundaries of the tales themselves, but Scott's continued employment of the fable of Gandercleuch throughout three series of *Tales* and his willingness many years later to accept Lockhart's suggestion that he use it a fourth time to unite two highly disparate stories[22] show that he never lost his personal fascination with this particular articulation of the relationship of teller and tale. Opposing theories of fiction are here set against each other. On the one hand, the stories appear to be validated by an internal thrust towards coherence and inevitability that commands the reader's acquiescence. On the other hand, the insistence that these are *tales*, shaped by an authorial hand, requires that they be seen as fictions, made rather than found, with aesthetic and moral meanings that need to be read and interpreted.

It may of course be asserted that Scott's choice of an historical setting, his use of a background of events whose public outcome was well known, automatically imposed severe restrictions upon his narrative freedom. But the importance of the 'historicalness' of *Old Mortality* can be overstated. Actual events and characters certainly receive more extensive treatment in this novel than in any of its predecessors; the ability of the historical scenes to carry conviction – to make us believe this is how the Covenanters talked or how matters stood at Bothwell Bridge – makes a major contribution to the power of the overall narrative, and there seems no need to quarrel with David Daiches's view, put forward in his seminal essay of 1951, that *Old Mortality* is 'a historical novel in the most literal sense of the word' and 'as an accurate picture of the state of affairs at the time ... clearly Scott's best work.'[23] It is no less true of *Old Mortality* than of Scott's other novels, however, that public events are always subordinated to the demands of the total narrative design.

It is at the ends of the novels that historical pattern and narrative design are usually seen to be most closely attuned. It has become a commonplace of Scott criticism to argue that his heroes choose the winning side and so survive; or, less crudely, that the fortunate outcomes of his private plots are endorsed by their being in step with the patterns of history. As a generalization this view has some validity, and yet examination of the endings of individual novels reveals important variation among the ostensible similarities. Scott in *Old Mortality* has moved on from the ending of *Waverley*, where the separation of Edward from the Jacobite cause and his recommitment to the more 'progressive' side was fundamental to the satisfactoriness of the final outcome. It has already been suggested that, in toying with the idea of making the outcome for Henry Morton tragic, Scott was looking at an extreme alternative to clarify for himself what the proper ending should be, but the fact that he entertained such a possibility shows that he did not see any necessary connection between his hero's choosing the right side and his achieving personal happiness.

In this novel Scott presents history as the scene of moral action more continuously and consistently than in any of his previous works. Though his actions are capable of political rationalization, Henry Morton moves in and out of the stream of public events as a result of personal rather than political choices. His alignment with the winning historical side is not the principal reason for his surviving and winning Edith; indeed, that alignment is itself so underplayed in the concluding section of *Old Mortality* that the event which technically makes his return to Scotland possible – the accession of William and Mary – is presented as almost beside the narrative point. In *Waverley* Scott had been very comfortable with a hero who was temperamentally and politically 'ahead of his time,' using this happy anachronism as an endorsement of the final narrative outcome. But in *Old Mortality* he is more uneasy with this kind of solution and underplays both the final happiness of his hero and heroine and its historical endorsement. In the next two series of the *Tales* he would probe still further the problem of narrative and historical fit and, in *The Bride of Lammermoor*, finally face up to the implications of a situation in which a hero clearly more progressive than any of the other characters is nevertheless cut off from the future by being slightly but fatally out of step with the actual movement of historical events.

7

Rob Roy:
The Limits of Frankness

The publication of *Rob Roy* marked a crucial stage in the relationship between Scott and the publisher Archibald Constable. Their association, which commenced in 1802 with the publication of the *Minstrelsy*, had had its ups and downs over the years, the most important breach occurring in 1808–9 when Scott ceased to contribute to Constable's *Edinburgh Review*, actively involved himself in the founding of the rival *Quarterly*, and helped set up the firm of John Ballantyne and Co as a publishing house complementary to the printing firm run by James Ballantyne. Although the Ballantyne publishing venture had its successes – notably *The Lady of the Lake* (1810) – most of its efforts turned out to be losing propositions, and Scott was happy in May 1813 to seal a new treaty of alliance between himself, the Ballantynes, and Constable, under the terms of which John Ballantyne and Co would be wound up and Constable would take over a portion of the unsold stock. Constable was not, however, given exclusive rights to Scott's future works; that would have too severely restricted the negotiating room for the striking of individual bargains. And in any case, Scott's somewhat shaky credit needed the firmer support that bills drawn on London publishing firms such as Longman and Murray could supply. In 1813, when the new agreement was signed, and again in 1814, just at the time Constable published *Waverley*, Scott and the Ballantynes were under severe financial strain, but although the active support of Constable helped them through on both occasions and although Scott regarded him as the shrewdest judge alive of the market for books, no absolute commitment was made even then as to the future works of the Author of *Waverley*.

Waverley had been published by Constable with a share going to Longman; *Guy Mannering*, however, was published by Longman with a share going to Constable. This meant that the management of the sales of *Mannering* lay in Longman's hands, an arrangement Scott subsequently came to regret. For *The Antiquary* Constable was once more put in control, and Longman relegated to the kind of purely financial interest he had had in *Waverley*; but the Ballantynes were reluctant to see Constable's influence become all-powerful and strongly encouraged Scott in his move to John Murray and William Blackwood with his next work, *Tales of My Landlord*. Once again he felt that the performance of his new publishers failed to live up to the Constable standard and, as already noted, he took personal offence at Blackwood's attempt to get him to revise *The Black Dwarf*. He was also annoyed at the attacks on the *Tales* in *Blackwood's Magazine*: 'Mr. Blackwood in holding the door of his puritanical magazine open to all sorts of abuse on Mr Jedidiah has no particular title to expect a continuance of his favours' (*L* IV, 431).

For the next novel a return to Constable was once more indicated. The idea of giving him 'a smell' (*L* I, 514) of what was to be *Rob Roy* was broached between Scott and the Ballantynes in April 1817, just four months after the December 1816 publication of the *Tales*, and the bargain was struck in the first week of May. As a condition of the contract Constable was required not only to offer a large advance but also to take another substantial instalment of dead stock. He came magnificently up to the mark and committed himself to a first edition of 10,000 – an amazing figure considering that by the end of 1817 the first seven printings of *Waverley* itself amounted to only 9,500. Completion of *Rob Roy* was delayed by the severe attacks of stomach cramp Scott was suffering in the autumn of 1817, but when it was finally published on 31 December 1817, its popularity amply lived up to Constable's expectations; indeed, a second impression of 3,000 was needed within a fortnight of publication.[1]

There is no doubt that these complicated dealings with a series of publishers were primarily motivated by financial considerations. But as always Scott showed himself quick to take literary advantage of a chance offered him by circumstance. If one of the attractions of the Gandercleuch framework of the *Tales* was its usefulness as a device for avoiding the offence to Constable that would be given by allowing the name of the

Author of *Waverley* to appear over an alien imprint, it would, neverthe-less, be a mistake to think of it primarily in these terms and to fail to give due weight to Scott's seizure of the narrative opportunities afforded by the introduction of Jedediah. And although Scott himself acknowledged that *Rob Roy* could not be offered to Constable as a continuation of the *Tales* – 'because there might be some delicacy in putting that bye the original publishers' (*L* I, 514) – there is no doubt that, once the decision to resurrect the Author of *Waverley* was made, he took an especial delight in the prospect of new twists in the anonymity game that thus opened up.

The reappearance of the Author of *Waverley* is deliberately underlined at the outset of *Rob Roy*. Not only is his name rather than Jedediah's on the title page, but the preliminary Advertisement offers a whole series of joking excuses for his resurrection after he had taken formal farewell of his readers in *The Antiquary*. He appears here in an ostensibly editorial capacity, but – unlike Jedediah, who could have 'revised, altered, and augmented' (*Tales* I, 20) but refrained – he takes an extremely activist position, speaking of changes 'so numerous that, besides the suppression of names, and of incidents approaching too much to reality, the work may in a great measure be said to be new written.'[2] By attracting attention to the Author's presence the Advertisement invites the initiated Waverley reader to place the new novel in relation to the Author's earlier performances and to set it off against Jedediah's *Tales*; by raising the issue of editorial practice it also extends the web of allusion back to the earliest achievements of Walter Scott, antiquary and ballad collector. In the repertoire of Scott's frameworks the *Rob Roy* Advertisement stands at one extreme on the line that runs from connecting bridge to boundary marker, its relationship to the narrative it introduces being of the most minimal kind. No reader of *Rob Roy* has ever wasted much time in wondering which details have been tampered with by the Author of *Waverley*. The slightness of the introductory fiction makes it easy to recognize that what is in question here is not an attempt to exert control over the narrative that follows, to require it to be read as a reflection of the Author of *Waverley*'s sensibility rather than of Frank Osbaldistone's. The framework's importance lies in the simple fact of its intrusion of itself between the reader and the tale. It signals that what follows is a separate literary text and invites the reader to relate it to others in the growing sequence of which it is a member.

The reading of that text is not a comfortable experience. Although the narrative design appears conventional, there is a persistent sense of disturbance at deeper levels, and the satisfactions of a romance story ending in marriage are modified by the presence of much that is dark, violent, and unredeemed. The hero, though young, courageous, and quick to take the offensive, is repeatedly involved in scenes of conflict and bloodshed not as actor but as powerless witness; the formally comic plot, complete with garrulous servant and other stock characters, is productive all too often of loss, betrayal, and death, while particular pieces of comic business generate as much pain as laughter; individual segments of the plot are arbitrarily negated and robbed of their ostensible point by subsequent revelations; the private action, though played out against important historical events, remains stubbornly separate from them. And all this is embodied in a first-person narrative marvellous in its eyewitness fidelity but resolutely resistant to the opportunities for commentary, analysis, and moralization implicit in the retrospective memoir form. Frank Osbaldistone, as protagonist-narrator, is frank indeed, but the connotations of his surname – bones, bleakness, and stoniness – tell us something rather different about the underlying meaning of the text. Although Frank's memory replays for him in the sharpest detail the scenes and voices of his youth, he lacks or represses access to memory in its other, more active mode as that mediating and interpreting faculty which connects present to past and endows experience with new meaning. Memory in this novel, far from being the redemptive power celebrated by the Romantic poets, manifests itself as a tormenting gift to the widowed and apparently childless old man who writes this story for Tresham, his business associate, and partner in the haunted house of Osbaldistone and Tresham.

To approach *Rob Roy* in this way is to take seriously as essential elements in its meaning features which criticism has traditionally attributed to weaknesses in overall design and execution.[3] The apparent dullness of perception in the narrator, the tension between the pattern of action as recorded in a plot summary and the actual experience of reading the novel, the seeming inconsequentiality of certain sequences of events and of such notoriously arbitrary occurrences as the killing off of Sir Hildebrand and six of his sons in a couple of pages or so – these features deserve consideration as possibly intrinsic to the meaning of the novel rather than as mere excrescences and incongruities.[4] The power of *Rob Roy* over the minds of generations of readers, the challenge and opportunity it has seemed to offer novelists as various as Thackeray, Charlotte Brontë, George Eliot, Hardy, and James, would seem to call into question the standard critical practice of detaching Diana Vernon, Nicol Jarvie, and Andrew Fairservice from the text and celebrating them in their own right while at the same time holding the text defective for releasing them so readily into independent life.[5] It may perhaps be essential to the meaning of this narrative that it should be so richly creative of characters and decline to hold them in check by any net of significant plotting or meditative commentary. Though the novel is filled with voices and peopled by characters who love to talk – all faithfully rendered by the ventriloquial powers of the narrator – it is, in fact, the silences that reverberate in the reader's mind, those agonized moments within the action when the words will not come, those still places in the narration when the clear opportunity for retrospective amplification remains unexploited.

Frank Osbaldistone does make occasional Waverley-narrator observations on the difference between the public situation as it was fifty years since and as it is at the time of writing, but these are so infrequent as to serve merely to underline his normal practice of eschewing generalization.[6] Such analytical and interpretative restraint on the part of the narrator could, of course, create awkward problems in an historical novel, but such difficulties are, in practice, easily circumvented. The semi-serious apparatus of edited memoirs implies a nineteenth-century perspective that the trained Waverley reader could be expected to deploy for himself, and Frank's detailed transcription of everyday life in the Northumberland wilderness, commercial Glasgow, or the fringes of the Highlands provides ample concrete materials on which the reader can exercise his talents for historical comparison. Within the fiction itself the role of Waverley historian is amply supplied – projectively rather than retrospectively – by Nicol Jarvie. Possessed of an insight into the social and economic conditions of Glasgow and the Highlands, understanding the political realities affecting Scots-English relations, he is able both to analyse the current situation and to look forward to what the future is likely to hold. Jarvie's shrewd foresight fills in the historical gap between 1715 and the 1760s; where Frank's is the observer's, his is the interpreter's vision, and he delights to discourse on what he sees and draw appropriate inferences and morals.

It is thus only at the level of personal memoir that the absence of interpretative commentary presents a problem. It is obviously tempting to posit a somewhat unthinking employment of first-person narrative as an off-the-peg device, to speculate that Scott merely wanted to avoid the awkwardness of such contemporaneous narrative strategies as letters and diaries and intended no special emphasis to fall on the distance between the now of narration and the then of the action itself.[7] But this is hard to reconcile with his persistent fascination with the processes of change, so specifically emphasized by the sixty-years-since subtitle of *Waverley*, or with his subtle and sympathetic explorations of the condition of middle age in novels such as *Guy Mannering* and *The Antiquary*. Scott could not but be aware of the temporal dimension of his chosen narrative method, and it is therefore arguable that any thinness we detect in this novel is that of the ice over which the narrator skates – that the apparent shallowness represents a deliberate turning away from the depths below.

The narrator is, after all, presented as being far from unselfconscious about the literary possibilities intrinsic to the memoir form. Frank expresses an almost Jamesian wariness about the 'seductive love of detail, when we ourselves are the heroes of the events which we tell' (1, 6),[8] and exhibits a sophisticated pleasure in the narrative intricacies of Sully's memoirs – 'told over to him by his secretaries, being himself the auditor, as he was also the hero, and probably the author of the whole book' (1, 7–8). Disclaiming personal vanity as a motive, he makes a half-hearted attempt to argue a moral status for his story by asserting a providential interpretation:

The recollection of those adventures ... has indeed left upon my mind a chequered and varied feeling of pleasure and of pain, mingled, I trust, with no slight gratitude and veneration to the Disposer of human events, who guided my early course through much risk and labour, that the ease with which he has blessed my prolonged life, might seem softer from remembrance and con-trast.   (1, 3–4)

But that 'I trust' fails to carry much conviction, and the reference to 'remembrance and contrast' points to precisely the dimension that is missing from the narrative which follows. It is left to his friend and partner Tresham to supply the interpretative meditation:

> Others bequeath to the confidents of their bosom portraits of their external features – I put into your hands a faithful transcript of my thoughts and feelings, of my virtues and of my failings, with the assured hope, that the follies and headstrong impetuosity of my youth will meet the same kind construction and forgiveness which has so often attended the faults of my matured age. (1, 5)

It may be that Scott did not fully develop the possibilities inherent in the first-person memoir form, but the choice of a single narrator and a retrospective angle of vision can hardly have been accidental. As autobiography the narrative certainly seems to have limitations, but it is surely worth asking whether those very limitations are not important clues to the meaning of the text as psychological portrait.

Even if the choice of a first-person perspective was initially dictated by a desire for that immediacy of effect afforded by the straightforward transcription of observed actions and setting, a wish to present remarkable men and events and unfamiliar locales in direct and uncomplicated forms, it is hard to escape the feeling that the limitation of Frank to this kind of camera-eye function takes on enhanced – one might almost say, newly discovered – significance as the narrative unfolds. This unreflecting narrator reveals himself as having been an unreflecting young man, caught up in a self-regarding pattern of behaviour that prevents him from responding fully to the complexities of the situations in which he is involved or the motivations of the people with whom he has to deal. At the same time the apparent arbitrariness of the plotting sharpens the reader's need not just to understand the forces generating the particular occurrences to which the young Frank responds in his egotistical and ad hoc fashion, but to make sense of the entire action. The pressure of the narrative method to supply such overall meaning thus increases as the novel progresses, but the reader finds that he must himself be far more active in the process than he is likely to have anticipated.[9]

The characteristic combination of inconsequentiality in the plot with a shying away from narrative expansion on the part of the narrator is operative at the very moment that ought to provide the climax to the plot of banishment and quest, Frank's reunion with his father:

Owen was not alone, – there was another in the apartment, – it was my father.

The first impulse was to preserve the dignity of his usual equanimity, – 'Francis, I am glad to see you.' – The next was to embrace me tenderly, – 'My dear – dear son.' – Owen secured one of my hands, and wetted it with his tears, while he joined in gratulating my return. These are scenes which address themselves to the eye and to the heart, rather than to the ear. – My old eye-lids still moisten at the recollection of our meeting; but your kind and affectionate feelings can well imagine what I should find it impossible to describe.   (III, 258–9)

The notation of what occurs here is precise and powerful – the surprise at the father's reappearance, the deliberate suppression of emotion between father and son and its transference to the faithful Owen, the embrace and the brief words that mark the renewal of the familial bond. The under-stated force of the dramatic moment is rendered stronger by the absence of any glossing commentary, yet the lack of such editorializing remains remarkable and the text itself deliberately underscores the gap. It is not that Frank is unmoved in old age by what he so precisely recalls – 'My old eye-lids still moisten at the recollection of our meeting' – but that he deliberately leaves to his audience the responsibility for narrative ampli-fication: 'your kind and affectionate feelings can well imagine what I should find it impossible to describe.' The scene addresses itself 'to the eye and to the heart, rather than to the ear.'

It is almost as though something of the mediating role performed by Owen within the action is being required of Tresham, and of the reader, in response to the narrative. Owen is repeatedly shown as the conduit of feeling between father and son, as interpreter, substitute, and even parodic counterpart for the elder Osbaldistone, filling in his master's silences, explaining his intentions, and acting for him. It is Owen who puts into the language of arithmetic a comically simplified version of his master's moral code: 'Mr Francis seems to understand the fundamental principle of all moral accounting, the great ethic rule of three. Let A do to B, as he would have B do to him; the product will give the rule of conduct required' (I, 28). He answers Frank's questions as to what banishment to Osbaldistone Hall means: 'You have ruined yourself, Mr Frank, that's all' (I, 52). And though there are comic overtones to Frank's discovery of Owen disgraced and bedraggled in the Glasgow prison, the episode brings home very forcibly to him what his father might have suffered as a result of his own desertion.

The Glasgow reconciliation appears to resolve the conflict between arithmetical father and poetical son that began in the London counting house early in the story. The father's mocking critique of the verses that fluttered from the pages of a notebook intended for the numbers not of poetry but of trade seemed a harmless comic puncturing of the son's youthful vanity, but it was not without an element of cruelty. The father's sharp tongue picked with equal quickness on false quantities, false rhymes, and false sentiments, while the faithful Owen attempted in vain to smooth matters over. Even when the son glimpsed the feeling that lay behind the father's desire to have him share his life and work, Owen waited in vain for the required message: 'My acquiescence stuck in my throat; and while I was coughing to get it up, my father's voice summoned Owen. He hastily left the room, and the opportunity was lost' (I, 49).

It is easy to see the antiphonal relationship between these opening scenes and the reconciliation in Glasgow. Yet if the embrace and few words of reunion restore the broken bond, they do not quite erase the memory of the forfeited opportunity and the words choked in the throat. Frank's journey into the Highlands in search of his father's missing documents ought to be the connecting link between the two moments, initiated as a kind of expiation for the earlier denial of filial loyalty and making possible a coming together in love and shared commitment. But the whole purpose of that exercise in commercial knight-errantry is vitiated at the very moment of reconciliation by the information that the papers are not needed, that the father's reappearance upon the scene had been all that was required to restore the firm's credit. This apparent perversity of plotting calls into question the entire significance of Frank's journey into the dark world of the MacGregors, deprives the reunion of any practical connection with that journey, and thus renders the meaning of the reunion itself problematical. The fitness of Frank to be his father's partner and heir is still in doubt, especially since his next reported actions are to join the Hanoverian army and then set out to claim his other inheritance of Osbaldistone Hall. It is true that he has his father's acquiescence and even encouragement for both these decisions – father, son, and political situation have all changed to some degree since that moment when Frank's suggestion that he might choose a military career drew from his father the response 'Choose the d—l' (1, 40) – but it is hard to forget that earlier remark or the fact that Osbaldistone Hall was not only the place of Frank's banishment but the embodiment of everything from which his father had separated himself.

The pattern of reconciliation in the father-son strand thus receives little reinforcement, and the earlier failures of communication remain unexorcised. And if one looks to the later consequences of the reunion, matters are equally disturbing. The pattern promises to be very satisfactory: the use of the new money to restore the ancient family property ought to promise dynastic restoration, a new future for the young man in whom ancestral right and commercial wealth are combined.[10] Yet that young man becomes the old one who tells this story, addressing it not to his descendants but to his business partner and providing no sign or glimpse of the future implicitly promised by its narrative of disinheritance and reclamation, exile and reunion. While it is clearly a mistake to read *Rob Roy* as though it were *Waverley*[11] – this is an essentially private story affected by historical circumstances but not embodying an emblematic resolution of historical conflict – the failure to elaborate the conventional outcome even in the private action remains none the less disconcerting. The story of father and son ends in reconciliation and inheritance, and these are reinforced by marriage in the second major plot strand, but the reconciliation is muted; the reclamation of Osbaldistone Hall becomes possible only after an amazing series of deaths and a final episode of special anguish and violence; the marriage itself is never directly presented but reported only – and in terms, finally, not of joy but of grief:

How I sped in my wooing, Will Tresham, I need not tell you. You know, too, how long and happily I lived with Diana. You know how I lamented her. But you do not – cannot know how much she deserved her husband's sorrow.   (111, 346)

However much Tresham may be imagined as knowing, the reader is not fully informed on these matters; as early as 1821 Nassau Senior complained in his review that 'How Mr. Osbaldistone "sped in his wooing"' remained 'mysterious.'[12] What has been powerfully imaged throughout the novel is Diana Vernon's role as the unattainable one, the vision, meteor, apparition, lost Eurydice of this quest. What makes her loss so poignant is the very specificity of Frank's act of witness to the living, breathing humanity, the free vitality of the girl of those early scenes at Osbaldistone Hall – quick-witted, beautiful, energetic, honest, careless of convention, and always just out of reach. For the reader, her transformation into the chastened figure of the final scenes is never reversed; the marriage remains unrealized in the narrative; she is the dead lost one and her childless old husband can only testify to what she was.

The pattern of the pursuit of the beloved echoes that of the father-son strand of the plot: silence, dumbness, or ineffectuality characterize the moments of crisis; recovery cannot erase the memory of earlier loss, nor achieved peace the memory of earlier violence. Most of the high points in the love story are, in fact, moments of conflict or parting. For all the openness of Diana's manner and the freedom of her talk, she remains surrounded by mysteries in which Frank has no share and is always partly in the power of those dark forces associated with the shadowy realm behind the library tapestry to which, even on the night he returns to Osbaldistone Hall as rightful heir, Frank cannot penetrate. The successive moments of parting from Diana become increasingly painful, forming a kind of hierarchy of loss. When she first urges him to leave Osbaldistone Hall to interfere in Rashleigh's machinations on his father's behalf, the scene begins with much romantic rhetoric: 'Every thing is possible for him who possesses courage and activity' (II, 53). Frank seizes her hand and presses it to his lips, but the 'rat behind the arras' (II, 58),[13] that reminder of the world of mystery from which he is shut out, drives him from the library 'in a wild whirl and giddiness of mind,' a 'chaos' (II, 58) of murderous emotions. The next meeting quickly becomes a quarrel, but Diana will not allow him the luxury of jealous anger and compels his assent to the calmer feelings of friendship: 'I sunk ... my head at once, fairly *overcrowed*, as Spenser would have termed it, by the mingled kindness and firmness of her manner' (II, 80). Her words of farewell seem final indeed: 'Adieu, Frank; we never meet more – but sometimes think on your friend Die Vernon' (II, 86). But it is hard for the experienced novel reader, only part-way through volume two and confident of that 'cork-jacket, which carries the heroes of romance safe through all the billows of affliction,'[14] to take this as too tragic or ultimate a gesture. The hero sets off on his quest accompanied by his comic squire, and it is difficult to believe he will come to any serious harm or suffer any absolute loss. But what in fact follows in the story of Frank and Diana is a series of re-enactments of this moment of parting. Each time, despite the constraints under which she finds herself, Diana continues to play the active role while Frank remains to some degree wordless or powerless, and the whole sequence takes on the quality of nightmare, very much of a piece with the actual dream recorded near the end of the book.

When Frank next encounters Diana in the darkness near Aberfoyle, the figure who was hidden at Osbaldistone Hall no longer lurks behind the arras but rides beside her and directly controls her freedom of action. Frank has himself experienced his share of horrors by this point. The darkness seems to be fast overpowering the light; unreason and violence have taken over from good sense and prudent action. Diana, again taking the initiative, gives him the papers he has been seeking on his father's behalf, but although the moment of receiving from the hands of the beloved the means of saving his father ought to be extremely positive, it concludes in fact with words of parting far more absolute than her farewell at Osbaldistone Hall: 'for *ever* – there is a gulf between us – a gulf of absolute perdition – where we go, you must not follow – what we do, you must not share in – farewell – be happy' (111, 177). These words are quite different in tone from the romance terminology she had used earlier in the encounter in a vain attempt to elicit some response from Frank by recalling the special language of their happy times together. But he responds neither to the private code nor to the sterner language of farewell. Far from his seizing her in an embrace, it is she who bends her face to him and leaves her tears on his cheek as he stands in stunned silence:

Heaven knows, it was not apathy which loaded my frame and my tongue so much, that I could neither return Miss Vernon's half embrace, nor even answer her farewell. The word, though it rose to my tongue, seemed to choke in my throat like the fatal *guilty*, which the delinquent who makes it his plea knows must be followed by the doom of death. The surprise – the sorrow, almost stupified me. I remained motionless with the packet in my hand, gaz-ing after them, as if endeavouring to count the sparkles which flew from the horses' hoofs. I continued to look after even these had ceased to be visible, and to listen for their footsteps long after the last distant trampling had died in my ears. At length, tears rushed to my eyes, glazed as they were by the exertion of straining after what was no longer to be seen. I wiped them mechanically, and almost without being aware that they were flowing, but they came thicker and thicker – I felt the tightening of the throat and breast, the *hysterica passio* of poor Lear; and, sitting down by the wayside, I shed a flood of the first and most bitter tears which had flowed from my eyes since childhood. (III, 178-9)

It is the catching of the concrete details which is the most remarkable feature of this altogether remarkable account, the stress on the physical processes of sight and hearing. The straining after the last sparkles of the horses' hoofs as the vision is swallowed up by the darkness expresses a clinging to the actual as a means of avoiding the implicit. In seeking to prolong Diana's physical presence Frank postpones confronting either the pain of loss or the meaning of the strange feeling of guilt associated with his inability to speak in this moment of crisis. And Frank the narrator repeats the process, capturing the experience but declining to offer construction or interpretation. The account of all his physical reactions is sharp and detailed, but the comparisons invoked, first for the choked silence and later for the hysterical tears, have an incongruity and hyperbole out of proportion to any significance openly acknowledged in the text. Just why Frank should define his silence as like that of a guilty man or compare his first tears since childhood to the anguish of the old Lear is not immediately easy for the reader of the memoirs to say. Frank himself offers no further commentary; narrator follows actor in mechanically wiping away the tears and continuing the journey (then physical, now narrative) on which he is already embarked.

Frank has already used the image of the guilty criminal when describing his appearance at breakfast the morning after his drunken quarrel with Rashleigh and again in recounting Diana's summons to him that same morning when she required him to explain his conduct: 'I followed, – like a criminal I was going to say to execution; but, as I bethink me, I have used the simile once, if not twice before' (1, 292). But nothing in any of these passages explains why Frank should be repeatedly overwhelmed by feelings of guilt when called upon to apologize, explain, or, finally, bid farewell to his beloved, why the guilt he feels should be associated with that of the condemned criminal, or why he should be self-conscious about using a comparison which might otherwise have passed unnoticed as a mere cliché. Again, the 'transcript' is supplied, but the 'construction' is left to the reader. What Tresham already knows, however, and what the reader of *Rob Roy* eventually discovers, is that the narrator who uses the guilty-man simile to evoke the feelings of his youth has himself been several times under suspicion, compelled to undergo cross-examination, and made aware that his life or freedom is at risk. He has also witnessed two episodes in which men are condemned to death and summarily executed in nightmare parodies of judicial procedure.

If the murder of the hapless Morris at the hands of the pitilessly vengeful Helen MacGregor is the episode which haunts Frank above all others, he has also seen Rob Roy himself take on the roles of judge, jury, and executioner in the death of Rashleigh:

The window of the carriage, on my side, permitted me to witness it. At length Rashleigh dropped.

'Will you ask forgiveness for the sake of God, King James, and auld friendship?' said a voice which I knew right well.

'No, never,' said Rashleigh, firmly.

'Then, traitor, die in your treason!' retorted MacGregor, and plunged his sword in his prostrate antagonist. (III, 338)

Though Rashleigh, Frank's chief enemy, is slain, it is by no heroic act of Frank himself, and the death, like that of his minor enemy Morris, is horrible both in its manner and in its suddenness. Frank may have wished both men dead, but had either been at his mercy, he would certainly have drawn back from the mock-judicial slaughter which they suffer. Clearly, too, he sees himself as in some sense implicated in the two deaths – by his thoughtless teasing of Morris and the clumsy naïveté of his interruption of Rashleigh's most cherished designs – much as he is ignorantly responsible for repeated complications of Diana Vernon's difficulties. These, together with the troubles caused his father, are no doubt some of the items covered by the reference to 'the follies and headstrong impetuosity of my youth' in Frank's opening address to Tresham. Within the narrative itself the blame is neither measured nor acknowledged in any explicit way, but its effects can be registered in those choked silences at moments of crisis, moments whose anguish seems out of all proportion to anything that youthful folly and impetuosity might be expected to unleash.

The absence of complex reactions in the young Frank can be in part attributed to his being stunned by the sheer pace and horror of the events in which he is caught up. Bloodshed, violence, powerlessness, and loss become the characteristics of an entire series of episodes which, if they come to seem to the reader like enactments of each other, must also appear so to Frank himself. The ambush of the English soldiers, the killing of Morris, the escape of Rob Roy and consequent shooting of the soldier who lets him go, the death of Rashleigh – these form a tormenting sequence of experiences, each intensifying the horror of the others and all capable of being replayed in that faithful memory of Frank's over and over again. Fused with the similarly recurrent experiences of his apparently doomed pursuit of Diana Vernon, they become near the end of the novel the materials of an actual nightmare in which something of what underlies the calm surface of the narrative is finally allowed full expression:

I remember a strange agony, under which I conceived myself and Diana in the power of MacGregor's wife, and about to be precipitated from a rock into the lake; the signal was to be the discharge of a cannon, fired by Sir Frederick Vernon, who, in the dress of a cardinal, officiated at the ceremony. Nothing could be more lively than the impression which I received of this imaginary scene. I could paint, even at this moment, the mute and courageous submission expressed in Diana's features – the wild and distorted faces of the executioners, who crowded around us with 'mopping and mowing'; grimaces ever changing, and each more hideous than that which preceded. I saw the rigid and inflexible fanaticism painted in the face of the father – I saw him lift the fatal match – the deadly signal exploded – It was repeated again and again and again, in rival thunders, by the echoes of the surrounding cliffs, and I awoke from fancied horror to real apprehension.   (III, 325–6)

The notation employed here is not very subtle, perhaps because of Scott's desire to make abundantly clear the paradigmatic nature of this dream, its status as model for the crisis sequences within the action proper. After each disastrous episode Frank, as actor and as narrator, has simply picked himself up and gone on. After the apparently traumatic encounter with Diana near Aberfoyle he reports: 'I recovered, however, sooner than might have been expected, and without giving myself time accurately to examine my motives, I resumed the path on which I had been travelling when overtaken by this strange and unexpected apparition' (III, 180–1). He cuts off his account of the curses of the dying Rashleigh by announcing that he chooses to 'dwell no longer on so hideous a picture' (III, 343). The motives cannot so safely be left unexamined, however, nor the pictures so easily exorcised. They persist in re-emerging in unaccountable sensations of guilt, and they trouble his dreams: Frank speaks of Morris as setting up 'the most piercing and dreadful cries that fear ever uttered – I may well term them dreadful, for they haunted my sleep for years afterward' (III, 122).

The guilts and horrors of the past recur – unconsciously in sleep, consciously (and obsessively) in narration – precisely because of Frank's inability or refusal to confront them and their meaning. The absence from the narrative of reflective and meditative passages is not accidental but integral; autobiography is here transformed into a ritual for keeping full understanding at bay. This evasion of interpretation is embodied within the narrative itself in a series of variations on the theme of transposed, deflected, or unexpressed meaning. This is a novel full of both words and silences, of plain-speaking and secrets, of communication and the failure to communicate, of letters that go astray and documents that seem to be vital but turn out not to be. The characters speak to each other in codes, sometimes as a matter of personal idiosyncrasy – as in Nicol Jarvie's employment of the terminology of weaving – and sometimes as a means of expressing feelings and attitudes that cannot be stated openly and unselfconsciously: Owen's translation of morality into the terms of arithmetic offers a comic example of this, while Frank's entire courtship of Diana is carried on as a kind of verbal jousting with a good deal of agile switching among the lexicons of hunting, farriery, heraldry, and chivalric romance. To speak in codes and images, however, is to engage in something more than a game; the meanings which are thus controlled and rendered safe are always liable to spring into active and dangerous life. Imagery will not necessarily stay put in the metaphoric realm: the cliché of the condemned man comes to awful life; the idea of some mysterious secret haunting Osbaldistone Hall turns into the actual figure of a man dressed to imitate a picture, and when that man is taken for a ghost, real violence follows; Frank and Diana quarrel and the metaphoric gauntlet thrown down between them is concretely represented by the physical presence of the glove on the library table. Frank's response to this instability is to tell, report, describe with marvellous specificity, but not to interpret. The fidelity of the narrative to surface detail – perhaps even the act of narration itself – is a way of keeping in the light and avoiding the dark meanings that seem literally to be manifesting themselves in this interchange between metaphor and actuality.

For Bailie Nicol Jarvie, memory is a fortunate possession that supplies continuity and meaning to his life in the present by connecting it so fruitfully with the past, with his father the deacon or the old wife by the fire at Stuckavrallachan. Memory for Frank is nearer to that obsessive sense of irrecoverable loss which devastates Helen MacGregor. Unwilling to change the metaphors or probe their meaning, afraid to read the lesson of his dreams, he finds himself perpetually compelled to reproject his earlier experiences precisely as they occurred, no more able to rid himself of them than he was able as a young man to rid himself of the incubus of Andrew Fairservice, no more capable of moving on from experience to explanation than he was of speaking at those moments of separation and anguish within the action itself. Not only does the activity of narration thus possess, in the end, as little efficacy as the quest through the Highlands for the papers that would save his father or the girl whose possession would ensure his own happiness, but the inability of the narrator to release the meaning from his story, to find words of solution, can be seen to have been prepared for and symbolized by the action itself. The link between action and narration is not, as we might initially expect, effected through explanation and interpretation but rather through repetition and reinforcement. The narration, in fact, far from illuminating the action, can itself only be understood by reference to that action.

Tresham, the sympathetic friend to whom the story is addressed, may look like a not very important piece of conventional narrative apparatus, but his invocation at the outset and intermittently throughout the story signals the need for continuous audience participation in narrative analysis. The link between Tresham and the reader is, however, far from simple. Tresham's response is never presented, and he seems, in fact, to have failed to supply that saving attention by which the listening friend can activate the process of narrative release. This is not, after all, the first time Frank has told Tresham his story – he speaks of 'the narratives to which you have listened with interest, as told by the voice of him to whom they occurred' (I, 4) – but the necessity to repeat the story a final time in written form remains compelling. Tresham retains the stance of wedding guest; Frank's marinerlike need to narrate is unassuaged, and, as in Coleridge's poem, there is a deliberate disjunction between 'moral' and story, between the tentative opening assertion of a providential interpretation and the experience of the narrative itself. The paradoxical effect of the unanswered calls to Tresham to supply 'construction' is to compel the reader to recognize that he must himself respond.

Rob Roy demonstrates the inability of narration alone to release the meaning of past experience or to provide a bridge between past and present selves. Indeed, in so far as narration attempts to set down the details of past events as though they were occurring at that very moment before the mind's eye, it seems to involve a denial of distance, a deliberate exclusion of the kinds of comparative measurement that would be made possible by registering change and difference. Frank Osbaldistone possesses not hindsight – with all its potential for definition – but merely the capacity to re-see. Scott's other novels are full of story-tellers, but nowhere else does he give the entire text over to a single protagonist-narrator committed to direct recall. Since there is no suggestion that irony is to be invoked to supply perspective – no occasion for the kind of doubt about the narrator's motivation that is necessary to a full understanding of, say, *Henry Esmond* – the inadequacy of Frank's grasp of his own experiences, his failure to process them so as to extract their meaning, forces the reader to establish his own bearings in respect of a text whose consistency of narrative method and singleness of focus deprive him of obvious markers. The image of the haunted and haunting figure of the older Frank, telling his story again and again, has a powerful impact once it has been disentangled from the ostensibly comic surface of the text, but it heightens rather than resolves the problem of what to make of the story and its narrator.

The discomfort that accompanies an engaged reading of *Rob Roy* is a measure of the reader's response to the interpretational challenge of a text that forgoes narrative doubleness – that interchange between differing perspectives which is supplied in *Waverley* by the combined visions of the youthful protagonist and the wise historian-narrator, in *Redgauntlet* by the pattern of dialogue embodied in the opening exchange of letters. For Darsie and Alan, listening is as active and creative a role as telling, and within *Redgauntlet* as a whole the kind of telling that reaches after meaning and self-understanding is sharply distinguished from the repetitive recapitulation of those whose very skill as tale-tellers ties them inescapably to a particular moment in time. In *Waverley* and *Redgauntlet* the youthful protagonists are employed sometimes as observing witnesses and sometimes as the objects of observation; we see with them but also look at them. In *Rob Roy* the older Frank certainly closes up the time gap so that we are able to look through the eyes of his younger self, but we are given little opportunity to view him objectively. Instead of the dialogue of Darsie and Alan that images salvation through friendship, *Rob Roy* offers a monologue that actually has more in common with those narratives of Pate-in-Peril and Nanty Ewart that enact the captive condition of men locked in their own pasts.

We are thus left at the end of the novel with a bleak conviction that frankness alone is not enough – to register without distortion what passes in front of the eye and ear will not tell the whole story. *Rob Roy* deliberately challenges the easy assumption of conventional romance that the frank and extrovert youth possessed of 'courage and activity' will escape both physically and psychically unscathed, and proclaims instead not only that there will be wounds but that they will remain unsalved unless some means of accommodation and compensation is found. In Frank Osbaldistone it presents a portrait of a dreaming boy who survives but does not in the process attain wisdom. Frank never comes into imaginative possession of himself in the way that Edward Waverley and Darsie and Alan eventually do, and what seems to haunt him is the suspicion that the universe he inhabits may in fact be absurd rather than providential – this despite his initial glib assertion of the orthodox view. The action of the novel, which is to say the course of Frank's early life, repeatedly shows that right results as often occur in spite of good intentions and right actions as because of them, and that separation and transience rather than reunion and permanent happiness are the norms of human experience. Yet Frank persistently shies away from reading such lessons into his own experience. He simply tells his tale once more, deaf to all except the sound of his own voice, substituting detailed description for analytical questioning, narration for interpretation. *Rob Roy*, in fact, is a novel about a man who, like Scott himself, cannot quite make sense of his own life, even though the outward pattern of that life has been a fortunate one.

The Heart of Midlothian:
The Pattern Reversed

Blackwood and Murray had brought out the first series of *Tales of My Landlord* in 1816, but Scott's disillusionment with them as a publishing team had only been confirmed by his satisfaction with Constable's handling of *Rob Roy*. Not only, therefore, did he come to terms with Constable for the second series of *Tales of My Landlord*; he also transferred to him the rights for the first series, beginning with the fifth edition of 1819. Henceforward, indeed, until the crash of 1826, all his novels appeared over the Constable imprint.

The new tale, *The Heart of Midlothian*, retained the Gandercleuch framework, the Author once more giving place to Jedediah, but in certain respects it seemed closer to *Rob Roy*, its immediate predecessor, than to the first series of *Tales* – as if, in fact, it were offering a kind of antiphonal response to the deployment in *Rob Roy* of key elements in the Waverley design. Frank Osbaldistone, abstractly considered, had fitted the pattern of the dreaming boy: a dabbler in poetry who rejects a place in his father's office, proposes to embark on a military career, and finds himself exiled to a region which seems in some respects to be the very country of romance. He had also embodied a variation upon Scott's favourite point-of-view figure, the Englishman travelling in Scotland, and his role as a narrator reporting the events of many years earlier made it further possible to see him as a version of the narrator-as-historian, thus combining narrative functions divided among separate figures in Scott's earlier fiction. In practice, however, these familiar devices are associated with Frank in surprisingly negative terms. His gifts as a poet do not seem impressive and his romantic dreams are only very sketchily dressed out; his discontent with the idea of a commercial career seems to be a matter of adopted attitude rather than innate impulse, the expression of the generational conflict with his father as much as of romantic temperament. As an observer of the Scottish scene he lacks the imaginative engagement of Edward Waverley or Harry Bertram. As an historian he is possessed merely of information rather than of the enhanced perception of hindsight.

To insist, however, that Frank Osbaldistone represents a severely limited version of a recurrent Scott type is by no means to say that the novel in which he appears is a failure. The tale Scott wanted to tell in *Rob Roy* was far more sombre than that narrated in *Waverley*, and its young hero had to be denied his predecessor's imaginative fulfilment; the potential for insight of dreaming boy, traveller, and historian is presented as partially blocked in Frank's case. The apparently successful outcome of his quest for liberation, worldly fortune, and love and for his rightful place in society is undercut by the irony of his failure to achieve wisdom. He is left at the end of the novel with no apparent future, only a past he does not really understand.

The standard elements of the picaresque plot of the youthful traveller in Scotland were pushed in *Rob Roy* to an extreme that constitutes a disturbing commentary on the Waverley model. And in his next novel Scott probed still further the potential of that model by standing it on its head. In *The Heart of Midlothian*, plans for which were well under way in the autumn of 1817 before *Rob Roy* was finally through the press, he took as his protagonist not an educated young man of good family but a young woman of humble origin, and set her upon a journey that led not from England to Scotland but in the opposite direction. Jeanie Deans is marked off from the outset by the absence of any tinge of the romantic in either her appearance or her perspective; at the same time those figures possessed of any significant degree of romantic sensibility are pushed to the melodramatic fringes of the text. In George Staunton, indeed, the figure of the travelling Englishman eager for excitement and the indulgence of his romantic appetites has become an anarchic and destructive force, incapable of reassimilation into the fabric of society.

The evidence that Scott was employing, deliberately as well as instinctively, a repertoire of motifs built up in the course of his earlier novels is too ample to require much elaboration. By this point in his career he had become highly self-conscious about his ongoing dialogue with the reader of the Waverley Novels.[1] The Gandercleuch framework of *The Heart of Midlothian* and the other series of *Tales of My Landlord* allowed him to express this dialogue overtly, but the creation of his own subgenre of the 'Scotch' novel also allowed the Author of *Waverley* to engage in a more subtle interaction with his audience, to take for granted a familiarity with certain forms of plot, types of character, categories of incident, subjects for description, and so on, that could be exploited in various ways, each instance sharpened in its significance by the echoing presence of the full repertoire as it existed in the novels taken as a loosely related sequence. When, for example, particular emphasis was placed on Jeanie's lack of the handsome appearance of the traditional heroine or hero, or on her want of familiarity with any literature beyond the Bible and a few religious tracts, or on her innocence of anything resembling a taste for the picturesque, the author could safely expect his audience to make the appropriate comparisons with Edward Waverley, Harry Bertram, or Frank Osbaldistone.

Jeanie Deans is the heroine of truth. She has no need to search for a father or an identity – her paternity and her selfhood are never in doubt. She is not concerned to define and locate her own situation in terms of literary analogues: that is left to Madge Wildfire. She is never found in disguise or decked out in clothes that shadow forth a different identity; the stress on her adherence to her Scottish dress and to such symbolic elements in that dress as her plaid and her maiden snood constitutes something more than the telling detail of a brilliantly realistic portrait. It is Madge Wildfire, Staunton, and Effie who appear in different guises and whose inconstancy and lack of any stable core of being mark them off from Jeanie. The role-playing and costume-changing that were harmless episodes in the growth of Edward Waverley and some of Scott's other young heroes become in *The Heart of Midlothian* dangerous signs of instability of character and failure of moral integrity. Staunton and Effie are possessed of the kind of imaginative responsiveness that was a positive quality in Scott's earlier heroes and heroines, but it avails them nothing. This is, as the references to Milton, Bunyan, and *Measure for Measure* indicate, a puritan fable – one in which Scott denies the imagination the kind of pre-eminence he had assigned it hitherto.

Scott was now moving into new fictional territory, turning away from the personal saga of the man of imagination caught up in the strangeness of historical action and regional disparity and towards a more intensive concern with moral questions. The allusions to earlier literary forms and texts remain for the reader to pick up, but whereas in *Waverley* literary allusion and romance patterning were employed to tell the story of a young man who was of romantic temperament and himself deeply read in the works invoked, in this novel they are employed to tell the story of a young woman who is not merely a stranger to imaginative projections but literal-minded to the point of comedy.

The ribbon of contrastive allusion that connects *The Heart of Midlothian* to its predecessors is not designed merely to afford delight to those initiated in the Waverley game; it is a matter of substance. The inversion of many of Scott's favourite patterns and motifs helps to underline the fact that, by the use of this new novel to carry Scotland into England, the matter of Scotland and her national identity is being brought into the forefront of the action. Like Henry Morton in the first series of *Tales*, Jeanie herself is compelled into a self-consciousness about her Scottishness quite distinct from the pride in her descent from honest and God-fearing folk that she has learned from her father. Her appearance and conduct must do credit to her native country as well as to herself. Scottishness is everywhere at issue – not merely among the dissatisfied citizens of Edinburgh, their national pride offended by the compounded insensitivity of the British court in dealing with the Porteous affair, but also on the road to London and in the capital itself. Jeanie is handed on from one Scot to another, finally arriving at the home of her kinswoman at the sign of the thistle. What seems to the Scots like the natural fellow-feeling of exiles is interpreted by the English as clannishness – Queen Caroline assumes that Jeanie must be not merely a Scotswoman but a Campbell, so warm is the Duke of Argyle in her cause. The suppressed hostility detectable in the murmurings of the inhabitants of Wilmingham against Jeanie and Madge Wildfire bursts out in the violence of Harabee that delights in the hanging of Meg Murdockson and costs Madge her life: 'Shame the country should be harried wi' Scotch witches and Scotch bitches this gate – but I say hang and drown.'[2] In the face of such animosity even the powerful Mr Archibald, surrogate for his employer the Duke of Argyle, can do nothing.

In the early part of *The Heart of Midlothian* the detail of Scottish history is close to the narrative surface. Though on the scale of historical importance the Porteous riots cannot be said to equal, say, Sheriffmuir or

Prestonpans, they assume a central position here, event dominating over character at certain points in a fashion very different from *Waverley*'s avoidance of the detail of major historical episodes. In this respect *The Heart of Midlothian* is closer to *Old Mortality* than to any of its other precursors. The characteristic Waverley method is to play out the protagonist's fictional story against the background of an historical action, and though historical characters may be briefly encountered and individual incidents, such as Waverley's rescue of Colonel Talbot, based on historical anecdotes, no extended use is made of the lives of actual men and women. In *The Heart of Midlothian* not only are the public events fully displayed – especially through the extensive treatment of the Porteous affair and the historically very astute portrayal of the situation of the Duke of Argyle as Scotland's spokesman at the court of George II – but Jeanie's story goes beyond even Henry Morton's in its historicity in that it is based on that of the real Helen Walker. The novel's factual origin may have helped to push Scott towards presenting Jeanie with an amplitude that gives the reader access to the inner workings of her mind and feelings. She is a distinctly new figure in Scott's fiction, and he lavishes on her presentation an attention denied to his earlier youthful protagonists. In the process the balance of characterization shifts from the typical to the individual, from the conventional to the realistic, in ways that help account for this novel's popularity with critics who have little sympathy for the emblematic rather than psychological characterization found in those Scott novels that place a more overt reliance on romance conventions.

To speak of Helen Walker is to engage with Scott's sources – an ancient and honourable activity, but one that rarely yields substantial critical rewards. The impulse to find an original for Tully Veolan or Dandy Dinmont gripped even his earliest readers, and Scott himself gave such enterprises a certain legitimacy by his January 1817 review of the first series of *Tales of My Landlord* and, from 1829 onwards, by his new introductions and notes for the *magnum opus* edition. But Scott's own annotations and commentaries are themselves deceptive: what look like historiographical often turn out to be rhetorical devices; the citing of sources and invocation of parallels becomes a special version of the trope of amplification. Even in *The Heart of Midlothian*, for which he himself identified (in the 1827 Introduction to *Chronicles of the Canongate*) the actual germ from which his narrative sprang, the relationship between the raw material and the workings of the historical imagination is very difficult to assess, and it is not even possible to trace the way in which two separate factual strands – the story of Helen Walker and the account of the Porteous riots – came together as essential elements in a complex narrative design. Mary Lascelles, in her examination of Scott as retriever of the past, has recently attempted to confront this problem by carefully scrutinizing both the letter from Mrs Goldie that supplied Scott with the Helen Walker story and the subsequent recensions of the story in which Mrs Goldie was involved,[3] and it is not necessary to reconsider the material she has so perceptively treated – beyond, perhaps, re-emphasizing the extent to which Scott's historical understanding and novelistic imagination have totally transformed the narrative kernel with which he began. What is clearly of primary importance is Scott's choice in this novel of an actual heroine of the people rather than a fictional hero of good birth and the accompanying increase in historical matter in both public and private plots.

In combining the Walker and Porteous elements Scott was committing himself to 1736 as the date of his narrative. This was almost thirty years after the Act of Union, and it was clearly of symbolic importance to him that two very different assertions of Scottish independence should have been brought together at a moment when a particular phase of Scottish history came to a climax. In a letter written during the composition of the novel he spoke of the desire to break the Union of 1707 as being 'for thirty years ... the predominant wish of the Scottish nation' (*L* v, 75). Though it would certainly be an over-simplification to allegorize the novel so as to read the Porteous riots as the emblem of Scotland's hostility to the Union and Jeanie's successful pleading with the Queen as the Union's vindication, an element of this pattern certainly inheres in *The Heart of Midlothian*. As a novel about violence and rebellion it is connected to *Old Mortality*; as a meditation on the Union it is linked to its successor *The Bride of Lammermoor*. The three series of *Tales of My Landlord* that appeared between 1816 and 1819 have, in fact, closer affinities than has generally been recognized, and they can be seen as a kind of national trilogy marked off from the rest of the Waverley sequence. Many of Scott's actions and writings – from the dedication of the *Minstrelsy*, through the building of Abbotsford, to the annotation of the *magnum opus* edition – took much of their impetus from his yearning to assert a continuity between the old Scotland and the new. But while his commitment to the Union settlement and his belief in the economic, social, even moral advantages accruing to Scotland are not in doubt, it remained impossible for him to exorcise completely the fear that the incorporating Union of 1707, as distinct from the 1603 Union of the Crowns, constituted an absorption of Scotland into the body politic of England. It is that fear which haunts the three series of *Tales of My Landlord*.

During the later months of 1817 and the first part of 1818, when *The Heart of Midlothian* was in progress, these issues were very much at the forefront of Scott's mind. He had been directly instrumental in persuading the Prince Regent to send down a commission for the opening of the crown room in Edinburgh Castle and the investigation of the locked chest in which the regalia of Scotland were supposed to have been deposited in March 1707, upon the adjournment of the Scottish parliament. Article XXIV of the Act of Union stipulated that 'the Crown, Sceptre, and Sword of State ... continue to be kept as they are within that part of the United Kingdom now called Scotland,'[4] and Scott believed that had the rumours about the removal of the regalia to London been proved correct at any time during the crucial thirty-year period after 1707, the action would have provided a substantial element in the Scottish population with a pretext for demanding a revocation of the Union. The regalia symbolized the power and independence lost when Edinburgh ceased to be the seat of government, and though the importance, both symbolic and actual, of the separate Scottish legal system steadily increased to fill the vacuum, the abolition of the Scottish parliament continued to be felt as a national injury, cutting off the Scottish people from direct contact with their rulers. As Mrs Howden says in the fourth chapter of *The Heart of Midlothian*, 'When we had a king, and a chancellor, and parliament-men o' our ain, we could aye peeble them wi' stanes when they were na gude bairns – But naebody's nails can reach the length o' Lunnon' (1, 100).

Scott was himself a member of the commission that entered the crown room on 4 February 1817 and opened the chest to reveal the regalia present and intact. He seems, in fact, to have orchestrated the entire ritual, and his fascination with the regalia made him think of using them as the basis for one of the tales in his new work. 'As I maintain a correspondence with Mr. Jedediah Cleishbotham,' he told Lady Louisa Stuart on 16 January 1818, 'I intend to recommend to him a tale founded upon an earlier adventure of these same Regalia' (*L* v, 55). He sketched out for her the story of the conspiracy for their concealment during the Cromwellian period when the local minister and his wife assisted in smuggling them out of the besieged Dunottar Castle and in hiding them under the floor of the church, where they lay secure throughout the Commonwealth – threats of violence and torture notwithstanding. 'I think this may be made a capital story & Jedediah without any sacrifice of his own opinions may make his peace honourably with his presbyterian friends if he can make a lively picture of a good divine of that persuasion & his good dame' (*L* v, 56). The same story, with added emphasis on the unfairness of the rewards distributed at the Restoration to the various participants in the conspiracy, was repeated in a letter to Croker of 7 February 1818 in which the opening of the regalia chest was described – though Scott naturally made no mention of his plans for using it in a tale.[5] The next day he mentioned the story to Daniel Terry as a possible subject for a play, but added: 'it would interfere with the democratic spirit of the times, and would probably – "By party rage, / Or right or wrong, be hooted from the stage" ' (*L* v, 78).

It is not clear exactly why or when Scott abandoned his plans for a regalia story; having passed the plot on to Croker he perhaps felt some hesitation about using it in Jedediah's next work. As late as the end of April 1818 the plan was still to have *The Heart of Midlothian* occupy only the first two and a half volumes or so, and, as Scott told Daniel Terry, to devote 'vol. 4, and part of 3d' to 'a different story' (*L* v, 135).[6] As that first tale developed, however, something more than a change of narrative scale took place. It had been described to Terry as 'a Bourgeoise tragedy' (*L* v, 135), and in sending Ballantyne the final pages of volume II Scott commented: 'The whole story must be mournful. There is no way of changing the tone that I can discover for it is a mournful story' (*L* v, 67). But while the ending for Effie in the novel as completed remains 'mournful,' that can hardly be said of Jeanie's story.

What seems to have occurred in the process of writing the novel is that Jeanie's journey expanded in the telling until the 'weight' of her personal moral achievement called for a more positive emphasis to be given to the conclusion as it affected her own future – and, by extension, that of Scotland. Critical dissatisfaction with the novel tends to dwell on the problem of volume IV, and readers familiar with the text only in later editions frequently assume that this volume consisted merely of the Knocktarlitie pastoral. It is necessary to remember, however, that at the end of volume II of the first edition Jeanie has still not left Scotland, that volume III ends with her interview with the Queen, and that the first third of volume IV is taken up with her return to Scotland, a sequence integral to the shape and meaning of her journey as a whole.[7] It is only by recognizing that the process which transformed the shorter structure into the longer is one of expansion rather than addition that we can engage with the problem of the ending in historical and generic as well as structural terms. Scott could, after all, have easily 'filled out' a fourth volume by writing the regalia story in which he was so much interested.[8]

It is highly unlikely that Scott could ever have contemplated finishing his story, as some modern readers would have preferred, at the end of Jeanie's successful pleading with the Queen. Journeys in his fiction rarely follow the unidirectional pattern of the simple picaresque. Coming home to the father or the place of the fathers is an essential element in his characteristic design; the meaning of the journey inheres not in arriving at any particular goal but in coming to terms with the experience of the voyage and carrying that understanding forward into the life that extends beyond the narrative climax. *Waverley* is not finished at that moment in the Lake District when Edward thinks the romance of his life is over; no more is *The Heart of Midlothian* complete when Jeanie's eloquence wins Effie's pardon from the Queen. London cannot provide a conclusion; it is after all a Vanity Fair rather than a Celestial City, and to take Jeanie's quest as a straightforward Bunyanesque pressing-on towards eternity involves in any case a misreading of the text. It is Madge Wildfire who develops the analogy between Jeanie and Christiana, and though the comparison works to enhance the moral seriousness of the journey, it also serves as a defining contrast. Jeanie's personal salvation is not at issue: the triple temptation in her father's house, in the prison with Effie, and in the courtroom is already behind her before she sets out. If anyone's soul is at stake it is Effie's, but she must save that for herself. All Jeanie can do is buy time. Her most urgent concern is therefore with this world rather than with eternity.[9]

The journey out and back allows the Independent's daughter to come into full independence, but it is the very reverse of an exercise in self-assertion. Determined to vindicate her faith in authority and providence,

Jeanie is distinguished from everyone else in the novel – including her father and Butler – by her lack of egotism and by the absence of any impulse to self-dramatization. She is no rebel and has nothing in common with Staunton, Effie, or the Porteous mob. Though she leaves without her father's permission, she is superstitiously careful to obtain a blessing from him; though she cannot win Butler's approval for her plan, she uses her farewell visit to secure his acquiescence; she even extracts from the reluctant Dumbiedikes a gesture of goodwill in the form of money for her journey. Yet in the very process of winning these partial acquiescences Jeanie does inevitably disturb the customary order of her own small world. The dominant male figures – including Ratcliffe – are reduced to ancillary roles. Even the Duke of Argyle's intervention extends only as far as her introduction to the Queen; after that her own words must do the work.

Formerly quiescent and dutiful, a listener rather than a talker, Jeanie frees herself by her radical action and dominates for a time over her masters. She is herself undaunted by the paradoxes involved in her journey; its aim is essentially restorative – to save Effie's life and bring her back within the circle of the family – but she does not shy away from the disruption necessarily involved. She seeks rather, through the totally unaccustomed act of writing, to impose a new order on the future – as she tells Staunton, she wants 'To prevent farder mischieves, whereof there hath been enough' (IV, 22). Her letters are masterpieces of persuasive rhetoric, instinctively phrased so as to reinstate a hierarchy shaken by her own assertion of the right of independent action. 'This is eloquence' (III, 326) says the Queen after listening to Jeanie's plea, and the same could be said of what she writes. She seeks to remove the winning of Effie's pardon from the realm of the extraordinary – the Queen is 'not muckle differing from other grand leddies'; the Duke of Argyle is 'ane native true-hearted Scotsman, and not pridefu'' (IV, 23). If the disruptive effects of Effie's defection from the ordered ways of St Leonard's are to be diminished rather than reinforced, the heroic nature of her elder sister's efforts must be underplayed. The good fortune has been achieved 'under the Great Giver, to whom all are but instruments' (IV, 23), and the talk of other providential blessings – the promised cattle, a school for Butler – is directed towards controlling through language the perception of recent events and projecting a future ordered, harmonious, and unremarkable. By refusing in her letters to take personal credit for what has occurred, Jeanie uses them to give back authority to those to whom it has traditionally belonged.

There is, however, no letter to Effie. Jeanie pleads with her father to be gentle with the recovered lost sheep, but she does not herself have the chance to try whether, spoken in time and face to face, her own words can draw Effie back into the circle of light. The return journey exposes Jeanie to an actual hanging such as Effie has escaped, and she watches helplessly at the bedside of the dying Madge Wildfire, Effie's half-crazed counterpart. But these victims cannot serve as scapegoats for Effie; in withdrawing from the family to regions where Jeanie's word can have no power she commits herself to wilfulness and isolation. Effie and Staunton reject authority in favour of the individual will and are thus pushed beyond community. Jeanie does not arrive too late for the pardon – itself associated with a sentence of exile – but Effie has already gone beyond the point at which the pardon could reclaim her. In their farewell meeting Effie insists that she is 'a banished outlawed body' and refuses to listen to her sister's plea: 'O Effie, dinna be wilfu' – be guided for anes – we will be sae happy a'thegither!' (IV, 196) She cannot 'Come hame to us, your ain dearest friends' (IV, 197); she is already married to Staunton, and a smugglers' vessel waits in the darkness to carry her off. Winning the pardon thus stands isolated as a vindication of Jeanie's faith that authority can comprehend justice and mercy. But for those who stand outside the community of belief of which Jeanie is the centre, her action can have no efficacy.

It would be easy to turn this novel into a kind of feminist tract by insisting on the importance of the act of sisterhood in which Jeanie engages. Her initial refusal to be false to herself by lying – read by Effie as rejection – is transformed by the heroic action of the journey into an affirmation of sisterhood that comprehends even the Queen. Such a reading would stress that royal authority is embodied in a woman and note that the worst danger and deepest anguish Jeanie must endure are occasioned by two women who are themselves almost quintessential victims of male oppression. But this would be to politicize sexually a text concerned with human values in a wider sense.[10] That Jeanie is a woman makes her task more difficult, her actions more heroic, and her success in wresting justice from authority all the more significant. But she never for a moment considers that the necessity of responding to a higher duty liberates her from the ordinary obediences of everyday. Unlike Mrs Dolly Dutton, she is perfectly willing to conform to the mandates of the Duke of Argyle and his surrogate Mr Archibald on the journey homewards, and she is quite ready to accommodate herself to the Highland strangenesses of Knocktarlitie. It is precisely because Jeanie believes in the hierarchy she temporarily subverts that her action carries meaning, transcends the impulses of one individual, and has significance for the community. By requiring that authority be true to itself, that the King's face be given the opportunity to give grace, she affirms the conservative as opposed to the revolutionary vision.

In compelling London and the Court to fulfil their responsibility towards one particular Scottish subject and recognize her own and her sister's humanity, Jeanie vindicates in this one instance the power arrangements regarded with such hostility by the Edinburgh citizenry of 1736: the Court is obliged to register Scottish feelings and desist from treating the inhabitants of North Britain as alien barbarians requiring to be taught their lessons by bloodshed. The narrative clearly requires this kind of reading in respect of Jeanie and Effie, and Scott also saw it as capable of extension into a larger political meaning. By expanding the emphasis on Jeanie's Scottishness at various points in her journey he moves deliberately towards establishing her as a nationally emblematic figure and transforming her achievement into a general vindication of the Union of 1707.

In *The Heart of Midlothian* an action that begins in violence and defiance ends with the violent and defiant destroying each other while leaving the moderate and humane to survive and even flourish within a political order that promises continuing economic and social progress. As always in Scott, the nineteenth-century narrator shows himself in no doubt as to the advantages of the current state of Scotland over its earlier condition, and this novel dwells less on the charms of certain aspects of the old social order than do some of his other texts. At the same time there is a confidence expressed – most powerfully through the portrait of Jeanie – in the enduring strength of certain moral values associated with the old Scotland, as well as a determinedly positive attitude towards the increasing 'civilization' of Scottish life. Where Scott gets into difficulties is in his attempt to make a narrative of the 1730s and '40s image forth his political vision of the overall pattern of Scottish history during the whole of the second half of the eighteenth century. He seeks to bring off the transition from historical narrative to political emblem by a fully orchestrated shift of mode – by projecting the Knocktarlitie episode as a pastoral expressive of Jeanie's attainment of a restored but transformed harmony and by associating that harmony with the idea of Union, especially of Union juxtaposed against the alternatives of extended feudalism, violent rebellion, or anarchy. But the specifically historical problems prove not to be readily susceptible of the technical solution provided by the move into pastoral.

The transition itself could not be more clearly signalled. Journey by land concludes with a crossing over water necessitated as much by symbolic as by actual geography. A quotation from Alexander Ross's *Helenore: or The Fortunate Shepherdess* is followed by the statement, 'They landed in this Highland Arcadia, at the mouth of the small stream which watered the delightful and peaceable valley' (IV, 163). The same kind of signalling introduced the Charlieshope episode in *Guy Mannering*, but there the evocation of the texture of life at a precisely defined time and place gave historical substance to the deployment of pastoral interlude in the moral allegory of Harry Bertram's proving. In the Knocktarlitie episode, however, the stylization accompanying the generic shift combines with the introduction of a somewhat strenuously comic tone to make the episode conform more closely to the simple contrastive pattern of traditional pastoral than to the more complex strategies of the historicized pastoral Scott had himself originated. This implausible Arcadia, where cows, pasture, and even ministerial livings flow from the beneficent hands of the Duke of Argyle, is threatened not by the economic facts of agricultural life in eighteenth-century Scotland – so sharply evoked in the earlier presentation of Davie Deans's struggles to establish himself as a farmer – but by incursions of such traditional pastoral figures as alien robbers; the faint historical ripples that reach it carry no import for the Butlers.

The episode, of course, is not entirely without historical specificity – there is talk of the banning of the kilt and the abolition of heritable jurisdictions after the '45 – but the narrative as a whole seems to view these matters almost as lightly as does Duncan of Knockdunder, the comic representative here of the power of the Duke of Argyle. Scott continues to take Jeanie herself seriously; the realistic touch supplied by her incipient jealousy at Effie's social elevation and the brief sketch of the rationalizations that allow her to keep Effie's gifts of money a secret are instances of his continuing engagement with her character. But he seems to stop taking history seriously – or rather, he sacrifices historical faithfulness to a particular moment in time in favour of a generalized attempt to project a larger design.

Given the status of this novel as one of a sequence of texts, the reader inevitably looks for something like the picture of the painful consequences of the '45 that makes Edward Waverley's return to Scotland so moving. That Argyle was a supporter of the government, his people and lands relatively secure from the most severe depredations of 1746, is no justification for the absence of any adequate recognition within the text of the bloodshed and violence of the exercise in suppression by which, in the aftermath of Culloden, the British government imposed its lesson on Scotland. And even if the reader's expectations are confined to those generated by the structure of this novel as separate text, the weight and detail assigned to the opening sequence of the Porteous riots clearly call for something over and beyond the absorption of the '45 and its consequences into the private melodrama of the Stauntons.

One brilliant page of dialogue between the Duke of Argyle and his daughters conjures up the culminating events of the earlier rebellion of 1715 and its significance for subsequent Scottish history (IV, 46–7), but the '45 is deprived of even this kind of realized presence in the narrative. Two passages – eighty pages apart, very similar in wording, and of roughly the same length – are virtually all the reader is given. The first reads:

After the breaking out and suppression of the rebellion in 1745, the peace of the country, adjacent to the Highlands, was considerably disturbed. Marauders, or men that had been driven to that desperate mode of life, quartered themselves in the fastnesses nearest to the Lowlands, which were their scene of plunder; and there is scarce a glen in the romantic and now peaceable highlands of Perth, Stirling, and Dumbartonshire, where one or more did not take up their residence.   (IV, 248)

Even on this brief, partial, and deliberately generalized evocation of the turmoil in the Highlands and adjoining regions, the image of later peace and tranquillity is superimposed by the nineteenth-century narrator. In the second passage, reporting Sir George Staunton's inquiries, the 'Marauders' have become 'banditti' (IV, 334), but since Donacha dhu na Dunaigh, the 'prime pest of the parish of Knocktarlitie,' is said on both occasions to be not a genuine product of the '45 but a tinker turned robber to take advantage of the fact that 'all police was disorganized by the civil war' (IV, 248), Scott allows him the dignity neither of history nor of the sentimental romance evoked by Staunton's Italianate vocabulary. National tragedy is reduced to the private action of the murder of Sir George Staunton by his son, and only minimal gestures are made towards integrating personal violence and lawlessness with the pattern of public events in the manner of the Porteous-riots sequence.[11]

The whole episode, indeed, is allowed to spiral downwards. Duncan of Knockdunder's plan to hang Staunton's murderer in front of his wife's window – 'which would be a creat comfort to her in the morning to see that the coot gentleman, her husband, had been suitably afenged' (IV, 363) – carries with it none of the horror associated with hangings, actual and anticipated, earlier in the novel. What could have been a powerful image of an obsolete code of violence and vengeance becomes a kind of black comedy. Duncan Knock is a comic Highland eccentric – smoking during the sermon, hanging people outside windows – with whom Jeanie can be expected to cope. His dark counterpart, the 'pest' Donacha dhu, is a nuisance unlikely to disturb those who live peaceably in the fertile valley, stay away from romantic waterfalls and smugglers' coves, and do not yearn for those lost children that only romance can recover.

The melodrama associated with Staunton in the final sequence is not in itself a problem. It is entirely consistent with his earlier presentation as an habitual poseur who feels his own reality only when playing some literary part. As in the later exploitation of the same convention by Hardy in the portrayal of Alec D'Urberville, the method is particularly effective in a scene such as that at Muschat's cairn, where the role-playing is mounted for an audience unfamiliar with the conventions that govern it – Jeanie cannot distinguish between a devilish fine performance and the genuinely diabolical, any more than Tess Durbeyfield, unread in cheap fiction, knows quite what to expect from a young man with 'a well-groomed black moustache' and a 'bold rolling eye' who greets her with 'Well, my Beauty.'[12] But in the last part of *The Heart of Midlothian* the patterned simplicities of melodrama combine unhappily with the smoothing out of historical reality in the pastoral presentation of the Butlers, and the entire balance of the novel is disturbed. The romance convention of the rediscovery of the lost heir is here turned into a bitter joke; pastoral abundance as the reward of virtue is trivialized, and the idealized portrait of Highland life simply does not work as a response to those dark images of gallows, prison, and mob that dominated the opening.

In order that the prosperity of the Butlers may stand for the overall tendency rather than the particulars of Scottish history in the second half of the eighteenth century, Scott chooses not to look too closely at the Highland world of the 1740s. He supplies no historical articulation of the connection between the Knocktarlitie Arcadia and the actual discontent and ferment of the Edinburgh of 1736. Jeanie's success in staying the bloody hand of punishment – and in making London recognize the humanity of the Scots – can only have emblematic significance if the bloodshed of 1745 and '46 is displaced and, in effect, ignored. In refusing to take the history of the 1740s seriously Scott shifts the emphasis away from his historical and on to his moral and political fable. The final stress falls on Jeanie's imperviousness to violence, so that she is reassimilated to those stylized literary counterparts from whom she had earlier been discriminated – Christiana and the Lady in *Comus* – and on the Union as a solution to centuries of national violence. Peace and prosperity are presented as the natural outcome of both the private and public plots, and rebellion is displaced by a revitalized authority.

George Levine has recently reminded us of the way in which Scott uses happy endings and other 'tricks ... from the romancer's bag' to 'do the work of history itself,' thus ensuring that the protagonist, 'having found the right side in large historical conflicts, is rewarded personally with the success of the winning party.'[13] Although these comments are not specifically applied to *The Heart of Midlothian*, they seem on the surface to capture something of what happens in that novel. But, as the discussion of the ending of *Old Mortality* has already suggested, it would be uncharacteristic of Scott to make uniform or uncritical use of any formula, even his own. In *The Heart of Midlothian* it can, indeed, be argued that it is the private plot that endows the public with significance and value. It is not so much that Jeanie chooses the right side – the Union settlement – but that the virtues of her private actions are harnessed to the projection of a positive vision of that settlement. In the process the narrative shifts away from psychological and historical realism in the direction of stylization, validating the course of Scottish history in a way that is essentially ahistorical. What starts out as the most 'authentic' of Scott's fictions, clearly distinguished from the earlier Waverley Novels by its displacement or inversion of their characteristic devices, returns in the end to a reliance on the stylized convention of pastoral for the transformation of historical narrative into an act of historical interpretation.

The Bride of Lammermoor and *A Legend of Montrose:* The End of the Beginning

When the third series of *Tales of My Landlord* was published in June 1819, Scott was ill and believed by many people in Edinburgh to be actually on his deathbed. The new volumes were thus viewed from the first as something set apart, potentially destined to be the final contribution to the wonderful sequence that had begun with *Waverley* just five years earlier – and indeed, *The Bride of Lammermoor*, the longer and more important of the two new tales, has continued to enjoy a special position in the Scott canon as a work somehow different and distinct from both its predecessors and its successors. The perception derives to some degree from features genuinely present in the novel itself – most notably its heightened romance stylization – but it was reinforced by the major change in direction in Scott's career that occurred with the novel that immediately followed the *Tales*: *Ivanhoe*'s break with the established Waverley pattern served to throw the *Bride* into quasi-culminatory relief. The modern status of the *Bride*, however, depends still more on the biographico-critical myth woven by Lockhart out of the story of Scott's illness and on the subsequent elaboration of that myth by other writers. If the tale of the *Bride* is to be seen clearly both as a separate text and as an item in the Waverley sequence, it is important to free it from some of the encumbrances of that other tale – the legend of its composition.

The exact chronology of the writing of the novel is hard to establish either from the *Life* or from Grierson's edition of the *Letters*, but it seems possible that Scott began work on it as early as May 1818.[1] It was certainly under way by the early autumn of 1818 (*L* V, 181) but seems to have been set aside in favour of other tasks, and it was still not finished in March 1819 when Scott became gravely ill with a recurrence of his old gallstones problem. The agonizing pains caused by stomach cramps and the effects of the opiates, bleedings, and blisterings prescribed by his doctors left him desperately weak and, on occasion, almost delirious. Some of his family and friends clearly thought him near death. A remission in April permitted him to ride out at foot-pace on his pony Sybil Grey, 'the very image of Death on the pale horse' (*L* v, 355), but May brought another flare-up and the renewed double anguish of the ailment and its treatment. Determined to finish the volumes of *Tales* in spite of his indisposition, Scott began dictating – sometimes to John Ballantyne, sometimes to William Laidlaw – at the end of the first week in April, and the best evidence suggests that the *Bride* itself was finished and sent off to James Ballantyne by 2 May 1819.[2] Lockhart has a vivid description of Scott dictating from his sofa between groans of anguish but nevertheless rising up from time to time to act out the parts in the dialogue: 'It was in this fashion that Scott produced the far greater portion of The Bride of Lammermoor – the whole of the Legend of Montrose – and almost the whole of Ivanhoe.'[3]

This account is not, in fact, particularly accurate for either *A Legend of Montrose* or *Ivanhoe*,[4] but since it has had the greatest impact on discussions of the *Bride*, it is particularly important to have the record straight for that novel. The incomplete manuscript of the *Bride* is in the Signet Library, and all that survives is written in Scott's own hand. Far from being a small portion of the text, this comprises approximately four-fifths of the whole. And since the last page ends in a catchword and carries on its verso holograph corrections for a subsequent page now lost, it is clear that the part set down by Scott himself was originally even more extensive. The manuscript thus offers little support for Lockhart's account of a text whose major portion was dictated, and since it does not differ notably from that of Scott's earlier works – it is written in his usual small, neat hand and shows no obvious signs of distress – it offers little confirmation for the alternative version of the composition legend proposed by Edgar Johnson: 'Page after page was written in a blurred trance of suffering in which he did not know what words he was putting down, images and dreamlike actions rising somehow out of unconscious depths of the imagination while he himself struggled through a drugged nightmare world.'[5]

The source of this latter version of the writing of the *Bride* is James Ballantyne's recollections as recorded in Lockhart's *Life*. It was Ballantyne who reported Scott's telling him that when the printed form of the work was first put into his hands 'he did not recollect one single incident, character, or conversation it contained'; Ballantyne hastened to add that he did not mean that Scott had forgotten the original anecdote on which the tale was based but that he could not recall 'a single character woven by the romancer, not one of the many scenes and points of humour, or any thing with which he was connected as the writer of the work.'[6] There is no need to doubt Ballantyne's word – 'you may depend upon it, that what I have now said is as distinctly reported as if it had been taken down in short-hand at the moment'[7] – but neither is there any reason to assume that because Scott, after a second bout of a near-fatal illness, could not recall what he had written, he had been in some kind of semi-delirious condition while actually writing it. So far as the manuscript itself goes there is every reason to believe that Scott had completed most of the holograph before becoming seriously ill, and even if one assumes that he did indeed dictate the final fifth of the novel in April 1819, his illness had by that time abated sufficiently for him to substitute the taking of hot baths for the frequent recourse to opiates that had been necessary earlier.[8]

The way in which the 'blurred trance' legend of the composition of the *Bride* has turned it into a kind of *lusus naturae*, detached from the rest of the Waverley Novels, is unfortunate for a variety of reasons, not least because it distracts attention from the historicalness of this text – the degree to which it is precisely embedded in a particular historical moment. What is more, to see the stylization and patterning of the novel and its elaborate use of symbolic imagery as the product of Scott's drugged condition is to fail to give due weight to these features as part of an overall narrative strategy. In order to recognize the contribution made by the *Bride* to Scott's continuing exploration of an individual life's relationship to historical circumstance and (as in the earlier *Tales of My Landlord*) of the implications of the narrative act itself, it is essential to approach it as a controlled work of art rather than as a species of automatic writing.

If one begins by considering the historical aspects of the *Bride*, another immediate difficulty arises – the very extensive critical debate about the dating of the action. Though of Scott's own creating this is, in fact, a false problem, arising as it does from changes he made in the text subsequent to the first edition. It has, nevertheless, generated a good deal of confusion that must be cleared away if the precision and appropriateness of the original dating are to be appreciated.

Opinions about the date of the action have ranged widely: some critics and literary historians place the confrontations between Edgar Ravenswood and the Ashton family firmly in the seventeenth century, occasionally assigning them to the specific year 1695; others are quite clear that the period is after Queen Anne's accession in 1702 but before the Union of England and Scotland in 1707; a third group point out that a series of references to historical events make it certain that a later period in Anne's reign, some time after 1707, must be intended. G.M. Trevelyan places the novel 'a decade before the Union'[9]; Francis Hart also plumps for a pre-Union date, although there are suggestions in his discussion of a time-scheme somehow stretching beyond 1707[10]; Edgar Johnson, despite a cautious comment about ambiguities in the dating, seems to endorse two different dates, referring in his notes to a period in Anne's reign just prior to the Union but in his text to the novel's 'seventeenth-century world.'[11]

The debate is at one level quite unnecessary, since all the participants have depended upon texts derived from the *magnum opus* edition of the novel which Scott published in 1830 and since there are in such texts enough specifically datable references – including some to the Union itself – to make a post-Union date inescapable.[12] The truth of the matter is that while the manuscript of the novel, the first edition of 1819, and all subsequent editions for the next ten years set its events two or three years *before* the Union, the 1830 *magnum opus* edition transposes the action to two or three years *after* the Union. The change seems to have been prompted not by any dissatisfaction on Scott's part with the appropriateness of the original dating itself but by subsequent doubts on a purely technical matter – that of the exact status of appeals to the Scottish parliament against decisions of the Court of Session in the period between the accession of William and Mary and the coming into force of the Act of Union. Any error or confusion over such a question would have been highly embarrassing to Scott, so long a Clerk to the Court of Session, and it is not surprising that he would wish to alter something that could be said to reflect upon his professional expertise. Having decided on a clarifying – or evasive – transposition to a later date, one for which firm information was available, he went to some pains to include passages appropriate to a post-Union date in the revision he prepared for the *magnum opus* edition.[13] But he did not weigh fully the effect on the coherence of his novel of such a change, nor prune his new text of all the vestiges of the original period. Critics of the novel have, however, remained unaware of the crucial differences between the first and later editions and have therefore failed to grapple with the significance of the original dating for the meaning of the novel. In the text as originally composed and published the events are clearly pre-Union, though still within Anne's reign, and although a case for the appropriateness of the later dating can be made, and indeed has been made – implicitly at least – in the many positive valuations of the novel based on the *magnum opus* text, there is little doubt that the first version has considerably greater coherence than its successor. There is in the later version a general blurring of resonances and, more specifically, a loss of the original integration of the private plot with the public history of the dying moments of Scotland's identity as a separate nation.

It is certainly hard for readings which place much stress on the historical aspects of the *magnum opus* text to avoid significant distortion of the roles of both Edgar Ravenswood and Sir William Ashton. Undue emphasis tends to be placed on Ravenswood as the representative of an outworn feudalism, unable to survive in the new post-Union world.[14] When note is taken of his resemblance to other Waverley heroes, these attributes are customarily viewed as anachronistic or not quite integral to the major pattern of the work, in that they fail to ensure for him the survival granted to a Francis Osbaldistone or an Edward Waverley. Sir William Ashton, on the other hand, is sometimes seen as a representative new man, more in tune with the changing times.[15] What seems clear, however, from the deliberately chosen dating of the first version – carrying over with necessarily diminished clarity into the second – is that *both* Ravenswood and Sir William Ashton are in some sense out of step with the times and thereby rendered largely powerless.

The narrative perspective of both the first edition and the *magnum opus* versions of *The Bride of Lammermoor* is that of the early nineteenth century, and they both imply a consistent recognition of the advantageous developments that have occurred in the administration of Scotland – especially in legal matters – since the enactment of the Union. The story proper, however, belongs in the first version to a moment just before that crucial turning point in Scottish history, a moment when there existed 'no supreme power, claiming and possessing a general interest with the community at large, to whom the oppressed might appeal from subordinate tyranny, either for justice or for mercy.'[16] Edgar Ravenswood is thus compelled to function in terms of the old dispensation; his actions need to be seen in the context of the novel's sharply patterned version of late seventeenth- and early eighteenth-century Scotland. When he makes his vow of vengeance at his father's funeral, he is presented as being in a state of temporary disequilibrium, involved by his family loyalties in rituals and utterances in which his more rational self, his individual conscience, does not fully acquiesce. The Ravenswood of this moment is absolutely behind the times, speaking for a world that was already obsolete after the Revolution of 1689, a feudal past which has nothing to do with the world of the eighteenth century. But subsequently, when his more rational self – what Francis Hart calls his 'enlightenment'[17] – spurns violence and puts faith in moderate courses and legal redress, he is just as surely ahead of the times. His reasoned moderation is quite different from the conciliatory cunning practised by his kinsman the Marquis or by Sir William Ashton as a ploy in their political games. Ravenswood's predicament is clearly articulated in the depiction of the complex politico-legal situation in which he finds himself: redress is a possibility, but the processes are slow and positive results attainable only by political manipulation. After the Union, as Scott's *magnum opus* note later insisted, justice would have been more impartial; and the right of appeal to a forum where local Scottish prejudices had little influence would have rendered the Master of Ravenswood more completely the master of his own fate.[18] But in the first version of the novel, set before the Union, the degree to which Ravenswood is trammelled by actual historical circumstances serves to intensify the total pattern, working as mutual reinforcement with the rest of the imagery to define the inescapability – despite his possession of certain potentially redemptive characteristics – of the doom which overtakes him.

Sir William Ashton, on the other hand, is the pre-Union opportunist, the man of 1689 rather than 1707. A skilful fisher in the murky waters of Williamite Scotland, he is now running out of time and room to manoeuvre; the threat to the old ways of doing political business is already apparent, although in the first version the door has not yet actually been closed by the Union. Sensing that the old manipulative techniques will soon cease to be effective once the location of power shifts to London, Ashton scurries about in an attempt to salvage, protect, and solidify his earlier gains. He does not represent the new Scotland, the North Britain of the post-Union era, for in so far as the conflict between old and new enters in any direct way into the novel, it is articulated, as Donald Davie has pointed out, within the figure of Ravenswood.[19]

Where everything chimes so coherently together it might be expected that the first version would be the darker, but the reverse is, in fact, nearer the mark. In the text that Scott originally composed and published the final effect, despite the formal tragedy, is in historical terms quite positive: such circumstances of time and place as play a part in Ravenswood's fate are presented as the products of a particular situation of limited duration. In the later version the destruction of Ravenswood takes on an element of the gratuitous: the times have already changed; the great boundary-line of the Union has been crossed, and yet the outcome for Ravenswood must still be disastrous. It is true that the second version carries over from the first the mutual reverberation of many elements of characterization, parallelism with earlier works, and so on, which are integral to the novel's symbolic patterning, but the diminished historical consonance of the later text enforces a much grimmer irony than Scott had originally achieved or perhaps intended. Because a term is now placed to the corrupt legal and political situation of the first version, thus sharpening the distinction between the now of the narrative framework and the then of the narrated events themselves, the fate of Ravenswood and the Ashtons becomes clearly distinguished from the view of the future course of Scottish history implicit in the work as a whole. In both texts the hope that a shift in the political situation would offer to Ravenswood is distant and not fully realizable, but a date before the Union – when the promised change might prove to be just another swing of the see-saw of power – makes the failure of that hope more readily acceptable, keeps personal fate and historical fact more nearly attuned.

There was, of course, as Scott well knew, no miraculous overnight transformation in 1707, no immediate purging of all the old corruption or sweeping aside of the old networks of power and influence – he was himself a skilful exploiter of the system of patronage that continued into his own day.[20] The scene of activity shifted from Edinburgh to London, but many things long remained the same. Nevertheless, there is no doubt that in the course of the eighteenth century the administration of justice in Scotland became far more certain and equitable. This was partly a consequence of the existence of the right of appeal to the British House of Lords, where Scottish political loyalties could have virtually no effect on the decision, but much was also due to the focusing of national pride on the still-independent legal system of a country deprived of its parliament and of much else that had formerly given assurance of a separate identity. Scott himself epitomized this feeling of pride in the article he wrote for the *Edinburgh Annual Register* of 1808 on proposed changes to the Court of Session: 'Our system of real rights has attained a point of perfection unknown to any other country in Europe ... The personal rights of the subject are as well defined, and his character and *status* as securely protected, as they have ever been, under any government with which the history of the world has made us acquainted.'[21] Though Scott was fully aware that this happy situation had been only gradually attained, the presence of the Act of Union as a boundary between the old Scotland and the new was very important to his historical sense. The initial dating of *The Bride of Lammermoor* can thus be said to possess an appropriateness that the later version does not quite attain – for all Scott's care in domesticating his new chronology by inserted glimpses of post-Union sentiment about 'foreign' meddling with Scottish justice. The original world of the novel belongs with that 'auld sang' of which the last Scottish Chancellor spoke, with what Scott called 'brutal levity,' on the final adjournment of the Scottish parliament[22]: the darkness and tragedy do not spill over, as they do in the second version, into what Scott perceived as the greater brightness of the new post-Union day.

The textual changes in later editions that have made the dating of the action of the *Bride* into a critical problem should not deflect attention from the fact that the date was always intended to be an important *issue* in the novel. In choosing a moment just before the Union, Scott was deliberately shifting out of the time-frame proper to the kernel narrative on which he based his tale. The source of the *Bride* was a story often recounted by Scott's mother, Anne Rutherford, concerning the Dalrymple and Rutherford families in the seventeenth century.[23] Scott's summary of this anecdote in the introduction to the 1830 *magnum opus* edition includes the following note: 'If the last Lord Rutherford was the unfortunate party, he must have been the third who bore that title, and who died in 1685' (*WN* XIII, 242). In supplying such an identification and in further assigning the Dalrymple marriage to 1669, Scott was functioning in his favourite role as antiquary, glossing an oral original that was itself imprecise as to individuals and dates. As novelist, however, he moved beyond this kind of marginal annotation. By transposing the events to a period thirty-five years or so after the actual Dalrymple marriage he took full possession of the tale, transforming it into an historicized fiction in which private and public plots were in full consonance.

That Scott was entirely conscious of what he was doing in making this transposition and wanted to build it into the reader's experience of the tale is clear from the Pattieson-Tinto introductory chapter – even though, as so often in Scott's frameworks, the substance of his most serious narrative concerns is there articulated in comic terms. Tinto has none of the instincts of the historian, as is made clear by his treatment of the manuscript which is to be one of Pattieson's major sources. He has taken down the story from an 'aged goodwife ... well acquainted with the history of the castle, and the events which had taken place in it,' but his 'notes of the tale' as handed to Pattieson consist of 'a parcel of loose scraps, partly scratched over with his pencil, partly with his pen, where outlines of caricatures, sketches of turrets, mills, old gables, and dovecotes, disputed the ground with his written memoranda' (1, 35). His preliminary sketch for the 'history-piece' (1, 35) he hoped to base on the story shows a chamber in the castle 'furnished in what we now call the taste of Queen Elizabeth's age' (1, 29), while the figures seen there in passionate confrontation wear 'the Vandyke dress common to the time of Charles 1' (1, 30). An 'Elizabeth-chamber' (1, 35) had indeed once existed in the castle Tinto visited, but there is no evidence that the old woman's narrative referred to the time of Charles 1, and it seems entirely possible that in clothing his characters Tinto merely consulted his own taste. Pattieson, at all events, deliberately places his own version of the story firmly at the beginning of the eighteenth century rather than in the middle of the seventeenth.

The discrepancy between the periods of the sketch and of the associated tale draws the reader's attention to the difference between Tinto and his friend the tale-maker. Tinto yearns to create one of those early nineteenth-century 'history-pieces' whose nature is essentially ahistorical – a matter of striking settings and colourful costumes. His criteria are purely visual, his aim the production of notable contrastive effects. Pattieson, on the other hand, has the true historian's desire to go beyond the strikingly pictorial situation and ground it temporally, socially, and politically, and by so doing to make the date not a matter of aesthetic preference but an integral part of the total explanation of the narrative situation.

The broad outlines of this opening fable of composition provide a paradigm of Scott's art in *The Bride of Lammermoor*, establishing the deliberate historicization of the story as one of its crucial elements and the retention of an oral narrative kernel as the other. The 'aged good wife' who tells Tinto the tale stands in the composition allegory for that fidelity to the oral origins of this material that is documented in other terms in Scott's various accounts of his mother's Rutherford family legend. What these accounts, fictional and autobiographical, affirm is that in the course of its transmission, of its many tellings, this story has been assimilated to the oral tradition which in Scotland preserved ballad and tale alike and whose goal was stability of story rather than stability of text. As David Buchan, following Bernard Bronson, has reminded us, the ballad-makers carried in their heads 'not a *text*, but a *ballad*,'[24] and the act of recovery was with them an act of re-creation. With oral prose narratives, too, the outline of the story and the basic repertoire of incidents remained constant, but in the retelling the individual narrator supplied his or her own coloration.

All Scott's accounts of his mother's story emphasize the power she gave to its telling. When just embarked on the *Bride* in 1818 he told James Ballantyne:

The story is a dismal one, and I doubt sometimes whether it will bear working out to much length after all. Query, if I shall make it so effective in two volumes as my mother does in her quarter of an hour's crack by the fireside? But *nil desperandum*.   (*L* v, 186)

In the Introduction to *Chronicles of the Canongate* (1827) he remarked:

The female relative, by whom the melancholy tale was communicated to me many years since, was a near connexion of the family in which the event happened, and always told it with an appearance of melancholy mystery, which enhanced the interest.   (*Chronicles* I, x)

He also placed repeated emphasis on her direct contact with at least one of the participants, thus employing that mode of authentication so characteristic of the oral tradition – verification of the marvellous by an assertion of the provenance of a story rather than by substantiation of its details:

She had known, in her youth, the brother who rode before the unhappy victim to the fatal altar, who, though then a mere boy, and occupied almost entirely with the gallantry of his own appearance in the bridal procession, could not but remark that the hand of his sister was moist, and cold as that of a statue.   (*Chronicles* I, x–xi)[25]

In transposing his mother's tale into a novel Scott sought to enhance its attributes as narrative by deploying the *Tales of My Landlord* apparatus to its fullest extent. The preliminary chapter with its debate on narrative technique provides one way of insisting on the status of the *Bride* as *tale*, and within the narrative itself there are numerous references to the story's transmission by other tellers prior to its present narrator. Pattieson himself proceeds in accordance with the aim he enunciated at the beginning of *The Black Dwarf*, that of ridding his narrative of 'circumstances of exaggerated marvel' (*Tales* I, 34), and is prompt to psychologize away the apparently supernatural – by insisting that a man's own 'violent and unresisting passions' (I, 59) can be as powerful as any fiend or by analysing the envious and embittered feelings that drive an Ailsie Gourlay to assume the role of witch. Faithfulness to the existing tale requires, however, that the supernatural version remain alongside his own naturalistic account, and he gives full play to those characters within the narrative, such as Caleb and Alice, who see the hand of fate at work in the disaster that befalls the Master of Ravenswood. At one crucial moment, that of Ravenswood's vision of the dead Alice at the Mermaiden's Fountain, Pattieson is presented as being at a loss for a rational explanation, compelled to let the tale stand as transmitted:

We are bound to tell the tale as we have received it; and, considering the distance of the time, and propensity of those through whose mouths it has passed to the marvellous, this could not be called a Scottish story, unless it manifested a tinge of Scottish superstition. (II, 217)

The comment is that of the nineteenth-century pedant, but the opening commitment – 'We are bound to tell the tale as we received it' – belongs to the classic rhetoric of the oral tradition.

Confirmation that Pattieson's compulsive fidelity to his story offers a metaphor for Scott's own relationship to his materials is not far to seek. The summary of his mother's tale in the *magnum opus* introduction reveals that all its key incidents have been retained, the only substantial change occurring in the suitor's expiration in the quicksand rather than of unspecified causes during a self-imposed exile. And even here the new version remains technically faithful to the original, in that the fictional ending is reserved for a final chapter, allowing the penultimate chapter to conclude with the claim that readers 'who are read in the private family history of Scotland' would recognize in what had gone before 'AN OWER TRUE TALE' (III, 111). Scott's expansion and development of the details of his original can also be demonstrated from the *magnum opus* summary, brief though it is. Its report, for example, of the remark of the returned suitor, Lord Rutherford, to his former betrothed, Janet Dalrymple, 'For you, madam, you will be a world's wonder' (*WN* XIII, 242), is transformed within the novel from prophetic threat to a more complex expression of bitterness, regret, and self-justification: 'I have nothing farther to say, except to pray to God that you may not become a world's wonder for this act of wilful and deliberate perjury' (III, 84). The modulation here in the direction of increased psychological depth goes along with other novelistic features such as the expanded social and cultural detail of the portrayal of Wolf's Hope and the greater precision as to the historical moment.

Such increased specificity is often assumed to belong to a realism antithetical to romance, but in Scott's fiction the patterns of history and those of romance persistently reinforce each other, and in the *Bride* itself he pushes his special combination of historical detail and romance design to its furthest limits. The depictions of the castle of Wolf's Crag, the woods around Ravenswood Castle, the Mermaiden's Fountain, the grave-yard, the quicksands of the Kelpie's Flow, have a stillness, and idealization, an insistence on the emblematic, which make them comparable to motifs in a tapestry. And when the stillness turns to motion in the hunting episode or the race between the carriages of the Marquis and Lady Ashton, it is the shift in the narrative pattern which counts as much as the action itself: the hunt, for example, brings Lucy and Ravenswood together for the second time, marking this meeting with a more ritual-ized version of the pursuit, violence, and blood which had accompanied their first encounter. The landscape of the *Bride* belongs, indeed, as much to Spenserian romance as to Scotland at the beginning of the eighteenth century, and against these half-allegorized settings Scott plays out his scenes, arranging them in patterns of repetition and contrast which serve to heighten the novel's sense of entrapping unity.

Ravenswood is caught up in an historical situation in which his own ability to foresee or control the immediate future is severely limited. He is also caught up in a dream that is not of his own making. In the *Bride* the concept of dream as escape becomes a dark irony. Edward Waverley's day-dreams had been a mark of immaturity, but once channelled into right action the projective imaginative power associated with them becomes the source of wisdom and liberation. In the *Bride*, however, it is not the hero – the young man with the potential for action – who dreams, but the heroine. In so far as Lucy is the author of the parallel narrative generated by dream, Ravenswood is reduced to being a character within it. Lucy aspires to a dream-world composed of the stuff of ballad and romance: 'Her secret delight was in the old legendary tales of ardent devotion and unalterable affection, chequered as they so often are with strange adventures and supernatural horrors. This was her favoured fairy realm, and here she erected her aërial palaces' (1, 69–70). She takes on the part of Una or Miranda, or that of the patroness of some fanciful tournament 'raining down influence from her eyes on the valiant com-batants' (1, 70), and the 'ideal picture of chivalrous excellence which [she] had pictured to herself in the Master of Ravenswood' (1, 128) can be all too easily incorporated into this vision. Ravenswood is absorbed into the dreams of someone for whom the dream is all, since Lucy's actual condition – psychological, sexual, familial, social, and historical – pre-cludes direct action on her part. As the deliberately Gothic elements in the text indicate, the imprisoned Lucy could not be more distinct from the wandering heroes of Scott's earlier novels or from such active, and fortunately motherless, heroines as Rose Bradwardine, Diana Vernon, or, of course, Jeanie Deans. For Lucy the implications of being the daughter of a weak father – a source of comedy or, at worst, pathos in the earlier novels – are all tragic. Despite her identification with Miranda this is no Prospero's island; the Lord Keeper is no magus but a politican running out of time, a henpecked husband whose wife is about to return.

To a compassionate man Lucy's powerlessness and helplessness are almost irresistible. Ravenswood succumbs to her as surely as to the Kelpie's Flow. The pattern of his life modulates precisely into that of her dream vision of 'ardent devotion and unalterable affection, chequered … with strange adventures and supernatural horrors.' It is not that psychological realism is abandoned – Ravenswood is shown struggling against the impulse to remain, and his awareness of all the arguments against staying makes him sardonic and withdrawn even before the return of Lady Ashton stirs him into a renewed assertion of family claims. It is rather that surrender to Lucy's yearnings answers to something else within Ravenswood, that willingness to hold off from decisive action for a time which also expresses itself in his readiness to wait upon circumstance before committing himself to leave the country or to adopt a definite course of action against the Lord Keeper.

Ravenswood oscillates between the impulse to act in accordance with tradition – to 'requite … this man and his house the ruin and disgrace he has brought on me and mine' (1, 55) – and the more enlightened resolution to 'expostulate' (1, 144) with Sir William Ashton. His political views, as has often been pointed out, are advanced: 'I hope to see the day when justice shall be open to Whig and Tory, and when these nick-names shall only be used among coffee-house politicians, as slut and jade are among apple-women, as cant terms of idle spite and rancour' (1, 212). And he refuses to be daunted by Bucklaw's cynical response – 'That will not be in our days, Master' (1, 212) – insisting that 'It will be, however, one day' (1, 213). Rational about the past, long-sighted about the future, he is nevertheless unable to control his own contradictory impulses or dominate the detailed play of personal and political forces that determines his own immediate situation. Caught up within history, the man of historical vision is no more powerful than a naïve hero like Edward Waverley. Ravenswood may seem at times to carry his own Colonel Talbot with him, but as Bucklaw shrewdly observes: 'You are one of those wise men who see every thing with great composure till their blood is up, and then – woe to any one who should put them in mind of their own prudential maxims' (I, 214).

Ravenswood's persistent irritability, his alternation between heedless action and fatal lethargy, derives from competing visions of his own position. He succumbs from time to time to a kind of role-playing that belongs to the simplifying mode of melodrama – hence the dark clothes and sable feather, the initial vow of revenge, the challenge thrown down at the funeral. But on other occasions he shows himself capable of observing his own situation, analysing it, and offering himself wise counsel. At such moments he resists the stereotyped behaviour implicit in the traditional revenge code, rejects Caleb's prophecies, and attempts to separate out from Alice's predictions the good sense that lies beneath their Gothic articulation. The melodramatic instinct and the rational vision remain, however, quite separate: Ravenswood never integrates his impulse towards dramatic gestures with his capacity for analysis and judgment. Unlike those leaps for life made by Henry Morton, the crises of Ravenswood's life – from his father's funeral to Lucy's – remain strangely detached from what precedes and what follows them. They are utterances rather than actions, outbursts of inner anguish rather than revelations of a connective tissue capable of binding the present to the future.

Part of Ravenswood longs for a private solution to what at other times he recognizes as having wider social and political dimensions. The paradox of *Waverley* inhered in its demonstration that the world of history could be entered through romance; the *Bride* pursues instead the darker implications of *Rob Roy*. Ravenswood's bond with Lucy involves him in a retreat from history into a personal mythological realm in which the individual life is assimilated to the patterns of earlier literature or dream. For Ravenswood the outcome of the dream narrative in the *Bride* is controlled not by the dynamic of wish-fulfilment characteristic of day-dreams but rather by the predetermined workings of those night-dreams in which, do what he may, the protagonist is powerless to prevent what is clearly about to occur – or in which everything seems to have happened before.

Those effects which have generally been accounted for by the 'blurred trance' version of the novel's composition are, in fact, intrinsic to the tale itself and to its narrative purposes. In *The Bride of Lammermoor* Scott considers once again the situation of a young man of intelligence and imagination whose political attitudes and breadth of sympathy set him somewhat in advance of his contemporaries. Ravenswood's intelligence, self-awareness, and moral sense seem to carry with them the possibility of the kind of wise judgment and right action that would make him, within the normal limits of the human condition, a free man. But the social, political, and cultural realities – as articulated both directly and through the parodic Caleb Balderstone strand – restrict that freedom at every point. Burdened by a haunting sense of familial obligation and an obsolete code of revenge from which he cannot entirely escape, impoverished and politically powerless during the final stages of a corrupt administrative system, susceptible to the influence of the fatalism and superstition which characterize his culture, infatuated with a woman whose passivity and dependence are extreme – Ravenswood's ability to control his own destiny is less than that of any of his Waverley predecessors.[26] Like Edward Waverley he falls in love with the wrong woman, but here there is no alternative for him ultimately to recognize as the right choice. As in *Guy Mannering* and *Rob Roy* the love affair meets with the disapproval of those with power to command the heroine, but coping with the problem of the father offers on this occasion no solution, and the way is barred by a female figure as terrible and immovable as Helen MacGregor. What distinguishes the *Bride* from its predecessors is that Scott now moderates neither the implications of contemporary historical conditions nor the psychological incompatibility of the hero and heroine. Ravenswood is not ahead of his time in the fortunate sense which accrues to that phrase when it is applied to Edward Waverley, but simply out of step with his own historical circumstances and unable to escape the consequences.

This kind of appeal from the new work to the preceding Waverley Novels would have been almost automatic for its earliest readers, trained as they were in the anonymity game that made each succeeding text part of a mutually defining sequence. What can be called the Waverley context supplies the final element in the sense of entrapping design in *The Bride of Lammermoor*. For the initiated the distinctions between Ravenswood's situation and that of his precursors constitute part of the meaning of the tale. Certain narrative possibilities are foreclosed by this direction of attention beyond the text itself – just as they are by the allusions to *Hamlet*, *Romeo and Juliet*, or *Macbeth* that are signalled so prominently at certain points within the narrative – and taken in conjunction with the reiterated insistence that this is a story that has already been many times told, the effect is to endow its outcome with an inescapability that derives not merely from the necessities of character, circumstance, and history within the action but from necessities generated by the fact of narrative itself. Built into the *Bride* is the effect of inevitability proper to formulaic narratives in the oral tradition on first hearing – or to most novels on second reading. The impression that the story is already finished even as the reading is still in progress cannot be put aside. Though the reader may wish to immerse himself in the drama as it unfolds, to see the sequence of actions and choices as unique events witnessed in the process of their happening, the text everywhere resists this. The crisis of events – that confrontation of lover and mother watched by the cowering and appalled heroine which is depicted at the outset in Tinto's sketch – is present in the reader's mind throughout the tale. Unlike the prophecies about the Kelpie's flow and the wooing of a dead maiden, or the predictions of Blind Alice or her demonic counter-part Ailsie Gourlay, this 'future' outcome cannot be resisted or rational-ized away but is always waiting to be realized by the narrative as it moves forward.[27] The only freedom lies beyond the tale in the realm of history implied by the nineteenth-century perspective. But unlike the protagonists of *Waverley* or even of *Old Mortality*, Ravenswood and Lucy are not free to move forward into that realm. Instead they are cut off from the historical future by the most definitively closed of all of Scott's endings.

The intensity of interest in the narrative act itself exhibited throughout *The Bride of Lammermoor* does not carry over into its shorter companion piece, *A Legend of Montrose*. The framework of this second tale poses none of the technical questions characteristic of the Tinto-Pattieson debate but harks back more insistently to the relative simplicities of the minstrel framework of the *Lay of the Last Minstrel*. In Sergeant More M'Alpine we seem to have merely another 'appropriate prolucutor' – an elderly High-land soldier telling a story that deals with a military campaign in the Highlands – but, as with the *Lay*, what looks like a fairly mechanical deployment of the stepping-stone technique turns out to be as much a distancing as a connecting device. The most obvious opportunities offered by the situation of the Sergeant's return from the Peninsular campaigns to his deserted native glen are rejected: the ensuing narrative deals not with the Clearances but with the Civil War, and the Sergeant's access to this material is accounted for only by a somewhat perfunctory reference to the 'numerous Highland traditions, in which his youth had been instructed by his parents' (III, 146). Little is offered in the way of Highland coloration in the actual narrative, and no use is made of the special insights available to an old soldier. The connotations of the term 'legend' with respect both to oral tradition and to a heightened emphasis on supernatural detail are similarly – and deliberately – undercut by the way in which the reader is explicitly encouraged to treat 'the wild and wonderful ... with disbelief' (III, 147). The narrative voice, moreover, is that of an educated, nineteenth-century, Lowland historian whose rationalizing of the traditional and supernatural elements meets with little resistance from the kind of haunting of the written text by earlier oral versions that characterizes *The Bride of Lammermoor*.

This is not, however, to say that Scott has abandoned all interest in the relationship of teller and tale, framework and narrative. Not only does the small-scale experiment in narrative method conducted in the *Legend* involve the juxtaposition of opposing versions of a single stock-character type, but the story of the Sergeant and his sister constitutes a skilful and charming exercise in the sentimental mode. The soldier's return to his depopulated native glen where his sister alone remains, their decision to leave for Canada, the account of their residence in Gandercleuch – all this is designed to evoke a feeling response of an almost Mackenzie-like kind. This is a literary exercise in a familiar vein, a deliberate variation on the Deserted Village theme, and its specifically Highland features take the form more of local colour than of powerfully realized historical detail designed to evoke the specific experience of the Clearances. But if M'Alpine is a veteran who might easily figure in one of those gently regretful songs of exile composed as laments on the shores of Nova Scotia, the veteran in the main narrative is cast in quite a different mould. In the portrait of Dugald Dalgetty the sentimental gives way to the grotesque.

No one would want to argue that M'Alpine and Dalgetty are simply the same old-soldier stereotype presented in accordance with differing literary conventions. But it is much harder to be comfortable with the affectionate portrait of M'Alpine, its suppression of all awkward questions about the nature of his military exploits, once one has encountered Dalgetty. It is also much more difficult to accept without qualification the value of qualities such as courage, faithfulness, professionalism, loyalty to one's native place, pride in one's national identity, and so on. Dalgetty exhibits all these virtues, some of them inflated by his stupendous ego to monstrous proportions; he is also gifted with an energy and determination that would be wholly admirable were they not controlled by a narrow code of professional conduct rather than by standards more generously moral or humane. His concern for Ranald MacEagh arises almost exclusively from a consciousness of soldierly obligation, and even his beloved horse Gustavus, in whom the social affections are so highly developed, is the recipient in death of a somewhat grotesque expression of sentiment, his hide being destined 'in token of affectionate remembrance' (IV, 261) to provide a jerkin and trousers to go under his master's armour.

Thrown into relief by the framework's alternative version of the old soldier, the figure of Dalgetty is crucial to the ensuing narrative. For though the *Legend* opens with what seems like a reprise of *Waverley* – Lord Menteith, 'a young gentleman of quality, well mounted and armed,' riding slowly 'up one of those steep passes, by which the Highlands are accessible from the Lowlands of Perthshire' (III, 164) – it would clearly be a mistake to see this return to the situation and even the landscape of Scott's first novel as anything but another example of his art of self-allusion, his ability to exploit for new purposes the conventions he had himself established. The story that follows may take its outward shape in classic Waverley fashion from the young hero's experiences and end with his marriage, but the essential business of the novelist and his readers is not on this occasion with Menteith's growth and development, nor even with the revelation of the true identity of his disguised attendant, Anderson-Montrose, but with the figure who – in the adventure into the territory of the Campbells that occupies the Glennaquoich position in the narrative structure – takes over from the young hero the remainder of the perilous journey. There is nothing accidental about this usurpation: the sub-text of the classic Waverley plot ensures that the replacement of the gentlemanly hero by the veteran mercenary is fully registered. Dugald Dalgetty is not so much a character who gets out of hand as the story proceeds – a charge favoured by critics over-eager to release

Scott's more remarkable figures from the texts that produce them – as one who dominates from the start.[28] No description of the external appearance of a single character in Scott's previous fiction offers a precedent for the lovingly elaborated opening presentation of Dalgetty. He is a comprehensive emblem of warfare, every detail of whose equipment – from the 'bright burnished head-piece' to the 'case of pistols, far beyond the ordinary size' and his 'huge jack-boots' – speaks of his profession. A man of 'forty and upwards' with the 'countenance ... of a resolute weather-beaten veteran, who had seen many fields, and brought away in token more than one scar,' he stands in the path, possessing in 'every thing but numbers ... the advantage of those who seemed inclined to interrupt his passage' (III, 167–9).

There is no denying the delight that Scott as editor and annotator of his own works subsequently took in Dalgetty, his relish for the combination of the comic, the admirable, and the appalling in the Captain's make-up. He even chose to conclude the 1830 *magnum opus* Introduction in what was for him an uncharacteristically vaunting fashion by quoting Jeffrey's celebration of Dalgetty, complete with its Shakespearian analogies.[29] In the circumstances it is tempting to wonder how conscious he may have been at the moment of the tale's original composition that Dalgetty could be read as a gigantic caricature of his creator. Habitually silent about his greatest professional achievements, self-deprecating even when speaking of them to friends, Scott could not seem further removed from Dalgetty, especially since his own military aspirations had had to be satisfied by those early gallops with the Edinburgh Light Horse or transferred to the son who was just about to join his regiment as Cornet of Hussars. But in the Captain's national pride, his pedantry, his determination to re-establish himself on the paternal lands of Drumthwacket, his delight in his newly acquired knighthood (this in the year of Scott's own baronetcy), above all in his pride in his professional skill and lack of shame about being a mercenary – here, surely, is the potential for glimpsing an ironic image of Scott himself.

As in the case of such other figures as Jonathan Oldbuck it is not easy to distinguish between Scott's enjoyment of a joke at his own expense – a joke available to only his most intimate friends – and an impulse towards exorcism. By deliberately downplaying the Menteith-like aspects of his own personality – even to the extent of making Menteith himself appear somewhat priggish in his distaste for Dalgetty – while projecting at full melodramatic pitch his demonically energetic professional and mercenary side, Scott was once more confronting through narrative what he could not or would not come to terms with through analysis. With the artist's willingness to exploit in his work what as private individual he might not care to admit, Scott makes of self-consciousness or its absence a deliberate issue in this as in other of his tales. Dalgetty himself is presented as supremely unselfconscious, in no way hampered by the effect he has on others; he is totally free of the disabling sensitivity that affects Lovel, the loss of self-confidence that afflicts Waverley or Bertram when imprisoned, or the instinct for self-effacement that prevents Peter Pattieson from achieving anything other than a posthumous fame. Having so often dramatized the inhibiting of effective action that derives from self-consciousness, from gentlemanly sensitivity, and even from imagination itself, Scott here confronts the amoral force of a certain type of personal energy when released from such restrictions. Protected by his own anonymity and with Pattieson as intermediary, Scott allows himself through the twin versions of the soldier as professional that share the text of the *Legend* the opportunity not only to raise once again the issue of the controlling power of literary conventions but also to engage in disguised forms of self-analysis and self-revelation.

Such a giving away of himself always provoked in Scott the reaction of withdrawal and renewed disguise. At the end of *The Antiquary* he had taken formal leave of his readers and created for his next appearance the whole Gandercleuch framework of the *Tales*, removing all reference even to the Author of *Waverley* from their title-page. It is no surprise, therefore, to find him at this point once more beating a retreat. It is quite clear that with the completion of this third series of *Tales of My Landlord* Scott felt he had come to the end of one phase of his career as a novelist and needed to make some kind of new beginning. Though a dozen years later Lockhart was to persuade him to resurrect the world of Gandercleuch one last time in order to link together two stories into a fourth series, that could not have been foreseen in June 1819 when Scott composed the valediction terminating *A Legend of Montrose*. The Author of *Waverley*, reappearing here in his favourite role of Prospero, announces that 'like Horam the son of Asmar, and all other imaginary story-tellers, Jedediah has melted into thin air' (IV, 329). Since 'sufficient varieties have now been exhibited of the Scottish character, to exhaust one individual's powers of observation ... to persist would be useless and tedious' (IV, 329); the Author therefore declines to continue ('I retire from the field'), and though 'himself a phantom,' he takes the liberty of recommending in his stead 'a brother, or perhaps a sister shadow ... the author of the very lively work, entitled "Marriage"' (IV, 330).

This praise of Susan Ferrier, the daughter of an old friend and colleague, was added by Scott at the proof stage[30]; it is nicely symmetrical with the tributes to Maria Edgeworth and Henry Mackenzie included at the end of the *Waverley* Postscript. The experienced Waverley reader would have a sense of coming full circle, from seeing the Author of *Waverley* take up the torch from Edgeworth and Mackenzie to seeing him ostensibly pass it on to Ferrier. And though that reader, mindful of the earlier withdrawal in *The Antiquary*, might be forgiven for feeling a certain scepticism about the finality of this second farewell gesture, he would certainly register its rhetorical effect.

It was with a quotation from Prior – 'Now fitted the halter, now traversed the cart, / And often took leave, – but seem'd loth to depart!' – that the Author of *Waverley* made his not altogether unexpected reappearance on the title-page of *Ivanhoe*. Something had, nevertheless, come to an end with the third series of *Tales of My Landlord*, and the farewell can be allowed in some sense to stand. *A Legend of Montrose* marked the farthest extent of Scott's direct historical reach. Its mid–seventeenth-century date precluded, to be sure, the kind of personal links he had possessed to the period of *Waverley* – having himself talked in his youth with numbers of those who had been 'out' in the '45 – but the Civil War remained, nevertheless, just within the grasp of that oral tradition to which Scott had access through his mother. There was a sad appropriateness in Anne Scott's dying in the same week in December 1819 that saw the publication of *Ivanhoe*; the last of her son's works that she could have read would have been that third series of the *Tales* in whose genesis she played so important a role. Writing to Lady Louisa Stuart just a month after his mother's death Scott set out in almost diagrammatic form the kind of connections with the previous century and a half of Scottish history that she had provided:

> She had a mind peculiarly well stored with much acquired information and
> natural talent, and as she was very old, and had an excellent memory, she
> could draw without the least exaggeration or affectation the most striking
> pictures of the past age. If I have been able to do anything in the way of
> painting the past times, it is very much from the studies with which she
> presented me. She connected a long period of time with the present genera-
> tion, for she remembered, and had often spoken with, a person who perfectly
> recollected the battle of Dunbar, and Oliver Cromwell's subsequent entry
> into Edinburgh.   (L VI, 118)

In deciding to move on in 1819 to an English rather than a Scottish
story and to a moment that was not sixty but six hundred years since,
Scott was signalling to himself and his readers a major shift in direction[31] – a gesture he confirmed by arranging with Constable and Ballantyne for the reissue of the novels from *Waverley* to the *Legend* in the
collective form of *The Novels and Tales of the Author of Waverley* (1819).
Ivanhoe did not mark a definite break with the earlier novels: that is made
clear by the references in its Dedicatory Epistle to Jonathan Oldbuck and
Sir Arthur Wardour and by the echoes of the opening chapter of *Waverley*
in its discussion of the permanent aspects of human nature. Scott had not
abandoned his lifelong habit of keeping one foot on the old ground even
while stepping forward to the new. But in its Tintoesque pictorialism
and the patterned simplicities of its highly stylized narrative procedures,
Ivanhoe signalled a definite shift in the balance of historical realism and
romance design that had characterized the great sequence of Scottish
novels beginning in July 1814 with the publication of *Waverley* and ending
just five years later with the publication in June 1819 of *The Bride of
Lammermoor* and *A Legend of Montrose*.

Scott's special achievement in these novels lay in his narrative transformation of the raw material of seventeenth- and eighteenth-century
Scottish history. He validated anew for the nineteenth century the forms
of renaissance romance and, by his brilliant integration of literary
convention and historical detail, created a new fictional genre. He
employed standard plots, emblematic patternings, and such devices as the
pastoral interlude; he retained the kind of moralization of narrative

familiar in Spenser, Sidney, or Bunyan, thus endowing the adventures of individual Waverley heroes with something of a representative significance; he exploited all the pleasures which came from distance and the fascination of the remote and strange. But because he responded also to the impulse towards individuation intrinsic to the new Romantic – as opposed to the old romance – aesthetic, the remote and strange acquired historical and regional substance, constituting the Scotland of the early Waverley novels both country of romance and actual physical place. It was an achievement and a method that was to prove, in his own hands and those of his many successors, remarkably adaptable to other places and other times. In the process of making himself a novelist Scott had in fact arrived at a new kind of novel, and permanently affected the course of British, American, and European fiction.

Notes

I EDITORIAL STRATEGIES

1 Scott told James Ballantyne in January 1815, just after the publication of *The Lord of the Isles*: 'James, Byron hits the mark where I don't even pretend to fledge my arrow' ([John Gibson Lockhart] *Memoirs of the Life of Sir Walter Scott, Bart.* 7 vols [Edinburgh 1837–8] III, 328; subsequently referred to as *Life*).

2 *Minstrelsy of the Scottish Border: Consisting of Historical and Romantic Ballads, Collected in the Southern Counties of Scotland; With a Few of Modern Date, Founded Upon Local Tradition* 2 vols (Kelso 1802); the third volume was published in Edinburgh in 1803. Subsequent references to the *Minstrelsy* are incorporated within parentheses in the text.

3 *The Letters of Sir Walter Scott* ed H.J.C. Grierson, 12 vols (London 1932–7) I, 108–9; subsequent references to the *Letters* are incorporated within parentheses in the text, preceded by the abbreviation *L*.

4 See, for example, the headnote to 'The Souters of Selkirk,' in which Scott speaks of his office as Sheriff of Selkirk as having given him the opportunity to recover two extra verses of the song; or the note attached to 'Jamie Telfer of the Fair Dodhead,' which refers to Scott's ancestor, Auld Wat of Harden, and his wife the Flower of Yarrow (*Minstrelsy* I, 248, 92–3).

5 The dedication reads: 'To His Grace, Henry, Duke of Buccleuch, &c. &c. &c. these tales, which, in elder times, have celebrated the prowess, and cheered the halls, of his gallant ancestors, are respectfully inscribed by His Grace's much obliged and most humble servant, Walter Scott.'

6 *Scott on Himself: A Selection of the Autobiographical Writings of Sir Walter Scott* ed David Hewitt (Edinburgh 1981) pp 27–8; Dr Hewitt has retranscribed the

manuscript of the Ashestiel fragment, which was first printed as chapter 1 of Lockhart's *Life*.

7 By Scott's 'basic prose voice' I mean that used in most of his non-fiction prose and the general narrative of his novels. He was, of course, capable of moving away from this norm when seeking particular effects, but, as David Daiches has recently pointed out: 'In writing *Waverley* Scott was using his own voice, not inventing a special authorial voice, as most novelists do' ('Scott's *Waverley*: the Presence of the Author' in *Nineteenth-Century Scottish Fiction: Critical Essays* ed Ian Campbell [Manchester 1979] p 9).

8 Scott actually entertained the irascible Joseph Ritson – 'the most rigid of our British antiquaries' (*L* XII, 195) – for a couple of days in September 1801 and allowed him to examine much of the material which eventually appeared in the first two volumes of the *Minstrelsy*. Ritson had made repeated criticisms of Percy's editorial practices over the years and included a long critique, complete with parallel texts of 'The Marriage of Sir Gawaine,' in the introductory section of his *Ancient Engleish Metrical Romanceës* (3 vols [London 1802]). See Scott's discussion of the Ritson-Percy controversy in his 1824 'Essay on Romance,' *Encyclopaedia Britannica: Supplement to 4th, 5th and 6th Editions* VI (Edinburgh 1824) 435–56. The editorial careers of Ritson and Percy, as well as of Scott and his friend George Ellis, are fully examined in Arthur Johnston *Enchanted Ground: The Study of Medieval Romance in the Eighteenth Century* (London 1964).

9 For the contents of the various editions, see William Ruff 'A Bibliography of the Poetical Works of Sir Walter Scott 1796–1832' *Transactions of the Edinburgh Bibliographical Society* 1 (1938) 127–34.

10 *Edinburgh Review* 7 (1806) 368. Scott is here following standard eighteenth-century doctrine; see, for example, the essay 'On the Ancient Metrical Romances,' in which Percy argues: 'As many of these contain a considerable portion of poetic merit, and throw great light on the manners and opinions of former times, it were to be wished that some of the best of them were rescued from oblivion' (*Reliques of Ancient English Poetry* 3 vols [London 1765] III, viii).

11 'I have recoverd three Covenanting Ballads – The defeat of Montrose at Philiphaugh – the Battle of Bothwell Brigg & the preceeding Skirmish at Drumclog or Loudoun hill. They are all as you will readily suppose, indifferent enough the genius of the sect turning them rather towards psalmody but they will afford room for some curious notes' (*L* I, 161; see also

1, 157). In preparing the final text of 'The Gallant Grahams' Scott was able to make use of a printed copy sent him by Ritson (see *L* XII, 209, and *Minstrelsy* III, 171). 'Lesly's March' is not strictly speaking a ballad, but Scott needed it as the initial element in the powerful narrative unit he made out of the five poems and their accompanying editorial framework. It was readily accessible in Alan Ramsay's *Tea-Table Miscellany* (Edinburgh 1762), although Scott himself wrongly ascribed it to Ramsay's *Evergreen*; see M.R. Dobie 'The Development of Scott's *Minstrelsy' Transactions of the Edinburgh Bibliographical Society* 2 (1938–45) 71.

12 *The Poetical Works of Sir Walter Scott, Bart.* [ed John Gibson Lockhart] 12 vols (Edinburgh 1833–4) I, iv–v. This edition, prepared immediately after Scott's death, contains supplementary notes and introductory material by Lockhart.

13 For Muir, 'since some time in the sixteenth century Scottish literature has been a literature without a language' (*Scott and Scotland: The Predicament of the Scottish Writer* [London 1936] p 18). 'Every genuine literature ... requires as its condition a means of expression capable of dealing with everything the mind can think or the imagination conceive ... Scots has survived to our time as a language for simple poetry and the simpler kind of short story ... all its other uses have lapsed, and it expresses therefore only a fragment of the Scottish mind' (p 20). The effect on Scott of this situation, Muir argues, was that 'where he wished to express feelings of more than ordinary seriousness and range, or feelings modified by thought, he employed English, using Scots for the simplest purposes of humour and pathos. His Scots, it is true, was far better than his English, and he produced in his dialogue the best Scots prose that has ever been written. But as the Scots vernacular did not come out of a unity, he felt that it could not express a unity; so for the structural, the unifying, part of his work he relied upon English' (p 174).

14 The case made in eloquent sadness by Muir is repeated in angrier terms by David Craig in *Scottish Literature and the Scottish People 1680–1830* (London 1961); see especially pp 253–60. For a detailed examination of Scott's language, see Graham Tulloch *The Language of Sir Walter Scott: A Study of his Scottish and Period Language* (London 1980); the discussion of spoken and written Scots in the early nineteenth century (pp 171–81) is particularly illuminating.

15 The long poems that follow the *Minstrelsy* are, as Karl Kroeber has pointed out, notable for the absence of 'the dialect that looms so large in Scott's

novels' (*Romantic Narrative Art* [Madison 1966] p 174). This is not, however, true of the shorter poems; Thomas Crawford, in his article 'Scott as a Poet,' demonstrates the command of the vernacular exhibited in the lyrics and ballads; he also points to Scott's keen appreciation of 'the living variety of Scottish traditional modes' (*Études Anglaises* 24 [1971] 483).

16 See especially the letters of 27 March 1801 (*L* XII, 176), 17 October 1802 (XII, 219–25), 27 August 1803 (I, 196–9), 4 May 1804 (XII, 245–6), and 27 May 1804 (XII, 250–8).

17 The full title of the first edition is *Sir Tristrem; A Metrical Romance of the Thirteenth Century; by Thomas of Erildoune Called the Rhymer.* Edited from the Auchinleck MS. by Walter Scott, Esq. Advocate (Edinburgh 1804). Subsequent editions appeared in 1806, 1811, and 1819, and the 1819 edition was reissued as volume IV of the 1821 edition of Scott's *Poetical Works.* For an example of Scott's continuing determination to maintain the primacy of his own Thomas, see the ingenious passage inserted into the Introduction to the 1811 edition in an attempt to cope with the existence of a reference to Thomas von Britanie in a romance of Gottfried von Strasburgh attributed to 1232. To permit Gottfried's Thomas and his own to be one and the same, Scott posits for Thomas of Erceldoune a lifespan of almost a century (*Sir Tristrem* [1811] pp x–xi).

18 It was Lockhart who finally responded, in the Advertisement to *Sir Tristrem* in volume V of the 1833–4 edition of the *Poetical Works* (iii–x), to the charges made by Richard Price in the 1824 edition of Warton's *History of English Poetry.* Price argued that the poem could not have been by Thomas of Erceldoune, that if it had been then he would have followed a foreign source, not vice versa, that Thomas von Britanie could not have been Thomas of Erceldoune, and that the language of the poem had nothing peculiarly Scottish about it. Lockhart readily conceded the case for the poem's dependence on French originals and acknowledged that the Rhymer and Thomas von Britanie were not one and the same, but he maintained Scott's claims for attribution of the original version of the Auchinleck poem to Thomas of Erceldoune, and begged the question of the Scottishness of the language by asserting a preference for Scott's opinion on such a topic rather than that of Mr Price.

19 There is a detailed account of Mrs Brown and her ballads in David Buchan *The Ballad and the Folk* (London 1972) pp 62–73.

20 For a full discussion of Scott's editorial methods, see Dobie 'The Development of Scott's *Minstrelsy*,' which clearly demonstrates that Francis Child and T.F. Henderson were not justified in charging that Scott introduced into the ballads numerous and substantial alterations and additions of his own. The continued use of T.F. Henderson's edition of the *Minstrelsy* (4 vols [Edinburgh 1902]) has helped to perpetuate the accusations of editorial licence despite Dobie's excellent work. Scott's reliance on his own memory for particular ballads may have supplied unintentional minor verbal 'improvements,' but he followed his copies with considerable faithfulness, and while he felt free to combine them to create a poetically superior text, he did not habitually engage in sophistication of that text with interpolations of his own passed off as part of the original. For a recent discussion of Scott's editorial methods, see [Charles G. Zug III] 'The Ballad and History: the Case for Scott' *Folklore* 89 (1978) 229–42.

21 *Sir Tristrem* (1804) p lxxxvii

22 References to the *Minstrelsy* in the notes to the *Lay* also helped emphasize the connection; see, for example, *The Lay of the Last Minstrel; A Poem* (London 1805) pp 251–2, 267, 274. It is worth noting that Scott continued to make additions and corrections to the notes of the *Lay* throughout his life; see Ruff 'Bibliography' pp 135–42, and, for a discussion of some of the changes, J.H. Alexander *The Lay of the Last Minstrel: Three Essays* (Salzburg 1978) pp 189–90.

23 *Lay* p v. In his 1824 'Essay on Romance' Scott defines the genre as 'a fictitious narrative in prose or verse; the interest of which turns upon marvellous and uncommon incidents' (*Encyclopaedia Britannica Supplement* VI, 435); he is refining Ritson's definition, 'a fabulous narrative, or fictitious recital, in verse, more or less marvelous or probable' (*Ancient Engleish Metrical Romanceës* I, v).

24 *The Poetical Works of Sir Walter Scott* 11 vols (Edinburgh 1830) I, xxvii. Subsequent references to this edition are incorporated within parentheses in the text, preceded by the abbreviation *PW*.

25 Neither the letter to Anna Seward of 30 November 1802 (*L* I, 162–6) nor those to Ellis of December 1802 (XII, 229–32) and 30 January 1803 (I, 174–5) contain any word about Gilpin Horner, though the 30 January letter gives a full account of the minstrel framework, mentions the title of the poem, and suggests that Scott was fairly well advanced with its composition.

Edgar Johnson, in *Sir Walter Scott: The Great Unknown* 2 vols (London 1970), points out, on the basis of a letter from Thomas Beattie to the Countess of Dalkeith at Bowhill, that the Countess herself did not receive the Gilpin Horner story till December 1802 (1, xx). Johnson is wrong, however, in suggesting that Scott was in possession of the story that same month; the letter to Laidlaw cited by Johnson as evidence is dated not 2 January 1803, but nearly three weeks later, 21 January 1803 (*L* 1, 169–71; National Library of Scotland ms 851, ff 268–70). This would explain the absence of Gilpin Horner from Scott's accounts of the poem up to the end of January 1803.

26 Scott did not keep the original manuscript of the *Lay*. In 1821 Archibald Constable noted on the manuscript of *Rokeby*, which had just come into his possession: 'The original M.S. of The Lay of the Last Minstrel was not preserved such things not having been thought important till the publication of Marmion when I desired Mr Ballantyne to preserve the manuscript for me' (Pierpont Morgan ms, MA448 VIIC). A fragment of the *Lay* did apparently survive: W.S. Crockett reported in the *Scotsman* of 16 February 1924 (p 8) that he had seen the manuscript of the Introduction and 92 lines of canto 1 and hoped it would soon be deposited in the National Library of Scotland. Unfortunately, the deposit was never made.

27 Scott seems to have engaged here in the kind of 'creative' remembering discussed by F.A. Pottle in his fine essay 'The Power of Memory in Boswell and Scott,' *Essays on the Eighteenth Century Presented to David Nichol Smith in Honour of his Seventieth Birthday* (Oxford 1945) pp 168–89.

28 For a detailed discussion of the notes of the *Lay* and their relationship to the text, see J.H. Alexander *Three Essays* pp 162–96. Dr Alexander writes particularly well on what he calls the 'poetry of scholarship' (p 187) in the notes.

2 VARIATIONS ON A METHOD

1 Scott himself makes this connection in his account of the completion of *Queenhoo-Hall* in the 1829 General Preface to the *magnum opus* edition of his novels (*Waverley Novels* 48 vols [Edinburgh 1829–33] 1, xvii; subsequent references to this edition are incorporated within parentheses in the text preceded by the abbreviation *WN*).

2 *Life* 11, 144

3 *Edinburgh Review* 12 (1808) 2

4 A letter from Thomas Longman of 13 January 1807 (NLS ms 3876, ff 8–9) shows that Scott briefly considered a separate anticipatory publication of the epistles, but the scheme foundered that same month on Scott's insistence that Constable be given a share in the venture. The epistles were, however, an integral part of the poem, for which an agreement with Constable was reached on 30 January 1807 (Thomas Constable *Archibald Constable and His Literary Correspondents* 3 vols [Edinburgh 1873] III, 6). Lady Abercorn's letter to Scott of 18 February 1807 (NLS ms 3876, ff 28–9) shows that she had been sent the opening of canto I together with its preliminary epistle, and the evidence of the manuscript (NLS Adv. ms 19.1.16) indicates that composition of the later epistles and the cantos that follow them was, allowing for the normal processes of revision, continuous and sequential.

5 *Marmion; A Tale of Flodden Field* (Edinburgh 1808) p 16; subsequent references are incorporated within parentheses in the text.

6 Karl Kroeber sees the epistles as concerned with 'how permanence encompasses change, and how the present relates to the past' (*Romantic Narrative Art* p 171).

7 William Erskine was Scott's closest friend from their law-student days until Erskine's early death in 1822; he is the key figure in the two great 'origin' stories, that of the *Lay* and that of *Waverley*, and Scott was unwilling to proceed with any poem or novel without his approval. Urging Erskine to come and see him in late September 1809, Scott insisted, 'I cannot find the heart to proceed unless I have your *signetur*' (NLS ms 1750, f 100); and in October 1815 he chided him affectionately, 'You have used me very shabbily in not coming to see me & my works at Abbotsford and in not telling me what you think of my works at the Ballantyne's' (NLS ms 1750, f 157).

8 John Pikoulis has made the case for the integral nature of the *Marmion* epistles with particular force: 'The long introductions to each canto, far from being conventional pieties, underpin the poem firmly and persuasively, while the introduction of the poet in *propria persona* at his task of writing the poem has the effect of making Scott at least as important a figure in the poem as anyone else ('Scott and *Marmion*: the Discovery of Identity' *Modern Language Review* 66 [1971] 742).

9 *The Lady of the Lake; A Poem* (Edinburgh 1810) p 4; subsequent references are incorporated within parentheses in the text.

10 *Collected Letters of Samuel Taylor Coleridge* ed E.L. Griggs, 6 vols (Oxford 1956–71) III, 291

11 In a letter to Lady Abercorn of 29 June 1810 Scott commented: 'As for my lover I find with deep regret that however interesting lovers are to each other it is no easy matter to render them generally interesting. There was however another reason for keeping Malcolm Graeme's character a little *under* as the painters say for it must otherwise have interfered with that of the King which I was more anxious to bring forward in splendour or something like it' (*L* II, 354).

12 Writing in his journal in December 1825, Scott summed up the effect of the Williamina affair: 'Broken-hearted for two years – My heart handsomely pieced again – but the crack will remain till my dying day' (*The Journal of Sir Walter Scott* ed W.E.K. Anderson [Oxford 1972] p 43; subsequently referred to as *Journal*).

13 The phrase actually comes from the account of Edward Waverley's childhood in *Waverley; or 'Tis Sixty Years Since* 3 vols (Edinburgh 1814) I, 45. For the affinities between Scott's own boyhood reading and Edward's, see the 1829 General Preface (*WN* I, v–vii).

14 *Scott on Himself* p 26

15 *Journal* pp 42–3

16 George Crabbe *Tales* (London 1812) pp [79]–80

17 *Annual Register, 1781* (London 1782) p 177; Scott first encountered an excerpt from *The Library* during his boyhood reading of some odd volumes of Dodsley's *Annual Register*. For a fuller discussion of the affinities between Crabbe and Scott, see my article 'Scott and the Dreaming Boy: a Context for *Waverley*' *Review of English Studies* 32 (1981) 286–93.

18 *Rokeby; A Poem* (Edinburgh 1813) p 38; subsequent references to *Rokeby* in this chapter are incorporated within parentheses in the text.

19 Lockhart's note, *Poetical Works* (1833) IX, 126, n 1; the twelve lines quoted by Erskine, beginning 'A face more fair you well might find,' occur in stanza 5 of canto III of *Rokeby*.

20 Lockhart's comments in quoting from this letter to Maria Edgeworth confirm the association of Scott with both his heroes; see *Life* III, 42.

21 In addition to using remembered details from earlier visits to the home of his friend Morritt at Rokeby, Scott made a special visit there in 1812 and sent Morritt requests for exact details of scenery, local names, etc; see *L* III, 40–1, 88, 202.

3 *WAVERLEY*

1 The account of the composition of *Waverley* in the General Preface to the 1829 *magnum opus* edition (*WN* I, xi–xii, xvi–xviii) speaks only of the first seven chapters composed in 1805 and makes no mention of any continuation in 1810. I agree, however, with Claire Lamont that the letter to Morritt written immediately after publication of the novel in July 1814 is likely to give a more accurate sense of just how much had been written before the manuscript was mislaid; Scott there speaks of having 'written great part of the first volume' (*L* III, 457) before the disappearance. See *Waverley; or 'Tis Sixty Years Since* ed Claire Lamont (Oxford 1981) pp xxiv–xxv. The three phases of composition – seven chapters in 1805, most of the rest of volume I in 1810, volumes II and III in 1814 – are collapsed into two stages in all of Scott's accounts (the letter to Morritt, the 'Postscript, which should have been a Preface' to the first edition, and the 1829 General Preface). This may be a further example of 'creative' remembering: a single setting-aside followed by rediscovery after a nine-year interval makes a particularly satisfying story.

2 *Waverley; or, 'Tis Sixty Years Since* 3 vols (Edinburgh 1814) I, 40. Subsequent references are incorporated within parentheses in the text.

3 For a discussion of *Waverley*'s employment of eyewitness reports as a bridging device between past and present, see Wolfgang Iser *The Implied Reader: Patterns of Communication in Prose Fiction from Bunyan to Beckett* (Baltimore 1974) pp 88–90.

4 The temporal perspective is established precisely in the opening chapter: 'By fixing then the date of my story Sixty Years before this present 1st November, 1805 ...' (I, 7). The account of the subtitle in the 1829 General Preface is somewhat perplexing: 'About the year 1805, I threw together about one-third of the first volume of Waverley. It was advertised to be published by the late Mr John Ballantyne, bookseller in Edinburgh, under the name of "Waverley, or 'tis Fifty Years since," – a title afterwards altered to "'Tis Sixty Years since," that the actual date of publication might be made to correspond with the period in which the scene was laid' (*WN* I, xi). I have not seen any 1805 advertisement, however, and it is hard to escape the feeling that Scott's memory is playing him false here: since the period between 1805 and 1745 is sixty years, the use of the word 'fifty' in the title would have been deliberately misleading. What Scott

may in fact have been recalling is a discussion that could have taken place in 1814 about changing the wording to *seventy*. Lockhart fudges the issue in his biography by quoting selectively from the General Preface on this point (*Life* II, 52), but what is clear is that in 1814 and in all subsequent editions the date of narration is firmly identified as 1805 and the subtitle appears as *'Tis Sixty Years Since*. The manuscript of *Waverley* is divided between the Pierpont Morgan Library and the National Library of Scotland, but since the first fifty-three pages do not survive, no light can be thrown on the issue of the subtitle from this source.

5 In the first edition Scott described Flora's appearance as 'like one of those lovely forms which decorate the landscapes of Claude' (I, 338). In the third edition he changed the comparison from Claude to Poussin at the suggestion of his friend Morritt. See *Waverley* ed Lamont, p xxix.

6 For a discussion of the 'elegiac' quality of Edward's return to Tully Veolan, see D.D. Devlin *The Author of Waverley: A Critical Study of Walter Scott* (London 1971) pp 66–9; see also Donald Davie *The Heyday of Sir Walter Scott* (London 1961) p 33.

7 William Gilpin *Three Essays: On Picturesque Beauty; On Picturesque Travel; and On Sketching Landscape: To Which Is Added a Poem, On Landscape Painting* 2nd edn (London 1794): 'I hold myself at perfect liberty ... to dispose the *foreground* as I please; restrained only by the analogy of the country. I take up a tree here, and plant it there. I pare a knoll, or make an addition to it' (p 68). Scott's use of picturesque formulae is discussed in Peter Garside's important article '*Waverley*'s Pictures of the Past,' *ELH* 44 (1977) 659–82.

8 Maria Edgeworth was quick to catch the element of staginess in this scene, but she did not register the element of irony; writing to the Author of *Waverley* on 23 October 1814, she commented: 'We did not like the preparation for *a scene* – the appearance of Flora and her harp was too like a common heroine, she should be far above all stage effect or novelist's trick' (*Maria Edgeworth: Chosen Letters* ed F.V. Barry [London 1931] p 224). Robin Mayhead draws an interesting parallel between Flora's 'decorative landscaping' and 'that lucid orderliness of mind co-existing so oddly with the obsession with the Stuart cause which she admits to have been hers since infancy' (*Walter Scott* [Cambridge 1973] p 25). Peter Garside ('*Waverley*'s Pictures' p 674) shows that Flora's transformation of the landscape has an historical as well as an aesthetic dimension: 'Flora's framing in a Poussin

setting could then express the artificiality of her historical ideology, rather than its disinterestedness.'

9 Francis R. Hart, in *Scott's Novels: The Plotting of Historic Survival* (Charlottesville 1966), is one of the few critics to stress the danger of accepting 'Flora's tragically limited vision' (p 20). D.D. Devlin typifies the opposite view; for him she is 'the most intelligent person in the novel' and 'alone "places" Waverley' (*Author of Waverley* p 63).

10 For a stark formulation of the kind of reading of *Waverley* that curtails its design to this simple recovery pattern, see Robert C. Gordon *Under Which King? A Study of the Scottish Waverley Novels* (Edinburgh 1969): 'The hero begins as a loyal servant of George II, deviates into Jacobitism, is disillusioned, and returns to peace and sanity' (p 13). George Levine, in *The Realistic Imagination: English Fiction from Frankenstein to Lady Chatterley* (Chicago 1981), offers a more complex reading of the novel's pattern that gives some weight to the closing sequence of the action, but for him too *Waverley* 'follows the familiar pattern of disenchantment' articulated in a work like *Northanger Abbey*, though Scott's parody lacks the 'normative force' of Jane Austen's (p 83).

11 Robert Kiely, in *The Romantic Novel in England* (Cambridge, Mass 1972), sees *Waverley* as 'one of the narratives in which Scott tries most explicitly to define the romantic sensibility and its relation to the world of social and moral responsibility' (p 141). Professor Kiely's reading of the initial stages of Edward's dark journey is extremely perceptive, especially his analysis of the source of Fergus Mac-Ivor's attraction for Edward, but in taking the Lake District episode as climactic he dismisses as relatively unimportant what are, in fact, the final stages of a continuous journey. According to this interpretation Edward is made to see his experiences up to Clifton 'as somehow not real, as a dream or an adolescent phase to be outgrown' (p 147).

12 For the fullest discussion of Scott's passive heroes, see Alexander Welsh *The Hero of the Waverley Novels* (New Haven 1963).

13 An especially heavy stress not on irony but on romantic patterning can also distort interpretation of the novel; Mark M. Hennelly's article 'Waverley and Romanticism,' *Nineteenth-Century Fiction* 28 (1973) 194–209, rightly emphasizes the importance of the return to Tully Veolan but pays little attention to the part of Edward's journey which intervenes between the

Lake District and that return – 'The remainder of Waverley's adventure oscillates between England and the Lowlands' (p 208). Professor Hennelly's insistence on vacillation and oscillation followed by coalescence leads him to underplay the progressive aspects of Edward's education: 'The dialectic has wound down to a single focal point; Romance and Realism have coalesced; and the pariah has become messiah and rehabilitated the ravaged kingdom' (p 209).

14 Francis Hart sees 'Waverley's commitment to the romance world of historic involvement' as 'a morally constructive ordeal' (*Scott's Novels* p 30), but George Levine maintains that, since in Scott's fiction 'the creative imagination does not reveal truth, its primary function is entertainment' (*Realistic Imagination* p 87). Levine's emphasis on the realist impulse in Scott's fiction is extremely useful, especially in the face of continuing assumptions that the romantic surface of Scott's fiction is symptomatic of a fundamental lack of seriousness. But I would argue that in stressing Scott's 'refusal to "believe in" creative imagination' (p 87), Levine too readily accepts Scott's public statements and the attitudes manifested on the borders of the fiction as representative of what goes on inside the novels themselves.

4 GUY MANNERING

1 *Familiar Letters of Sir Walter Scott* ed David Douglas, 2 vols (Edinburgh 1894) I, 326

2 Ibid, p 328

3 Scott may already have had in mind the possibility of becoming a judge of the Scottish Court of Exchequer; he was to solicit the Duke of Buccleuch's assistance on this matter in December 1816. See *L* IV, 309–14, and *Life* IV, 46–9.

4 *Familiar Letters* I, 329

5 *Waverley* 3rd edn (Edinburgh 1814) vi–viii

6 Junius was for Scott, as for many others, the quintessential anonymous author; he is invoked in the Advertisement to *Rob Roy*, where the Author of *Waverley* remarks that 'every anonymous writer is, like the celebrated Junius, only a phantom' (*Rob Roy* 3 vols [Edinburgh 1817] I, v).

7 *Chronicles of the Canongate* 2 vols (Edinburgh 1827) I, xxii. Subsequent references are incorporated within parentheses in the text.

8 *Life* III, 327

9 See *L* III, 498.

10 *Life* III, 272

11 *The Lord of the Isles* (Edinburgh 1815) p 275

12 The stanzas were sent to Lord Montagu in proof on 27 December 1814; see *L* III, 534.

13 Early and late Scott loved to quote the Marquis of Montrose; see, for example, his letter to Lady Abercorn of 9 September 1809: 'He either fears his fate too much / Or his deserts are small / Who dares not put it to the touch / To win or lose it all' (*L* II, 239). See also his quotation of the same stanza in the 1830 Introduction to *The Lady of the Lake* (*PW* IV, iv).

14 *Scots Magazine and Edinburgh Literary Miscellany* 76 (1814) 932–3; Lockhart (*Life* III, 325) makes the juxtaposition even more dramatic by quoting the two items as though they formed a single paragraph.

15 For a large part of the novel Bertram is, of course, known as Captain Brown. It seems, however, preferable to call him consistently by his rightful name rather than to employ an awkward formulation such as Brown / Bertram.

16 *Guy Mannering; or, The Astrologer* 3 vols (Edinburgh 1815) I, 279. Subsequent references are incorporated within parentheses in the text.

17 Scott must have been aware that Gilpin singles out the tract of country through which Bertram and Dinmont have been travelling as an example of a region which though 'barren' is able none the less to 'amuse the eye' of the picturesque tourist (*Three Essays* p 55). For Gilpin's specification of roughness as essential to the picturesque and his rejection of smoothness, see pp 26–33.

18 The manuscript of the novel (in the Pierpont Morgan Library, New York) reveals that the episode of Mannering's Edinburgh visit was originally much longer and included character sketches of a number of unnamed Edinburgh notables whose identity the reader was left to guess: John Clerk of Eldin, Lord Monboddo, Adam Ferguson, and John Home. This more extended account had allowed Scott to balance Mannering's doings against the badger-baiting, fox-hunting, and salmon-spearing of Bertram's Liddesdale stay, and he no doubt enjoyed the joke of setting off the portraits of the Edinburgh literati against the sketches of their rural counterparts Tam o' Todshaw, Will o' the Flat, and Hobbie o' Sorbietrees. The decision to omit the section from the printed text probably derived from a feeling that it was a trifle self-indulgent and involved a private Edinburgh

game not readily accessible to an English audience – Scott's own version of High Jinks. For a transcription of the omitted section and a commentary upon it, see my article 'Guy Mannering in Edinburgh: The Evidence of the Manuscript' *The Library* 32 (1977) 238–45.

19 Harry Berger, Jr 'The Renaissance Imagination: Second World and Green World' *Centennial Review* 9 (1965) 46

20 For a discussion of Pleydell as 'professional,' see Mayhead *Walter Scott* pp 77–8.

21 The use of *The Winter's Tale* quotation as epigraph was a second thought on Scott's part; in the manuscript he uses two lines from *Antony and Cleopatra*: ' – Give me to drink Mandragora, / That I may sleep out this great gap of time.'

22 Francis Hart considers this scene weakened by the pace of the narrative at this point: it becomes one of a series of 'brief incidents in a veritable barrage of recognitions' (*Scott's Novels* p 265). I would, however, argue that any disappointment felt by the reader derives not from a technical flaw but from Scott's deliberate portrayal of the continuing unease of father and daughter with each other, the fear of intimacy that prevents their being frank and openly affectionate and makes them both wish to have the interview concluded as quickly as possible. It is perhaps significant that Julia sees herself as a Jessica rather than a Perdita; see I, 275.

23 *More Talking About Shakespeare* ed John Garrett (London 1959) pp 85–6

24 'Of a surety, little Harry, we must speedily resume our studies' (III, 235).

25 *Life* III, 321

5 THE ANTIQUARY

1 'I have closed with Usher for his beautiful patrimony which makes me a great laird. I am afraid the people will take me up for coining. Indeed these novels while their attractions last are something like it' (Scott to John Ballantyne, 11 October 1817; *L* I, 522).

2 *The Antiquary* 3 vols (Edinburgh 1816) I, 306. Subsequent references are incorporated within parentheses in the text.

3 *Life* IV, 12. Most of the contents of the *Reliquiæ* are printed in two articles by Mary Monica Maxwell Scott: 'Gabions of Abbotsford. A Hitherto Unpublished Fragment by Sir Walter Scott' *Harper's Monthly Magazine* 78 (1889) 778–88; 'Sir Walter Scott and his "Gabions"' *Nineteenth Century* 18

(1905) 621–32. See also the comments by Mary Lascelles in *The Story-teller Retrieves the Past: Historical Fiction and Fictitious History in the Art of Scott, Stevenson, Kipling and Some Others* (Oxford 1980) pp 51–2.

4 Francis Hart observes: 'What is needed for the recovery of the past, for the saving of its social orders, for the reinstating of its lost heir, seems ridiculously accessible. We wonder why it hasn't all been dug up before. Why now?' (*Scott's Novels* p 251) The answer for Hart lies in the thematic concern with the need to free ancient houses 'from their slavery to fraudulent pasts' (p 254).

5 For a sensitive discussion of this aspect of the novel, see the important article by Joan C. Elbers, 'Isolation and Community in *The Antiquary' Nineteenth-Century Fiction* 27 (1973) 405–23; Graham McMaster places similar stress on Scott's insistence on 'the inability of man to exist as a solitary being divorced from society' (*Scott and Society* [Cambridge 1981] p 161).

6 The song is in fact lost, however, since Elspeth dies at the end of the ensuing interview with Oldbuck and Edie.

7 Joan C. Elbers places particular emphasis on the role of Edie: 'In a novel organized around a series of contrasts between isolation and community Edie represents the value of sympathetic connection between man and man. And in a novel exploring the ways in which a sense of the past can destroy or nurture a sense of community he exemplifies the possibility of a life-supportive integration of past and present' ('Isolation and Community' p 421). For a perceptive analysis of Edie's role in the novel and of the source of the authority with which he speaks at certain key moments, see A.O.J. Cockshut *The Achievement of Walter Scott* (London 1969) pp 43–53.

8 It is significant that Scott, when revising his text for the *magnum opus* edition, chose to emphasize Lovel's gifts as a listener, adding the following sentences to the account of Oldbuck's surprise 'at the degree of attachment' (II, 6) he felt for Lovel: 'The riddle was notwithstanding easily solved. Lovel had many attractive qualities, but he won our Antiquary's heart by being on most occasions an excellent listener' (*WN* v, 216).

9 Edie registers Oldbuck's skill in making sense of isolated pieces of information: 'The de'il's in you, Monkbarns, for garring odds and evens meet – Wha thought ye wad hae laid that and that thegither' (III, 319). Edie is himself no mean 'reader' of physical signs; he can tell the time by the stars (II, 174) and recognize travelled earth (II, 219) as well as interpret the true cause of Lovel's unhappiness.

10 It is worth noting that in a novel in which most families are incomplete, or the normal relationships inverted or distorted, the Mucklebackits provide at the outset a kind of normative model. For all the dirt and confusion, their home is a place of warmth and plenty; three generations are present and Mucklebackit shows respect for his old mother while possessing in Steenie a loving and dutiful son.

11 A.N. Wilson, in *The Laird of Abbotsford: A View of Sir Walter Scott* (Oxford 1980), gives full weight to Oldbuck's capacity for love and fellow feeling: 'Antiquarian research is an amusing enough obsession to carry a disappointed man through life. But Oldbuck's stature as a man is measured by the depth of his sympathies, by his Christian charity' (p 70). Wilson's emphasis on the value assigned to friendship in the novel seems to me the right one, and he provides a brief but telling demonstration (pp 70–3) of the irrelevance of E.M. Forster's famous attack on the plotting. David Brown, in *Walter Scott and the Historical Imagination* (London 1979), is very shrewd about the tendency for antiquarianism to blind Oldbuck to the human implications of what he observes (pp 51–4), but he fails to register Oldbuck's capacity to move beyond this limitation of vision to new insight.

12 Those who see the plot of *The Antiquary* as damagingly incoherent fail to give due weight to the echoing and allusive structure common to most Scott novels. See, for example, Avrom Fleishman's comment in *The English Historical Novel: Walter Scott to Virginia Woolf* (Baltimore 1971): 'The Antiquary ... has the makings of a historical vision of the present, and almost survives its meanderings of plot and multiplication of secondary characters' (p 75).

13 The manuscript is in the Pierpont Morgan Library.

6 THE BLACK DWARF AND OLD MORTALITY

1 *Waverley, Guy Mannering,* and *The Antiquary* had all been published by Constable and Longman; the *Tales* were published by Blackwood and Murray.

2 *Tales of My Landlord, Collected and Arranged Jedediah Cleishbotham, Schoolmaster and Parish-Clerk of Gandercleuch* 4 vols (Edinburgh 1816) I, 18–19. Subsequent references are incorporated within parentheses in the text.

3 Scott himself supplied a teasing non-explanation of the title in his own review of the *Tales* in the *Quarterly*: 'They are entitled "Tales of my

Landlord:'' why so entitled, excepting to introduce a quotation from Don Quixote, it is difficult to conceive: for Tales of my Landlord they are *not*, nor is it indeed easy to say whose tales they ought to be called' (*Quarterly Review* 16 [1817] 441–2).

4 Ibid, pp 431–2
5 Ibid, p 442
6 Ibid, p 445
7 Ibid, p 464
8 *Ballantyne's Novelist's Library* 10 vols (Edinburgh 1821–4) VI, xx
9 *Novelist's Library* I, xvii
10 *QR* 16, pp 445–6
11 Scott was not, however, entirely satisfied with the management of the narrative in *Old Mortality*; he spoke critically of its 'carelessness as to arrangement of the story' in a letter to Joseph Train in December 1816 (*L* IV, 323).
12 *QR* 16, p 431
13 Ibid
14 In the manuscript of the novel (Pierpont Morgan Library) the preaching chapter (chap 5, vol III of the *Tales*) shows what is for Scott an unusual amount of revision, ranging from minor verbal improvements to substantial additions. For a discussion of the range and variety of Presbyterian eloquence in this novel, see Robert Hay Carnie 'Scott's Presbyterian Eloquence in *Old Mortality*' *Scottish Literary Journal* 3 (1976) 51–61; for a detailed analysis of the differing stylistic techniques employed by Scott for the speech of Kettledrummle, Macbriar, and Mucklewrath, see Peter D. Garside 'Old Mortality's Silent Minority' *Scottish Literary Journal* 7 (1980) 127–44.
15 John P. Farrell, in *Revolution as Tragedy: The Dilemma of the Moderate from Scott to Arnold* (Ithaca 1980), offers a succinct formulation of Morton's predicament: 'In its primary plot, *Old Mortality* concerns itself with Morton's inability to connect. His inner goodwill has no exchange value in a domain monopolized by fanaticism. He is a prisoner, most of all, of his conscience, because conscience, as an attribute of the moral self, has become caricatured as fidelity to an ideological program' (p 93).
16 For further comments on Cuddie's role in the novel, see Welsh *Hero* pp 233–4. Welsh sees the parallels between Cuddie and Morton as serving in some sense to 'subvert the precarious ambivalence of the hero by caricaturing it' (p 233). For further discussion of character parallels, see Mary

Cullinan 'The Possibilities of History: Scott's *Old Mortality*' *Philological Quarterly* 58 (1979) 321–35.

17 It is possible that 'resisting' is a misprint; the *magnum opus* edition reads 'unresisting' (*WN* x, 359).

18 Cuddie firmly believes that Mucklewrath prophesied the doom that overtook Claverhouse at Killicrankie: 'I heard it wi' my ain lugs ... foretauld to him by a man that had been three hours stane dead, and came back to this earth again just to tell him his mind' (iv, 161). In the *magnum opus* text Scott incorporates immediately after Mucklewrath's prophecy a brief addition designed to emphasise the element of wish-fulfilment in Claverhouse's death: 'he [Morton] often thought of it afterwards when that wish seemed to be accomplished' (*WN* x, 383).

19 For a discussion of the relationship of Claverhouse and Burley as expressive of the distinction between secular and religious fatalism, see Cockshut *Achievement* pp 139–43.

20 For Daiches Morton's survival has little carry-over for society as a whole; he sees 'no particular hope' implied in the elimination of the fanatics Burley and Claverhouse (*Literary Essays* p 109). For Alexander Welsh, however, Morton's survival signifies the coming into his own of 'the passive and loyal hero of the new era' (*Hero* p 235), while Avrom Fleishman speaks of Morton as returning to society at the end of the novel 'to expiate his rebellion, in one sense, and to claim his role in the new life of the nation, in a larger sense' (*English Historical Novel* p 67).

21 In creating Martha Buskbody with her demand for full details about 'the marriage – the marriage of the principal personages' (iv, 341), Scott was clearly having a joke at the expense of James Ballantyne, to whom he had written, when sending the final stanzas of canto vi of *The Lord of the Isles* at the end of 1815: 'You have now the whole affair, excepting two or three concluding stanzas. As your taste for bride's cake may induce you to desire to know more of the wedding, I will save you some criticism by saying, I have settled to stop short as above. – Witness my hand, W.S.' (*Poetical Works* [1833] x, 269n)

22 For a full discussion of the fourth series of *Tales of My Landlord* (1832) and Lockhart's editing of the Gandercleuch framework for that series, see Kurt Gammerschlag 'The Making and Un-Making of Sir Walter Scott's *Count Robert of Paris*' *Studies in Scottish Literature* 15 (1980) 95–123.

23 *Literary Essays* (Edinburgh 1956) pp 107–8

7 ROB ROY

1 For details of sales, see *Life* III, 296, and IV, 108.

2 *Rob Roy* 3 vols (Edinburgh 1818) I, vii. Subsequent references are incorporated within parentheses in the text.

3 See, for example, the comment by Edgar Johnson: 'And although the narrative begins in the tone of the mature man looking back on his past, Scott endows it with none of the haunting overtones of foreshadowing and reflective insight gathered from later experience that Dickens, for example, so subtly uses in *David Copperfield* and *Great Expectations*. Frank Osbaldistone might be recording these recaptured experiences from day to day for all that the supposed perspective on the past colors its presentation' (*Great Unknown* I, 604).

4 Critics of the novel from the earliest reviewers onwards have been troubled by the apparent inconsequentiality of the plotting; see, for example, Nassau Senior's 1821 *Quarterly Review* article (vol 26), especially pp 110–11, or the comments more than a century later by R.C. Gordon (*Under Which King?* espec p 78) and Avrom Fleishman (*The English Historical Novel* espec pp 69–70).

5 By the time of Lockhart's biography it had already become a critical commonplace to single out individual characters in the novel for particular mention; see *Life* IV, 108.

6 In preparing *Rob Roy* for the *magnum opus* edition more than ten years after its first publication, Scott indulged himself in an introduction of over a hundred pages and in six accompanying appendices. But since this material was almost exclusively concerned with Rob Roy and his children, it still did not amount to that overarching historical vision controlling all aspects of the narrative that occurs in *Waverley*.

7 David Brown says of Frank Osbaldistone: 'we are concerned with him only because he is our camera for observing the other characters' (*Walter Scott and the Historical Imagination* pp 93–4).

8 It is worth noting that in the *magnum opus* text of the novel Scott revised the phrasing here, changing 'detail' to 'narrative' (*WN* VII, 5), thus strengthening the emphasis on narration and Frank's marinerlike activity. The *magnum opus* text of *Rob Roy* shows, in fact, a relatively high incidence of verbal revision. Some changes are made to improve the cadence or to correct minor grammatical slips, but others are clearly intended to reinforce

the impression of Frank as someone disturbed by ineradicable memories of past experience. See, for example, the account of the death of Rashleigh, where Frank expresses his reluctance to dwell any longer on 'so hideous a picture' (1st edn, III, 343); in the *magnum opus* this becomes 'so painful a picture' (*WN* VIII, 377) – only a minor change, perhaps, but one which directs attention to the effect of the experience on Frank.

9 E.T. Channing in his 1818 review gave early expression to the discomfort created by the recurring stimulation and disappointment of the reader's engaged attention: 'Characters are brought forward, and sketched finely, and undertake a great deal and do little or nothing. The reader's curiosity is perpetually awakened by doubtful intimations, and he is extremely busy and ingenious to look into the mysteries of character and the bearings of plots, and after all he finds that very little was intended or at least accomplished, but an unfair excitement and baffling of his acuteness and eagerness' (*North American Review* 7 [1818] 159).

10 It is a pattern employed positively in other Scott novels such as *Guy Mannering* (1815) and, with modifications appropriate to its period, *The Abbot* (1820).

11 Donald Davie's comparison of the two novels – very much to the disadvantage of *Rob Roy* – is well known (*Heyday* pp 56–64). Francis Hart deals admirably with the problem inherent in such an approach and identifies very clearly the distinctive features of *Rob Roy* (*Scott's Novels* pp 36–42); he remains troubled, nevertheless, by 'Scott's apparent failure to recognize the possibilities of his first-person narrator' (p 42).

12 *QR* 26, p 111

13 For a discussion of the *Hamlet* allusion and its implications, see Welsh *Hero* p 198.

14 The phrase is Scott's own and comes from the opening chapter of *The Heart of Midlothian*, the novel that immediately followed *Rob Roy* (*Tales of My Landlord, Second Series* [Edinburgh 1818] I, 35).

8 *THE HEART OF MIDLOTHIAN*

1 For an important discussion of the 'sociability' of Scott as narrator, see Richard Waswo 'Story as Historiography in the Waverley Novels' *ELH* 47 (1980) 304–30.

2 *Tales of My Landlord, Second Series, Collected and Arranged by Jedediah Cleishbotham, Schoolmaster and Parish-Clerk of Gandercleuch* 4 vols (Edinburgh 1818) IV,

57. Subsequent references are incorporated within parentheses in the text.

3 See *The Story-Teller Retrieves the Past* pp 85–92.

4 *Scottish Historical Documents* ed Gordon Donaldson (Edinburgh 1970) p 275

5 A full account of the regalia, their history, and their restoration to view was appended by Scott to his *Provincial Antiquities and Picturesque Scenery of Scotland* (London and Edinburgh 1819–26). According to Peter Garside's note, 'Two Descriptions of the Regalia' (*Scott Newsletter* 2 [Summer 1983] p 9), this account was probably written in June or July 1819; it is numbered [i]–lii, and designed to be bound as the opening section of the work. It corrects certain inaccuracies in the story as retailed to Lady Louisa Stewart and Croker.

6 Grierson in his note to this letter (*L* v, 135), quotes Lockhart in identifying the proposed second tale as *The Bride of Lammermoor*, but there is in fact no evidence for such an identification. James C. Corson emends the note to refer to the regalia story (*Notes and Index to Sir Herbert Grierson's Edition of the Letters of Sir Walter Scott* [Oxford 1979] p 149).

7 The manuscript in the National Library of Scotland reveals that Scott was in some uncertainty as to where to end volumes I and II. He initially intended to include the first chapter of volume II in volume I, and considered carrying volume II up to the end of Jeanie's visit to Dumbiedikes that now opens volume III. But this would have advanced matters only one chapter and still left the English sections to be covered.

8 One of the earliest and most direct expressions of the view that Scott extended his novel to four volumes for mercenary reasons occurs in the November 1818 notice of the novel in the *British Review*: 'It is a poor device for so great an author; and if he had not been compelled by his mercantile engagement to spin out the thread of his story, with or without materials, so as to make out a *fourth* volume, and by that means secure the *fourth* thousand pounds, he would have scorned to introduce any part of the trash, of which he has composed the latter part of his work' (*British Review* 12 [1818] 404). For Robert C. Gordon, 'What follows [Jeanie's interview with the Queen] is a disaster which reveals perhaps as nothing else in the Waverley Novels Scott's capacity for an infantile disregard of aesthetic decencies' (*Under Which King?* p 94). But even Gordon acknowledges that the novel could not really end with the interview; he would like to add the chapter in volume IV in which Jeanie and her father are reunited and then the wedding of Jeanie and Butler. Avrom Fleishman (*English Historical Novel* pp 99–101) offers one of the most persuasive defences of the final

section of the novel, seeing it as inextricably bound up with the ethical movement that carries Jeanie from being a heroine of justice to a heroine of mercy and as intrinsic to the portrayal of the workings of historical process in this novel.

9 For Fleishman the Bunyan references underline the gradual education of Jeanie that leads her from the 'high idealism' of her opening stance to 'a broader conception of morality, one that admits of greater human sympathy than absolute principles usually allow' (*English Historical Novel* p 89).

10 'The story of these inner battles and of this struggle to save her sister show the rich humanity and simple heroism of a really great human being. Yet Scott's picture of his heroine never for a moment obscures her narrow Puritan and Scottish peasant traits, indeed it is they which again and again form the specific character of the naïve and grand heroism of this popular figure' (Georg Lukács *The Historical Novel* trans Hannah and Stanley Mitchell [London 1962] p 52).

11 David Daiches, in his 1948 introduction to the Rinehart edition of the novel, notes: 'The more monstrous and theatrical the end of Sir George Staunton, the more explicit becomes the point that the age for acceptable heroic action on the physical level is over ... The writing in this part of the novel may be less convincing, and the situation less grounded in that earthy sense of character that furnished Scott his finest creations, but in terms of the general plot pattern this part of the action is perfectly appropriate' ([New York 1948] pp xii–xiii). Robin Mayhead (*Walter Scott* pp 58–9) makes an interesting case for seeing the 'poetic justice' of Staunton's end as an element in the book's varied and complex exploration of different concepts of justice, but even he feels that the moralistic emphasis of the later chapters seriously weakens the novel. John P. Farrell, while not explicitly considering the question of the success or failure of the final chapters, does underline the rightness of Staunton's end in schematic terms; for him Staunton is a deliberately self-isolated figure who 'has rejected community in his reckless assertion of freedom, and the story of his end is Scott's argument against the autonomy of the self' (*Revolution as Tragedy* p 110).

12 Thomas Hardy *Tess of the d'Urbervilles* (London 1912) p 44

13 *The Realistic Imagination* p 92

9 THE BRIDE OF LAMMERMOOR AND A LEGEND OF MONTROSE

1 J.C. Corson (*Notes and Index* p 152) argues that the correct date of the letter in which the *Bride* is first discussed in detail (*L* v, 186) should be May 1818

rather than 10 September 1818 as suggested by Grierson. Since Scott did not complete *The Heart of Midlothian* till early July – since, too, his normal practice was to complete one novel before beginning another – such an early date for the commencement of the *Bride* seems somewhat surprising; it is clear, however, that whenever it was begun, composition was not very far advanced in the early autumn of 1818.

2 Frank McCombie points out, in his note 'The Completion of *The Bride of Lammermoor*' (*Notes and Queries* ns 23 [1976] 454), that the letter in which Scott told James Ballantyne 'My next parcel finishes the Bride' (*L* v, 392) is misplaced in Grierson's edition and was most probably written on 15 April. He also argues convincingly that the parcel of *Bride* manuscript sent to Ballantyne about 2 May with a note urging care with the printing must, in fact, have been the final section.

3 *Life* IV, 258

4 More than a third of the *Ivanhoe* manuscript survives in Scott's holograph in the Pierpont Morgan Library, and there are some holograph pages of the *Legend* in the Edinburgh University Library and one in the National Library of Scotland. As Grierson points out, George Huntly Gordon is on record as saying he transcribed the *Legend* for the press from Scott's own manuscript (*Sir Walter Scott, Bart. A New Life Supplementary to, and Corrective of, Lockhart's Biography* [London 1938] p 174).

5 *Great Unknown* I, 646; see also his later reference to its being written in 'drugged near-somnambulism' (I, 670). Johnson's account is very similar to that in John Buchan's *Sir Walter Scott* (London 1932) p 193: 'It was not the work of the ordinary Scott, but of a "fey" man, living in a remote world of pain ... It was the product of a drugged and abnormal condition, even as Coleridge composed "Kubla Khan" in an opiate dream, from which he was roused by an inopportune "person from Porlock."'

6 *Life* IV, 275

7 Ibid

8 See *L* v, 353, 357, 359, 361.

9 In his 1937 address to the Sir Walter Scott Society, reprinted in *Sir Walter Scott 1771–1832: An Edinburgh Keepsake* ed Allan Frazer (Edinburgh 1971); the quoted phrase occurs on p 27.

10 *Scott's Novels* pp 329 and 323

11 *Great Unknown* I, lxix, and I, 670

12 E. Owen, in 'Critics of *The Bride of Lammermoor*' *Dalhousie Review* 18 (1938) 365–71, castigated those commentators who failed to take account of the

obvious post-Union references, and Andrew Hook has more recently discussed the problem with particular perceptiveness and correctly dated the events as post-Union ('*The Bride of Lammermoor*: A Reexamination' *Nineteenth-Century Fiction* 22 [1967] 115); neither, however, seems to have been aware of the textual situation.

13 In addition to the long note on 'Appeal to Parliament' (*WN* xiv, 116) which he composed specially for the *magnum opus* edition, Scott made numerous changes in the text itself, referring, for example, to the House of Lords as 'a court of equity of which the Lord Keeper felt an instinctive dread' (*WN* xiv, 94) and making him object to the insult that would be offered to the Scottish courts 'through the intervention of what, with all submission, he must term a foreign court of appeal' (*WN* xiv, 286). One of the longer additions makes explicit the contrast between the pre- and post-Union political and legal situations and presents the Lord Keeper as basing his assumptions on the 'courts which he had himself known in the unhappy times preceding the Scottish Union' while remaining unaware of the 'high and unbiassed character of English judicial proceedings' (*WN* xiv, 100). For further examples of the differences between the two texts and discussion of the legal situation immediately before and after the Union, see my article 'Text and Context: Dating the Events of *The Bride of Lammermoor*' *The Bibliothek* 9 (1979) 200–13.

14 See, for example, Avrom Fleishman's comment: 'It is given to the old aristocracy to possess the chivalric virtues, the heroism, free spirit, and moral integrity which Scott recalls for his modern readers. He represents this chivalric survival in the person of the hero, the Master of Ravenswood' (*The English Historical Novel* p 68).

15 For David Daiches the *Bride* 'presents the conflict between the old and the new in naked, almost melodramatic terms: the decayed representative of an ancient family comes face to face with the modern purchaser of his estates' (*Literary Essays* p 113).

16 *Tales of My Landlord, Third Series, Collected and Arranged by Jedediah Cleishbotham, Schoolmaster and Parish-Clerk of Gandercleuch* 4 vols (Edinburgh 1819) 1, 42. Subsequent references are incorporated within parentheses in the text.

17 'His enlightenment extends to moral and political values as well ... He dislikes the petty politics of the time from the point of view of the enlightened humanitarian, *not* that of chivalric anachronism' (*Scott's Novels* p 316).

18 Scott's *magnum opus* note was technically inaccurate in stating that 'by the

articles of the Union, an appeal to the British House of Peers has been secured to the Scottish subject' (*WN* xiv, 116). This was not one of the articles of the Act of Union, probably because, as Sir George Clark suggests, the presence of bishops in the House of Lords made it 'a ticklish subject' (*The Later Stuarts, 1660–1714* [Oxford 1956] p 291). The privilege, however, was certainly assumed to have been conferred by the Union and was exercised immediately afterwards.

19 *Heyday* p 161

20 For a detailed account of Scott's active personal involvement in the 1818 negotiations that led to his baronetcy, see Peter Garside 'Patriotism and Patronage: New Light on Scott's Baronetcy' *Modern Language Review* 77 (1982) 16–28.

21 *Edinburgh Annual Register, 1808* (Edinburgh 1810) p 345

22 *Tales of a Grandfather: Being Stories from the History of Scotland* 2nd ser, 3 vols (Edinburgh 1829) iii, 316

23 Claire Lamont points out that the story of the Dalrymple-Rutherford tragedy was also in the repertoire of Scott's great-aunt Margaret Swinton ('Scott as Story-teller: *The Bride of Lammermoor*' *Scottish Literary Journal* 7 [1980] 116).

24 *The Ballad and the Folk* p 65

25 The same verifying detail is incorporated into the fabric of the novel at the point where Lucy's young brother is described as 'too full of his own appearance ... to pay much regard to any thing else; but he afterwards remembered to the hour of his death, that when the hand of his sister ... touched his own, it felt as wet and cold as sepulchral marble' (iii, 92).

26 Donald Cameron, in his important essay 'The Web of Destiny: the Structure of *The Bride of Lammermoor*,' points to the way in which the supernatural elements are integrated into the total pattern: 'A harmony and tension develop in the story between the portents of disaster and the historically-moulded psychological forces which determine the behaviour of the characters' (in *Scott's Mind and Art* ed A. Norman Jeffares [Edinburgh 1969] p 188).

27 For a perceptive commentary on prophecies fulfilled and unfulfilled in the *Bride*, see Cockshut *Achievement* pp 82–5.

28 Edgar Johnson is one of the few people to have challenged the conventional view that Dalgetty is a character 'whose vitality so takes over the story as to run away with the plot and run away from its theme' (*Great Unknown* i, 670).

29 *WN* xv, xviii–xix

30 The final paragraph, beginning 'I retire from the field' and including the recommendation of *Marriage*, was added by Scott in proof, at which time he also added the phrase quoted above: 'to exhaust one individual's power of observation' (NLS ms 3401, ff 329–30).

31 He had initially wanted to publish *Ivanhoe* under the name of its supposed narrator Laurence Templeton, thus confirming the innovative character of the new novel. He also insisted that it be printed on better paper than his previous novels – a requirement that led to a serious delay in the printing while the new paper was being obtained. Constable, unwilling to forego the advantages of the famous name, did, however, finally succeed in persuading Scott to allow the name of the Author of *Waverley* to appear on the title-page. For Scott's own account of these manoeuvrings see the *magnum opus* Introduction to *Ivanhoe* (*WN* xvi, iii–x).

Index